The Making of
American Whiteness

PHILOSOPHY OF RACE

Series Editor: George Yancy, Emory University

Editorial Board: Sybol Anderson, Barbara Applebaum, Alison Bailey, Chike Jeffers, Janine Jones, David Kim, Emily S. Lee, Zeus Leonardo, Falguni A. Sheth, Grant Silva

The Philosophy of Race book series publishes interdisciplinary projects that center upon the concept of race, a concept that continues to have very profound contemporary implications. Philosophers and other scholars, more generally, are strongly encouraged to submit book projects that seriously address race and the process of racialization as a deeply embodied, existential, political, social, and historical phenomenon. The series is open to examine monographs, edited collections, and revised dissertations that critically engage the concept of race from multiple perspectives: sociopolitical, feminist, existential, phenomenological, theological, and historical.

Recent Titles in the Series

The Making of American Whiteness

The Formation of Race in Seventeenth-Century Virginia

Carmen P. Thompson

LEXINGTON BOOKS
Lanham • Boulder • New York • London

Published by Lexington Books
An imprint of The Rowman & Littlefield Publishing Group, Inc.
4501 Forbes Boulevard, Suite 200, Lanham, Maryland 20706
www.rowman.com

86-90 Paul Street, London EC2A 4NE

British Library Cataloguing in Publication Information Available

Library of Congress Cataloging-in-Publication Data

Names: Thompson, Carmen P., author.
Title: The making of American Whiteness : the formation of race in seventeenth-century
    Virginia / Carmen P. Thompson.
Other titles: Philosophy of race.
Description: Lanham [Maryland] : Lexington Books, [2023] | Series: Philosophy of race
    | Includes bibliographical references and index.
Identifiers: LCCN 2022040495 (print) | LCCN 2022040496 (ebook) |
    ISBN 9781666923216 (cloth) | ISBN 9781666923223 (ebook)
Subjects: LCSH: White people—Virginia—History—17th century. |
    African Americans—Virginia—History—17th century. | Slavery—Virginia—
    History—17th century. | White people—Race identity—Virginia—History—17th
    century. | Virginia—Race relations—History—17th century. | Virginia—History—
    Colonial period, ca. 1600–1775.
Classification: LCC F235.A1 T46 2023 (print) | LCC F235.A1 (ebook) |
    DDC 320.56/9090755—dc23/eng/20220826
LC record available at https://lccn.loc.gov/2022040495
LC ebook record available at https://lccn.loc.gov/2022040496

*To my African ancestors, whose spirit has guided me
in telling the history of Whiteness in America.*

Contents

Acknowledgments

A book about American Whiteness does not develop in a vacuum but out of exhaustive study of the archival records of European explorers, colonizers and enslavers, details that show what they did in Africa and the Americas was indeed White supremacy. The publication of such a book was more than a decade in the making, and it came with a lot of personal and professional sacrifice and hardships. As a Black woman and historian who specializes in Critical Whiteness Studies, I am a part of the long legacy of other Black scholars who spoke truth to power. And I proudly embrace that heritage just as those before me, on whose shoulders I stand, have done and like others are doing. Thus, over these many years there are numerous individuals and organizations to thank. But first and foremost, I want to thank Jesus Christ, my Lord and Savior, without whom none of these efforts would be possible.

That said, many people and organizations deserve credit for this book. My scholarly mentor, David R. Roediger, whose close reading of my arguments and analysis over the years made this book better. My longtime friend and colleague, George Yancy, whose encouragement and unwavering confidence never let me forget the importance of this book to understanding Whiteness in America. Likewise, friends and colleagues at the Oregon Historical Society and the *Oregon Historical Quarterly* gave unwavering support and propelled the project to its ultimate completion. I polished many of the ideas in this book through conversations as a contributor to the *OHQ*, especially from my work as co-editor and contributor of the winter 2019 special issue on Oregon's history of White supremacy, which provided me the clarity of thought to define and explain Whiteness.

My understanding of precolonial West Africa, the transatlantic slave trade and the common cultural traditions and knowledge systems of those Black people was informed by the erudite scholarship of Jean Allman, whose writings, research and teachings expanded the scope and breath of my thinking on African culture as a force that sustained and continues to sustain Black people across the diaspora.

This book has benefited from the research of a long list of scholars whose work influenced my understanding of the connections between race, space and citizenship including Adrian Burgos Jr., Dianne Harris and Karen Gibson. Other scholars such as Patricia Schechter, Kim Williams and Avel Louise Gordly were a constant source of encouragement.

The long conversations with my pastor, friend and spiritual advisor, Reverend Doctor Leroy Haynes Jr., a scholar and author in his own right, invigorated me and gave me the encouragement to push through with the knowledge that God was always with me and would see me through to the completion of this book.

The list of family and friends who have faith in me is innumerable, and it is for them that I strive and persist in my scholarship. My mother, who does not quite understand the topic that consumes my days save for that I am writing a book. She, as only a mother can do, is proud of me no matter what and that unconditional love is a soul force.

It is hard to imagine writing this book without the love and emotional security I have from my spouse. It is what gives me peace of mind to write.

And to friends, cousins, nieces, nephews, my brother, aunts and uncles, you are the reason why I write. I love you more than words can convey.

Introduction

This book came about out of a lifelong quest to answer two questions that have befuddled me since childhood: why European people selected persons of African descent for centuries of enslavement, Jim Crow and other institutional forms of racism and terror and why the social order of America ranks Whites highest and Blacks lowest. Since elementary school, I have utilized my schoolwork to answer these questions and what I consider to be the most vexing problem in American history and society since its founding: what it means and meant to be White. Those questions have driven my scholarly work toward understanding the concept of Whiteness.

Whiteness is an expectation by White people (sometimes an unconscious expectation) that the government will enact and maintain laws and policies to benefit them. This practice, which has been effectuated throughout all institutions that govern American society, is White supremacy—the hierarchical ordering of human beings based on phenotypic or physical attributes that we call "race."[1] But the daily, ongoing expectations of privilege are Whiteness. On a day-to-day level, the system of White supremacy has repeatedly, since New World settlement, provided advantages to White people, as I demonstrate in the subsequent chapters. And the entrenchment of this system thereby encourages those of European ancestry to internalize their top ranking—that is, to embody White supremacy—and that embodiment of expectation, conscious or otherwise, is Whiteness.

For the past seventy years, leading U.S. historians and scholars have long accepted the notion of race and particularly Whiteness as having emerged slowly before settling into its institutional form after the passage of the 1705 law in Virginia (the first colony in what would become the United States) that made enslaved Black people chattel.[2] Similarly, scholars have largely agreed that the emergence of the racial categories of White and Black—which justified White privilege for the former and anti-Black racism and the system of enslavement of Black people by Whites for the latter—was not inevitable before the passage of the 1705 "slave law." Here, scholars regularly cite

1

Bacon's Rebellion as prima facie evidence of the absence of race and racial categories and exemplar of an interracial coalition between poor Whites and Blacks that existed in Virginia before the 1676 attack, as if to suggest that Whiteness and interracial harmony or affect could not simultaneously coexist.

This book challenges all of these longstanding ideas, the best of which were advanced by Theodore Allen, who claimed there was no functioning White racial designation when enslaved Africans arrived in Virginia in 1619 nor would there be such a thing called White people for another sixty years.[3] With extensive archival documentation on colonial Virginia, I correct Allen's theories, showing that Europeans' conscious embrace and exercise of their Whiteness was not only functioning before 1619, but it was already rolling at the settlement of England's first colony in North America. Specifically, my sources show what this sort of Whiteness looked like in the first half of the seventeenth century through their usage of time-honored systems of oppression against Native and African peoples that included conquest, genocide, land theft, enslavement and forced cultural change—launching an ideology I call "American Whiteness."

American Whiteness inextricably links the enslavement of African descended peoples to European colonization of indigenous lands in North America. The American form of Whiteness is historical and organic, deriving from English settlers' knowledge and interpretation of the principles of colonialism and expansionism (the bedrock and drivers of the international system of slavery), which they used to justify the original acts of colonization that made way for the United States of America.[4]

American Whiteness originated outside North America through European colonization efforts in West Africa during the fifteenth-century build-up to the transatlantic slave trade. At that time, there was no formal name for White supremacy, or even for race. Instead, European leaders defined their Whiteness by using oppositional language.[5] They employed terms like "heathen" and "uncivilized" when referring to Africans, as opposed to "Christian" and "civilized" when referring to themselves.[6] Thus, when European government leaders, church officials and explorers expressed their reasoning for expansion to the Americas, they used words such as "planting," "possessing" and "subduing," all within the context of colonization and enslavement.[7] These expressions, personalizing Europeans' expectation to rule over other people's bodies and lands, were all early forms of Whiteness and, by extension, White supremacy.

Along the same line, once in the New World, an exchange in 1612 between Virginia officials expressed the psyche of their Whiteness over concern about European settlers marrying Native American women. Without using the term, White colonial leaders referred to Native women as "savages" and their potential spouses as "Englishmen."[8] Similarly, the twenty-three enslaved

West African women, men and children listed in Virginia's 1624 census had the word "Negro" before or after their names, while a list of sixteen female and male European indentured servants documented in the same census were recorded using their full names without any racial designation, demonstrating a personal understanding of themselves as other than Negro, i.e., White.[9]

That said, internalized Whiteness and the concomitant anti-Black racism and the mass enslavement of Black people in Virginia was neither "peculiar" for Europeans, nor was it an "unthinking" decision. It was a conscious, calculated and intentional step in the high stakes, transnational enterprise of European empire building predicated on the enslavement of Black people just as it was in the international system of slavery.

With this in mind, an ironic characteristic of Whiteness is the inability of White people to fully perceive the historical depths of their Whiteness as well as the social, political and economic benefits of being White.[10] This is because Virginia was settled and America was "founded" for White people. Thus, it was from the unremarkableness of this deeply latent perspective of their Whiteness that American society was/is organized. Moreover, it was/is from the lived experiences of White people that American norms, values, standards and measures were/are established, all of which makes Whiteness strangely difficult for White people to recognize. Why is this? Because a fish does not know it is in water. That is, White people in America are generally incapable of perceiving the depths of their own Whiteness.[11]

Yet, those who are not White clearly know and sense that the perspectives of Whites are the standard in American society. Just as someone with a disability knows that the world is designed for people with certain ability, or women know that our society was organized to offer greater opportunity for people who are labeled as male, or someone who is not heterosexual knows that heterosexuality is assumed. It is the same way with White skin and supremacy in America. With this in mind, the goal of this book is to expose this blind spot by using American Whiteness as the model through which to explain the reality of White supremacy and Whiteness in America more broadly.

American racism and American Whiteness are both interdependent and mutually exclusive. This phenomenon has led to a great deal of misunderstanding and misinterpretation of what Whiteness and White supremacy is/are and why both are and have been the central feature and controlling variable in America's racial problems. This failure to speak truth to power and name American racism as the doppelganger of White supremacy embodied as Whiteness is not only a problem that beseeched early scholars of race; it also is one that confuses some contemporary writers.[12]

Whiteness, I maintain, is not a construction that explains the economic self-interest of differing classes of White people over non-Whites, nor is it a

North American phenomenon, but has its genesis in each European nation's initial decision to cross the Atlantic Ocean. As part of the consequences of European expansion to the Americas, Whiteness would severely impact the American continents and its peoples and its toll continues to be felt today. The chapters in this book are dedicated to explaining the manifestation of Whiteness in the United States.

I devote four chapters in this book to explicating the appearance and formation of American Whiteness with a wide range of primary sources, including county court records (deeds, orders and wills), estate inventories, government documents, statutes, travel logs and letters that demonstrate that European colonist in Virginia were not only aware of their Whiteness at settlement but had in fact adopted it before ever having arrived in Virginia.

Chapter 1 reconstructs the history of the emergence of Whiteness in the precolonial West African transatlantic slave trade and delineates its subsequent impact on the social organization of colonial Virginia's civil society. The chapter shows American Whiteness predated the British Empire and prefigured English colonization of the New World, first with the establishment of the English African Company in 1536 and then with the establishment of the Virginia Company of London in 1606.

The English African Company was established to explore the prospect of slave trading in West Africa in hopes of someday competing with and/ or surpassing their European counterparts, Portugal and Spain, who by this time had settled colonies in the Americas (Brazil and Santo Domingo) with enslaved African laborers who produced global commodities like sugar cane that helped make Portugal and Spain superpowers. Similarly, the formation of the Virginia Company of London, which was charted by England in 1606 specifically to colonize the area of United States that we call Virginia, marked the presence of American Whiteness before settlement, which at the time was home to various Native American groups.

Chapter 1 shows by 1660, American Whiteness was more than just functioning; it had matured, evidenced by the settlement of eight English colonies in North America and the development of the Royal African Company, an English mercantile company chartered in 1660 to trade in West Africa. Not long after this charter, England held a monopoly over the slave trade in West Africa for several decades, capturing, enslaving and transporting more Africans to the Americas than any other European nation in the entire history of transatlantic slave trade that sent untold millions of enslaved Africans to the Americas.

As stated earlier, Whiteness is an expectation (sometimes an unconscious expectation) by White people of privilege and advantage in laws and policies from the government: policies that were/are then effectuated through the institutions that order civil society. And nowhere were the expectations of Whiteness more present than in the international system of slavery and the public/private partnership between businessmen and the governments of European nations that sponsored and sanctioned slave trading and colonization in Africa and the Americas. It was in this mutual alliance that the expectation of American Whiteness was set and made manifest in the settlement of Virginia and in the social and political organization of colony.

Chapter 2 shows the American formation of Whiteness taking shape in the New World with the promises of land and social status made by English businessmen and the Virginia government to recruit White men and their families to the colony. The template for this practice mirrored the international system of slavery that also featured poor White men as temporary laborers.

In western Africa, poor White men volunteered to perform the arduous labor of colonization until their labor and standing was replaced by free and enslaved Africans. The duties of these men included voluntarily overseeing and assisting captured Africans in building slave castles and forts located on the ocean's shore until the European slave ships, manned mostly by poor White men, transported enslaved African women, men and children to European colonies across the Atlantic to places like Brazil and other locales in the Americas.[13]

The work of poor Whites in West Africa also included overseeing the slave coffles in the miles-long trek (sometimes hundreds of miles) of captured and enslaved Africans from the interior regions of Western Africa to the shore, where they were held until a sufficient supply of this human commodity had accumulated and was readied for transport on European slave ships sailing out of the continent. At the ocean's shore, White workers manned cannons that faced outward to the sea, guarding against the constant and consistent threat of other European nations and pirates looking to poach enslaved Africans or seize control of slave trading in the area.

Correspondingly, in the New World, and specifically in Virginia, most poor White men voluntarily immigrated to the New World as recruits who worked in labor programs sponsored by businessmen or the Virginia government or to join family and friends in colonizing Native American lands in the hopes of future benefits. Likewise, White women were recruited to Virginia in the early decades of the seventeenth century by these same entities to marry and procreate with these men: work that was equally important to the success of European colonization of the New World and to the making of American Whiteness.

Once in Virginia, White men and women temporarily traded their labor (both physical and domestic) to planters and their families in exchange for land and, most important, legal guarantees against their and their children's permanent bondage: a key characteristic of Whiteness that was established in the international system of slavery long before the arrival of enslaved

Africans in 1619. And although this accepted quid pro quo between poor, middling and upper class Whites in doing the exhausting work of colonization was sometimes to the point of death, the price of the ticket or benefit for all Whites, especially for poor Whites (women included), was Whiteness.

In this arrangement, as we learn in chapter 2, Whiteness was/is as much if not more an intra-racial struggle among and between various classes of Whites as it was/is an interracial one. And in chapter 3, we see the dynamics of this intra-racial tug of war and the contexts therein between various classes of Whites (women and men) beginning at settlement, being played out within the various institutions of Virginia and giving shape and form to political and ideological expression of Whiteness.

Of particular interest in this third chapter is the extent to which the reproduction of Whiteness both as an ideology and a matter of fact was affected by the access and proximity of White people to power in colonial institutions, a leading indicator of Whiteness. Specific sources from county depositories in Virginia show, for example, that it was indeed the struggles of poorer White men in the early seventeenth century for an elevated place within organized institutions (courts, churches etc.) and civil society where Whiteness as expectation was best understood.

As early as the 1630s, we see that Whiteness as expectation was as much a mix of White racial sensibilities predicated on the role and function of government and government-sanctioned institutions as any class interests in making American Whiteness. As an expression of values and as a historical force, the expectations of poorer Whites for a social and racial floor above Black people and Native Americans frustrated many British and colonial leaders. Even more significant to our understanding of American Whiteness, the expectation of poorer Whites for social, political and economic benefits and status above Blacks and Native people would overtake both the direction of public policy and the social customs of Virginia in the early decades of the seventeenth century and in the centuries to come.

The historical trajectory of the push and pull between all classes of Whites, but specifically the poorer ones, at settlement, is central to teasing out the nuances of American Whiteness exhibited by the White people who built the various institutions that came out of European expansionism and colonialism. And when, in its time, Black resistance to institutionalized American Whiteness manifested in colonial Virginia between European and African peoples as early as 1619 (as well at other junctures), we learn that poorer Whites were no more receptive to Black people's demands for freedoms and access to institutions than British and colonial leaders.

In light of the constant and consistent subjugation or threats therein experienced by early Africans in Virginia, chapter 4 uses indigenous African cultural forms as both a source and a methodology to uncover not only colonial Virginia's Black activist tradition but also to expose the character of American Whiteness and White supremacy since 1619, including the conditions of its historical emergence, its forms and its nature in relation and response to Black people in the colony.

This chapter begins with a reinvestigation of precolonial West African cultural traditions: traditions that very much influenced Black resistance strategies since European contact and beyond. In Virginia, Black people of various degrees of freedom utilized their prior skills and knowledge systems, including lineage systems, oral traditions and agrarian culture, to mitigate, survive and in, some instances, overcome White people's attempts to subjugate them and their children, and in doing so, expose the character of Whiteness since 1619.

The usefulness of indigenous African cultural ways as a source and methodology to reveal the interworkings of American Whiteness fills an evidentiary gap in U.S. historiography that has tended to reduce discussions about African cultural forms to debates on retentions and the degree to which they were manifest in the daily lives of African women and men in the New World. Although questions about the presence of African cultural traditions by those Blacks born in the continent and later captured, enslaved and shipped to the New World by Whites is one that has garnered a great deal of scholarly analysis, it would be an error to allow the retentions debate to arrest our studies away from its utility for revealing the character of Whiteness in colonial Virginia; the two are both mutually exclusive, interconnected and at once critical to understanding American White Supremacy.

The fact that leading historians exercised "immense physic and intellectual energies eradiating the significance of Nubia for Egypt's formation, of Egypt in the development of Greek civilization, [and] of Africa for imperial Rome" suggests a lot about the Black radical tradition as a source and methodology for understanding Whiteness and, more broadly, White supremacy.[14]

So effective was this effort by historians and governments to erase Blackness out of world history that today most students, media outlets and the general public across race and political lines more frequently than not speak of Africa not as the cradle of humanity, or the dawn of civilization, or even as the second largest continent holding nearly every mineral and precious metal known to exist, or that it has some of the oldest religious and cultural traditions as well as technological and artistic advances known to humankind. Instead, Africa in the main is discussed as if it were a backward "country" that made little if any contribution to human progress. The most natural consequence of centuries of this wanton misinformation, myth and outright lies was/is that the ideological, political and historical vocabulary of American Whiteness that has undergirded American history and society, including the rationale for Black enslavement, the American Revolution and the Civil War, as well as old and new forms of Jim Crow and White Nationalism.

Chapter 4 throws aside this White supremacist project and uses the common cultural traditions of pre-European contact West Africa to demonstrate not only the resilience of African people to survive enslavement and build community and create new cultural forms in the centuries-long quest for freedom and freedoms in America, but also to highlight the primary elements and character of American Whiteness since 1619.

With this in mind, a goal of this book is to expand the scope of analysis of sources and artifacts on colonial Virginia beyond the origins debate and open up the interpretation of archival sources and methodologies so to rethink what we "know" about race and Whiteness in America. And there is no better way of doing that than examining the records of European colonizers, settlers and enslavers in Virginia. The plethora of primary sources that are cited in this book tells us what European people before, during, at and after New World settlement thought of themselves in relation to Native and African people. European people's words and actions, including the laws and policies enacted specifically to oppress Native Americans and African people, organized the social order and Virginia's civil society along racial lines, which is Whiteness by any other name. The records of Virginia at settlement that are detailed in this book tell us what all went into the making of American Whiteness.

NOTES

1. A. Smedley and Brian D. Smedley, *Race in North America Origin and Evolution of a Worldview* 4th ed. (Boulder, CO: Westview Press, 2011), 20.

2. Prominent historians whose work established the acceptance of these ideas include: Theodore W. Allen, *The Invention of the White Race: The Origin of Racial Oppression in Anglo-America*, 2 vols., vol. I (New York: Verso, 1997); Edmund S. Morgan, *American Slavery, American Freedom: The Ordeal of Colonial Virginia*, 1st ed. (New York: Norton, 1975).

3. Allen, *The Invention of the White Race: The Origin of Racial Oppression in Anglo-America*, I.

4. Robin Blackburn, *The Making of New World Slavery: From the Baroque to the Modern, 1492–1800* (New York: Verso, 1997), 10–18, 33. I define the international system of slavery as the technologies of oppression and enslavement used by Europeans in the transatlantic slave trade. Among them were six key elements that overlap in various ways with other systems of domination such as colonialism and imperialism. The six key elements outlined by Blackburn as they relate to American Whiteness and to Virginia's growth and development include: religious intolerance and persecution, territorial expansion, colonial settlement, arrogant imposition on colonial and indigenous peoples, theological justification for enslavement, and racial exclusion.

5. Toni Morrison, *Playing in the Dark: Whiteness and the Literary Imagination* (Cambridge: Harvard University Press, 1992). Morrison in her reading of Whiteness indicates that it became defined by its opposite, Blackness. My analysis of seventeenth-century Virginia indicates that lower class Whites defined themselves in opposition to Blacks because of the impermanence of their bondage and, in doing so, sought to align themselves with elite Whites in using enslavement as a means to justify their higher social position. For the origins of the term "White" as a racial designation see *Oxford English Dictionary,* 2d edn. (*OED2*), Oxford 1989, 12:72; *A Dictionary of American English, On Historical Principles (DAE)*, Sir William A. Craigie and James R. Hulbert, eds., Chicago 1938, 4:2475–78.

6. Report on Angola drawn from the letters of Father Gouveia and Paula Diasde Novais, BNL, FG, MS 8123, cited in Ruela Pombo, *Angola Menina* (Lisbon, 1944); and Gomes Eannes de Azurara, "Chronicle of the Discovery and Conquest of Guinea," (1453). The first English translation of this work was by Raymond Beazley and Edgar Prestage, printed for the Hakluyt Society in two volumes, the first in 1896. See also William Waller Hening, ed., *The Statutes at Large; Being a Collection of All the Laws of Virginia, from the First Session of the Legislature in the Year 1619,* II: 283 (English translation at page 99).

7. Albert Bushnell Hart, ed., *Era of Colonization, 1492–1689* (New York: The MacMillian Company, 1908), 1586.

8. Regarding the opposition language European leaders used to differentiate themselves from Native peoples, see Correspondence taken from James City records, V: 2589, folio 61.

9. Annie Lash Jester, ed., *Adventures of Purse and Person, 1607–1625* (Princeton: Princeton University Press, 1956), 22, 27, 29, 34, 46, 49, 62. For an examination of the significance of the word *Negro* as a label of racial difference see Winthrop D. Jordan, *White over Black: American Attitudes toward the Negro, 1550–1812* (Chapel Hill: The University of North Carolina Press, 1968), Chapter II; Richard B. Moore, *The Name "Negro" Its Origin and Evil Use* (Baltimore: Black Classic Press, 1992), 33–55; and Cyril Bibby, "The Power of Words," *The UNESCO Courier* VIII, no. 11 (April 1956).

10. Peggy McIntosh, "White Privilege and Male Privilege: A Personal Account of Coming to See Correspondences through Work in Women's Studies," in *Critical White Studies: Looking Behind the Mirror*, eds. Richard Delgado and Jean Stefancic (1997: Temple University Press, 1988), 292. Also, see Matthew Pratt Guterl, "A Note on the Word 'White,'" *American Quarterly* 56, no. 2 (June 2004). One of the ways Guterl defines "Whiteness" is as an "inchoate conglomeration of factors that give group advantage to white people, often without showing it explicitly, but also including old-fashion, in-your-face racism, and color-blind things." I draw on his analysis when discussing the ways in which European immigrants held advantages over African persons in early seventeenth-century Virginia in areas such as good jobs and barriers against permanent bondage, and I use American Whiteness to explain and explore the consequences of this history since European settlement in Virginia.

11. McIntosh, "White Privilege and Male Privilege: A Personal Account of Coming to See Correspondences through Work in Women's Studies," 292.

12. Those writers include but are in no way limited to: Ibram X. Kendi, who does this in his 2016 book *Stamped from the Beginning: The Definitive History of Racist Ideas in America*, when he superbly explains the history of race in America since colonization but fails to explain White supremacy and to explicitly name Whiteness as central to American racist ideas. Similarly, Crystal Fleming argues in her 2018 book, *How to Be Less Stupid About Race: On Racism, White Supremacy, and the Racial Divide*, that White supremacy and Whiteness are new phenomena, thereby failing to acknowledge that White supremacist ideas were used to establish the colonies that became the United States and that they form the cornerstone to all conversations about American racism.

13. Brazil was a Portuguese colony beginning in the early sixteenth century that today has the largest number of African people outside the continent of Africa.

14. Cedric J. Robinson, *Black Marxism: The Making of the Black Radical Tradition* (Chapel Hill: The University of North Carolina Press, 1983; repr., 2000).

Chapter 1

The International System of Slavery and the Formation American Whiteness

When John Rolfe reported in a January 20, 1620, letter to Sir Edwin Sandys that "20. and odd Negroes" had been off-loaded from an English vessel at Point Comfort, Virginia, in late August 1619, his statement was more than just a casual comment penned to a friend about the cargo contained in this vessel. It told of Virginia's arrival into the fully developed yet growing international system of slavery that included Africa, the Americas, Western Europe and the Islamic world.[1] The decision made by Virginia leaders to participate in what we now know was a piracy that involved the "20. and odd Negroes" and to join their European counterparts in perpetuating a system of enslavement that included exploiting the labor of millions of Black people from West Central Africa—leading to the transformation of the regions social structures including its indigenous forms of slavery—was not unexpected or fortuitous, nor was it uncalculated. Rather, it was planned and premeditated, and it was precipitated by their bird's eye view of African enslavement being used by their European allies for more than just a means to create wealth and financial security.

The take-away by Virginia settlers from observing up-close the interworking of the international system of slavery would prefigure the social and racial structure of the colony and profoundly inform the trajectory and development of American Whiteness for centuries to come.

White settlers' early acceptance of the rightness of enslaving African people was the first step in the making of American Whiteness. Being an enslaver provided Virginia leaders a hegemonic and a racial way to view themselves against the African people who they enslaved. This positional conception of the White enslaver and the Black slave was contained in the rationale for enslavement to be used as a tool to advance the colonization of Virginia, a rationale that was carried by European enslavers like the Portuguese, who, for more than a century before, used Africans as slaves to advance their own colonial projects in places like São Tomé and Brazil. Thus, it should come as no surprise that the "twenty Negroes" that Rolfe was referencing as having arrived in late August 1619 were not the first enslaved persons imported to Virginia from West Central Africa, as many historical accounts have had us believe.

The muster (census) of 1619 shows "32 Negroes" (seventeen women and fifteen men) "in the service of seu[er]all planters, in the begininge of March 1619."[2] This fact confirms that Virginia's leaders were not as detached from the transatlantic slave trade during the early seventeenth century as many scholars have claimed.[3] Instead of the colony's involvement with the international system of slavery having occurred slowly, in the latter decades of the seventeenth century, and in isolation from England and other European colonies and countries, the subsequent decision to purchase a second group of enslaved Africans (the "20. and odd Negroes") in August 1619 reveals that Virginia's leaders were indeed early adopters of slave trading, importing more than fifty Africans into Virginia in 1619, even though European indentured servants outnumbered enslaved Africans by a whopping ten to one margin during this period.[4] More important to the making of American Whiteness, the purchasing of two groups of enslaved Africans in 1619 shows Virginia's leaders' belief in their propriety, like their European counterparts, to enslave Black people.

Two letters—one by John Pory, secretary of state of the colony, written on September 30, 1619, from Jamestown to Sir Dudley Carleton, English envoy to The Hague, and the other by the aforementioned Rolfe to Sandys, dated January 20, 1620—evidence this sense of propriety in the reporting about the dealings between European nations and colonies that led to the acquisition of the "20. and odd Negroes." First, a look at Pory's letter; it reads as follows:

> Having mett with so fit a messenger as this man of warre of Flushing, I could not but imparte with your lordship . . . these poore fruites of our labours here. . . . The occasion of the ship's coming hither was an accidental consortship in the West Indies with the *Tresurer,* an English man of warre also, licensed by a Commission from the Duke of Savoye to take Spaniards as lawfull prize. This ship, the *Treasurer*, wente out of England in Aprill was twelve moneth, about a moneth, I thinke, before any peace was concluded between the king of Spaine and that prince. Hither she came to Captaine Argall, then governour of this Colony, being parte-owner of her. Hee more for the love of gaine, the root of all evill, then for any true love he bore to his Plantation, victualled and manned her anewe, and sent her with the same Commission to raunge the Indies.[5]

The letter by Pory to the English envoy reads more like a normal debrief-ing on the usual course of events that occurred between European allies and rivals while slave trading than what one would expect from an anomalous event. Nonetheless, at the most basic level, his reflections show Virginia leaders were members of a select group of White men around the world who were participants in the international system of slavery. But with regard to their sense of propriety from their membership, the letter illustrates a level of self-assurance of their place within this group of dignitaries and bureau-crats who were representing their governments in the international system of slavery.

For example, the letter outlines the extensive network of officials from European governments Virginia leaders directly or indirectly interacted with (a governor, duke, prince and a king) in the seizure of a Spanish vessel that we now know contained the infamous "20. and odd Negroes."[6] According to Pory, colonial governments in North America (Virginia and West Indies) cooperated with imperial governments in Western Europe (England, Spain and Italy) to directly or indirectly back an orchestrated attack (consortship) against the ship we now know was the *San Juan Bautista* by the English ship the *Treasurer* and a Dutch vessel that hailed from England's seaport in Flushing.[7] What Pory ironically called an "accidental consortship" shows that the raid of the *San Juan Bautista*, which led to the acquisition of the "20. and odd Negroes," was carried out with public and private sector support by individuals at the highest levels of European and colonial governments and institutions.[8] These coordinated actions by disparate European nations and their representatives demonstrate the institutionalized logic of public policy initiatives and commercial investments in the enslavement and commodifica-tion of African people. But, more importantly, it shows that globally as well as in Virginia, there was a presumption of White hegemony over African people. And the substance of these presumptions, which I will expound on in chapter 2, was resultant of a conception of one's Whiteness that was already manifested in everyday life.

Additional evidence in Pory's letter illustrating how the conception of Whiteness was a byproduct of Virginia settlers' confidence in their position in the international system of slavery is found in the guidance provided by government officials residing outside the colony who helped them secure enslaved Africans. For example, Pory's letter was written to the English ambassador, Sir Dudley Carleton. Addressing the letter to Carleton confirms that Virginia settlers had direct access to world leaders via the aegis of the English government. As mentioned, Carleton was the English envoy to The Hague, which at the time was the seat of the Dutch parliament, government and Royal Court, located in the Netherlands. Trade relations between the English and the Dutch had been previously forged over several decades of mutual cooperation. Thus, it would make sense that England would use Carleton to leverage its diplomatic relationship with the Dutch to help aspiring settlers bring enslaved Africans to Virginia.

For more than thirty years, between 1585 and 1616, the English and the Dutch were trading partners in a variety of ventures. So much was this so that in the sixteenth century, England maintained its primary seaport in Flushing, which was located in the Netherlands. During this time, the Dutch were challenging Portugal's monopoly of the slave trading routes in West Central Africa, including the all-important Kongo-Angola region, which supplied the majority of enslaved Africans to Virginia and the Americas through the first half of the seventeenth century. As a result, the Dutch would often invade Portuguese trading networks in an effort to procure African people for sale across the Atlantic.[9] The Dutch ship the *Margarett and John* that brought "Mary a Negro Woman" to Virginia in 1622 likely was a case of this type of invasion, which frequently took place between European nations vying for control of established slave trading routes that would provide captured and enslaved Africans, to Virginia specifically and the Americas in general, throughout the history of the transatlantic slave trade.[10] Thus, the long-standing relationship between the Dutch and the English made it likely that Virginia officials in 1619 enlisted the services of its English diplomat (Carleton) to prevail upon the Dutch to facilitate the acquisition of African people for enslavement. Such endeavors between European nations participating in the international system of slavery helped to solidify the idea of the propriety of White people to enslave Black people, an idea that was steeped into the collective conception of Whiteness as a racial and a hegemonic marker of superiority on a global scale, as well as in Virginia and, later, the United States of America, in ways that would define the expectations of White people into the twenty-first century.

Evidence that Whiteness was seen as both a racial and a hegemonic marker of superiority is likewise found in the aforementioned January 1620 letter Rolfe wrote to Sandys regarding the events that led to the acquisition of the "20. and odd Negroes" in late August 1619. This letter shows the cooperative, though sometimes contentious, battles Virginia had with England and other European nations involved in the international system of slavery. In his letter, Rolfe stated the following:

> About the later end of August, a Dutch man of Warr of the burden of a 160 tunnes arriued at Point-Comfort, the Commandors name Capt Jope, his Pilott for the West Indies one Mr. Marmaduke an Englishman. They mett with the *Trier* in the West Indyes, and determyned to hold consort shipp hetherward, but in their passage lost one the other. He brought not any thing but 20. and odd Negroes, which the Govenor and Cape Marchant bought for victualle (whereof he was in

greate need as he pretended) at the best and easyest rate they could. He hadd a lardge and ample Commyssion from his Excellency to range and to take purchase in the West Indyes. Three or 4. daies after the *Trier* arriued.[11]

If we read Rolfe's January 20, 1620, letter to Sandys in conjunction with Pory's September 30, 1619, letter, together they suggest that the events described by Pory were not just an attack of the Spanish vessel for its slaves. It also characterizes the extent of the geopolitical acceptance in White hegemony over Black people among the European officials who, in their various capacities, represented their government in the international system of slavery. For example, Rolfe in his aforementioned letter to prominent Virginia settler Edwin Sandys informs us that "his Excellency" provided ample funds to hire a captain and first mate to raid the Spanish vessel that led to the eventual purchase of "20. and odd Negroes" by Virginia's governor.[12] Pory's letter, on the other hand, was written to his ranking superior, Sir Dudley Carleton, the ambassador of England, Virginia's mother country. In his letter to Ambassador Carleton, Pory also referenced Samuel Argall, Virginia's governor from 1617–1619, who was part owner of the English ship the *Treasurer*, the vessel involved in the pirated attack.

Additional evidence in the letter that supports the belief in White hegemony over Black people by those Rolfe referenced lies in the depth and breadth of influential leaders in Virginia government who supported slave trading, as evidenced by their ongoing collaboration with other European colonies active in the trade. For example, Rolfe tells us that the governor and the colony's merchant purchased the "20. and odd Negroes" that were obtained from the raid after the ship had stopped in the West Indies.[13] The governor that Rolfe was referring to, however, was not Argall (the one mentioned in Pory's letter) but George Yeardley, who was the governor of Virginia from 1619 to 1621 while Argall was temporarily in England, likely discussing slavery, among other things, with English officials.[14] Yeardley and his friend Abraham Peirsey would purchase the twenty Africans.

In all, the letters show that two of Virginia's governors (Argall and Yeardley) and high-ranking English officials fully supported and backed the decision to bring enslaved Africans to the colony. The first purchase of "32 Negroes" in March 1619 and the subsequent pirated acquisition of the "20. and odd Negroes" in late August 1619 together suggest that Virginia's entrance into the still expanding transatlantic slave trade was not an "unthinking decision," especially since at the time they had such a disproportionate number of European laborers. Instead, it was a well thought out one that reveals the top-down and global cooperation between leaders in England, Europe and Virginia who were agents in the international system of slavery. Thus, to understand the development of American Whiteness, one first needs to understand that it did not develop in a vacuum but through a collective process of sanctioning, legitimization and support at the local level by influential leaders like Rolfe, Pory and Sandys and through concerted efforts of transnational cooperation and backing like what occurred between governments in England, Virginia, the West Indies, Spain and the Netherlands. And despite whatever conflict that occurred between them, European people with interests in the international system of slavery all were united on one matter: the targeting of Black people for enslavement. This collective agreement between this confederation of colleagues on the social position of Whites as the enslaver and Blacks as the slave is of singular importance to understanding the development and persistence of Whiteness across time and space because it demonstrates how White people conceived of themselves vis-à-vis Black people.[15] And these conceptions, as I show in subsequent chapters, informed the basis of Virginia's social structure.

The details of Rolfe's description of the raid likewise provides insight into the comfort with which Rolfe and Sandys were with the conception of Africans as slaves and how the ease with which he spoke about them as "not any thing" when referencing enslaved Africans shows an already fully developed cognition of his Whiteness and its perceived superiority over Blackness. His characterization of enslaved Africans is important not only for what it says about Rolfe's state of mind regarding enslaved Africans in relation to himself but also the general state of mind of the person to whom the letter was written.

As stated in the beginning of this chapter, Rolfe's January 1620 letter about the August 1619 acquisition of enslaved Africans was written to Edwin Sandys, architect and namesake of one of Virginia's most noted labor programs that imported three thousand five hundred English immigrants to Virginia between 1618 and 1622 to work on contract for set periods of time. Rolfe and Sandys were both powerful men who were early settlers in Virginia, Rolfe being famously known today for his marriage to Pocahontas. As such, Rolfe's letter was more informal and candid on the matter of the raid and how he saw the station of Africans relative to him and Sandys and, by extension, the European workers Sandys was responsible for recruiting to the colony. In all, such candor demonstrates that the racial precepts of White supremacy (and for that matter, anti-Blackness) that were inherent in the international system of slavery were firmly planted in Virginia as shown in the certainty evidenced between him and Sandys of their perceived superiority over the "cargo" of Black people he characterized as "not any thing."[16] Both letters, Rolfe's and Pory's, spoke of their measurement of African people as commodities who were subject (subjects and subjected) to the prerogatives of White men who bought and sold Black women, men and children for specific uses and comforts or for gratuitous reasons, intimate and imaginary, that I will detail in later chapters. Such feelings and conclusions about the propriety of one's subjectivity relative to others, in this case Blacks, were/are the ingredients and drivers of Whiteness.

And yet, let us not let the number of enslaved Africans imported to the colony during this period distract our analysis of the decision to enter into the business of enslaving Black people in the first place; both were mutually exclusive and interdependent variables in the making of American Whiteness. Looking back in history, we know, on the one hand, from slave trade data, that North America received the fewest number of imports of enslaved persons, roughly five hundred thousand of the nearly twelve to twenty million people, through the entire span of the transatlantic slave trade.[17] Moreover, on the other hand, large disparities between the number of European indentured servants and enslaved Africans would remain constant throughout the seventeenth century. Still, despite their small numbers, Virginia leaders spent an inordinate amount of time and energy using the powers of government to hold the social position of African people below European indentured servants and poor Whites, as demonstrated in the years leading up to the enactment of the 1705 law that made all Black people in bondage chattel.[18]

In the buildup to the 1705 law, Virginia leaders were constantly making new laws and moving the goalposts on existing governing policies to ensure White racial hegemony over Black people regardless of their class or station. A few examples that I will expound on in greater detail in later chapters include a law enacted in 1640 whereby all Blacks were excluded from the requirement of possessing firearms, one in 1667 that declared baptism would not bring freedom to any Blacks, and a law in 1670 that deemed lifetime servitude the "normal" condition for every Black person.[19] With all this in mind, the numerical imbalance between European indentured servants and bonded and enslaved Africans in 1619 is not dispositive of the impending dialectics of race, especially constructions of Whiteness as superior to Blackness, that would take shape and hold firm for centuries to come. Instead, the actions of Virginia settlers throughout the seventeenth century against the relatively small numbers of African people as compared to indentured Whites point to an embracing of their Whiteness that is illustrated in subsequent chapters in the unprecedented roles and uses White settlers would have enslaved Africans occupy and hold in Virginia society within the context of their social status. Contemporary examples of such inclinations are still seen in the American psyche today though media depictions and visual and consumer culture and more.

Nonetheless, to grow the colony in the manner they had hoped before, during and after deciding to cross the Atlantic and invest their time, talent and treasure in colonizing Virginia, White men began embracing the principles and unfolding possibilities inherent in the racially motivated enterprise that involved the capture and enslavement of untold millions of Black people caught in the international system of slavery that had existed since the fifteenth century. And doing so meant maintaining their standing and cultivating alliances with various European interests who they knew were experienced in slave trading.

The process involved in developing these relationships and gaining acceptance as colleagues in the international system of slavery gave rise to and indeed shaped the development of American Whiteness. Moreover, the results of the interlocking business relationships among European people in the international system of slavery would be exponentially valuable to England and Virginia, and by extension the United States. It would not only create a perpetual and self-generating system of wealth into the late nineteenth century and beyond based on enslaving and subjugating Black people rather than European indentured servants and poor Whites.[20] It would also create an expectation by Whites of proprietary privileges in any number of areas in everyday life, which, over time, has produced various degrees of racial inequality in American society, like the wealth gap, into the twenty-first century.[21]

As a colony of England, many Virginia settlers in the early decades of the seventeenth century already had a conception of their Whiteness before immigrating to the New World because of their knowledge of England's slave trading exploits,e documented in travel narratives that discussed Africans not as people but as a monolithic entity called "Negroes" who were being bought and sold by White men. And though the narratives were written decades before Virginia settlers arrived in the New World with data generated from sources like the aptly named English African Company, formed in 1536 for the purpose of exploring the possibilities of slave trading in the continent, they nonetheless document the early ideas of what White men thought of themselves relative to the whole of these so-called Negroes that England was invested in going after.[22]

Travel writings, like today, are the monied elite's way of communicating taste, culture and trends to the masses that often come into being as popular thought, sentiment, feelings and views. Not so ironically, after the formation of the English African Company, travel writers began publishing the records of swashbuckling men who reported on the prospects of Africans as slaves. Such records would go on to frame for the masses how European people should feel and think about African people. For example, Richard Hakluyt, prominent writer of English seafaring ventures from the Middle Ages to the late sixteenth century, took to publishing the slave prospecting accounts of men like John Hawkins and his pursuits in Spanish America (1562–1563, 1564 and 1567–1568), most of which were financed by wealthy London businessmen.[23] We learn from Hawkins's documents that "Negroes were very good merchandise in Hispaniola, and that a store of Negros might easily bee had upon the coast of Guinea."[24] What was noteworthy in his characterization was not just Hawkins's projections about the prospects for acquiring slaves or how thoroughly commodified African people as a group already were in the eyes of White men in the sixteenth century, all of which were important to the development of American Whiteness. What was noteworthy in his statement is the way in which his pronouncement defines for the masses the objective relation between White men like him and the "very good merchandise" of "Negroes" he was reporting on. It is this sort of "transcendent characterization" of the subordinate social position of Black people, in this case as slaves, that sets the collective image of Whiteness and anti-Blackness across time and space.[25]

Like Hawkins, Edward Lopes, a Portuguese merchant who traveled to Angola in 1578 prospecting for Africans to enslave, also reinforced the characterization of African people as slaves and Europeans as masters when he wrote the following report about his slave prospecting enterprises: "Besides, there is also a greater Trafficke and Market for slaves, that are brought out of Angola, then any place else. For there are yearely bought by the Portugais above five thousand head of Negroes, which afterwards they conveigh away with them, and so sell them to divers parts of the World."[26]

On the surface, the accounts of both Hawkins and Lopes seem primarily concerned with simply reporting on the prospects for transatlantic slave trading in West Central Africa, which ultimately netted nearly a half million Blacks who left the continent as enslaved commodities headed toward the Americas.[27] But a deeper look into these passages reveals critical insight into the early history of the assumptions of White men about Black people and the common view that African peoples as a group were mere objects to be used for their personal and collective benefit, calling into question the generally accepted view that labor was the main reason that White people chose to enslave Black people.[28] In fact, by showing the historical links between European ideas about prosperity and the commodification of Black people to the growth of the transatlantic slave trade long before settlement in the New World in 1607, Hawkins's and Lopes's reports lay bare slavery (and for that matter, anti-Blackness) as the fundamental object through which expectation as Whiteness rests. And the public investment in slave trading at the founding of the English African Company in 1536 provides the context by which the choice of Whiteness was made inevitable for those choosing to settle in Virginia.

England's public investment in slave trading signaled to the slave trading world that it intended to be a major player in the international system of slavery. Equally, it also publicly communicated to English people a mandate for how they should think and feel about African people. Thus, the founding

of the English African Company in 1536 amounts to a government-backed
endorsement of the objectification of African people. This sanctioning
derived its social, political and economic coherence in the travel writings of
aspiring slave traders that ultimately stimulated the thinking of the masses of
White people. And yet, the important intervention that we are to take from the
founding of the English African Company in 1536 is that it establishes a pole
point in European people's stream of consciousness showing that they saw
African peoples as slaves and Europeans as masters over them long before
European settlement in the New World. This view was circulated globally by
European governments throughout the sixteenth century and was reinforced
nationally in the reports of slave traders active in the international system
of slavery.

Such examples are found in the writings of Englishmen like Master Thomas
Turner, who lived in Brazil but traveled to the West Central African country
of Angola to explore the market for Black people to enslave. In writing about
the potential for slave trading in the area being even more favorable than what
Lopes had reported, Turner in 1578 likewise illustrates the prevailing view
of White men as masters and Black people as slaves. According to Turner:

> Out of Angola that is said to bee yeerely shipped eight and twenty thousand
> slaves and there was a Rebellion of slaves against their Masters, tenne thousand
> making a head and barracadoing themselves, but by the Portugals and Indians
> chased, and one or two thousand reduced. One thousand belonged to one man,
> who is said to have tenne thousand slaves, Eighteene Ingenios, etc. his name is
> John de Paus, exiled out of Portugall, and heere prospering to this incredibilitie
> of wealth.[29]

As a result of Turner's writings other English merchants with designs on being
slave masters traveled to the Angola region to secure enslaved Africans. One
such merchant, Andrew Battell, traveled to the Angolan city of Benguela in
1589 to look for Black people to enslave.[30] Battell's account was giddy with
excitement about the prospects for African slaves when he wrote: "we laded
our ship with slaves in seven days, and bought them so cheap that they did
not cost one real, which were worth in the city of Loando twelve milreis."[31]

Battell's communication to English officials about the future of slave
trading in Angola expands our understanding of English participation in
the unfolding transatlantic trade prior to New World settlement. But more
importantly, the reports of Battell, Hawkins, Lopes and Turner historicizes
the characteristic of propriety found in American Whiteness that was held
by European men around the world who bet their future prosperity on the
enslavement and subjugation of African people, bets that would presage the
colonization schemes for the New World. That said, such speculations also

lay bare important feelings Whites had about the positional arrangement between Whites and Blacks in societies around the world, since the transatlantic slave trade that began in the fifteenth century would come to shape the social and racial structure of the New World. For centuries, this context would undergird American Whiteness.

The slave trading chronicles of men like Hawkins, Lopes, Turner and Battell and their message about the positional arrangement of Whites over Blacks was surely top-of-mind of the men who would colonize Virginia. So much so that some of the same men who helped colonize Virginia in 1607 also colonized Bermuda in 1609.[32] And, specific to the making of American Whiteness, these men were also responsible for bringing enslaved Africans to both colonies, Bermuda in 1616 and Virginia in 1619.[33] In fact, Bermuda was reported to have received the first imports of enslaved persons into North America in 1616. The record described those persons as an "Indian and a Negro."[34] Moreover, the aforementioned "20. and odd Negroes" were part of a larger shipment of enslaved persons who were divided between Bermuda and Virginia.[35] John Rolfe, the man mentioned at the beginning of this chapter as having written a letter to Edwin Sandys explaining how the "20. and odd Negroes" ended up in Virginia, not only participated in their capture but also had a hand in dividing the entire cargo of these Africans between the two English colonies. Rolfe's involvement in this venture makes sense given that he, like Sandys, was also one of the Virginia settlers who helped colonize Bermuda.[36]

The importation of enslaved Africans to Bermuda and Virginia so early in each colony's existence demonstrates European settlers had indeed internalized the message England inherited from the international system of slavery at the formation of the English African Company: that African people were slaves and White men were masters. Thus, both colonies were established with a full understanding of a belief in European superiority over African people.

This was likely the thinking of Daniel Tucker, who was the governor of Bermuda in 1616 and a resident of Virginia between 1608 and 1614, and the then governor of Virginia, Thomas Dale. As leaders of England's only North American colonies at the time, Tucker and Dale had to have worked together for Black enslavement to have subsequently appeared so early in each colony's history. Moreover, cooperation and alliance between Tucker and Dale was necessary to not only speed the growth and development of the areas, but more importantly to the making of American Whiteness, for communicating the social and racial hierarchy of both colonies to the resident settlers.

Thus, when Daniel Elfrith, the captain of the ship that delivered the "20. and odd Negroes" to Virginia in 1619 was also involved in bringing other enslaved Africans to Bermuda, we know that Tucker and Dale were successful in establishing a social and racial order of White over Black in the colonies during their administrations. For example, in 1618, a year before Elfrith brought the cache of twenty or so enslaved persons who were split between Virginia and Bermuda, Elfrith also had transported twenty-nine enslaved Africans to Bermuda, selling some to colony residents and some to the Earl of Warwick, England, Robert Rich.[37] So, whether enslaved persons were disembarking in Virginia or Bermuda or whether the two colonies split cargos containing enslaved persons, it is clear that colonial officials intended to establish the social structure of both colonies with the African slave as an important feature of the social order.[38]

Prominent leaders in Virginia, like Governor Thomas Gates, Secretary of State William Strachey and the aforementioned Edwin Sandys, who were responsible for the induction of African slavery into the colony regularly traveled between Virginia and Bermuda during the first few decades of its existence. In doing so, these men used their authority and power and their self-interest in African enslavement, as I will show in chapter 2, to organize the social structure of Virginia with White supremacy as the central feature that ordered European peoples relations with Africans and Native peoples. Part of that process included reproducing programs of subjugation that were used in the international system of slavery to structure their communities.

To be clear, Virginia's and Bermuda's leaders' overall knowledge of how to organize a society with enslaved Africans was ultimately grounded in the racial precepts that governed the international system of slavery but with a particularity that flowed from the pronouncements of the English African Company and reinforced in daily life from messages that were discussed in slave trading publications and accounts of European men active in the trade. Thus, the intercolonial slave trading ties that connected Bermuda and Virginia to England and to the international system of slavery demonstrate that colonial officials could approach their colonization plans with a presumption of racial hegemony over Black people in mind, which, as I show in subsequent chapters, was the driver of their economic messaging just like it was for their European counterparts nearly a century before them. That said, the intercolonial and emigrant history of Virginians and Bermudians in the New World puts to rest the notion that slavery had not been thought about in the initial settlement of English colonies.[39]

At a critical moment in England's colonization of parts of North America, some of its earliest maritime voyages were transatlantic slave trading voyages. Both Bermuda and Virginia embraced the tradition of transatlantic slave trading intending to create a White utopia with the African slave as the central feature of its social organization and economic structure. In doing so, Virginia and Bermuda expanded the trade routes of the international system of slavery, which began along the coast of West Africa, to their regions. These routes ushered into English colonies the then centuries old (but deeply transcendent for Black people and White people), deadly and inhumane experience known as the Middle Passage.

The voyage we call the Middle Passage began after slave ships were packed with a startling number of African women, men and children, upward of seven hundred persons, in individual spaces no bigger than a coffin.[40] The journey from Africa to the New World usually included a layover in the West Indies before arriving in Bermuda and/or Virginia. The overseas travel and intercolonial communication that connected England and its colonies into the broadening international system of slavery indeed occurred very early in their colonizing heritage and was done with little thought of the inhumanity of the project because successful efforts of the English African Company and travel writers projecting Black people as mere objects of commodity to be bought and sold by White men had already been firmly established in the minds of European immigrants long before their arrival in the New World.

Underlying the so-called Middle Passage was a system that historians quaintly call the Triangle Trade, which brought slaves and other commodities besides humans from Africa to Europe and the Americas. Instead of a system of mutual exchange and benefit between African and European leaders, this so-called trade program was more accurately an economic and structural system of branding and conditioning the view of Black people as slaves and Europeans as citizens, which ultimately was central to advancing the pace of European colonization of the Americas and the attendant ideas about race for centuries to come.[41] And while the horrors of Middle Passage turned Europe into a superpower and European men into masters, significant to the making of American Whiteness, it was also turning African people, in the minds of the White masses in the New World, into permanent slaves. With this in mind, the Middle Passage is a through-line that helps explain the historical contours of the racial and social structure of New World colonization schemes and colonial settlements, which was established with a transatlantic culture of White propriety over African people, propriety that had existed on a global scale since European contact with the continent of Africa and with African peoples. Such proprietary claims to resources and commodities, including humans, was/are the stuff of American Whiteness.

Another important influence besides the Middle Passage and the Triangle Trade that communicated the message of White supremacy and propriety over Africa and African people to the masses of Europeans were churches. Like it was with the formation of the English African Company, pronouncements from European churches about the backwardness of African people characterized for the populous the view that relative to Whites, Black people were of a lower human order and a lower social position. For example, by the first half of the sixteenth century, Portuguese explorers had a long-standing tradition of depicting African ethnic groups as heathens in need of Christianizing—an image that was emulated by the English in the latter half of the period. In fact, almost from the beginning of Portuguese contact with African peoples, the discourse of conversion to Christianity was often communicated in the same breath as the message of Black enslavement. So much so that priests were often a part of slave trading delegations. Not so ironically, many Portuguese officials believed or at least rationalized that Christianity sanctioned European men to enslave African people in an effort to "save" them from their backwardness.

In 1520, for instance, a Portuguese authority surmised that once African rulers and their courts had been converted to Christianity, the process of "redemption" would be manageable; redemption in this case turned out to be another word for "saving" via enslavement.[42] Also during this period, a Portuguese priest theorized that "converting the heathens would give them the opportunity to lead a Christian life as slaves in a country far removed from the temptations from their old environment."[43] Forty-three years later, in 1563, Father Gouveia, a Portuguese Jesuit missionary, indicated that "the only way seriously to convert a 'heathen' people to Christianity was by subjecting them to colonial rule," also a euphemism for enslavement and White supremacy during this time when used by Europeans in this part of the world.[44]

England's rivalry with Portugal over slave trading territories in West Central Africa during this period led English advisors to the queen to incorporate similar ideas about the use of Christianity to facilitate enslavement in their pre-colonization rationale. For instance, Sir George Peckham, a prominent English merchant and adventurer, wrote a lengthy treatise in 1583, called *The Advantages of Colonization*, to advise Queen Elizabeth I on colonial ventures. In it, he outlined three doctrines for England to follow in order to lay claim to the New World—the "Laws of Nations," the "Laws of Arms," and the "Laws of God." The "Laws of Nations" sanctioned trade between Christians and "Infidels or Savages"; the "Laws of Arms" allowed the taking of foreign lands by force; and the "Laws of God" enjoined Christian rulers to settle those lands "for the establishment of God's worde."[45]

These three doctrines, outlined in *The Advantages of Colonization*, were the ideological principles that guided England's ambitions for Virginia that included the taking of Native lands, the elimination of Native peoples and the exploitation of African people. But significant to the making of American Whiteness, it also provided the psychological distance for Whites to enslave African people and massacre Native people without guilt.[46] Thus, based on these three principles, which according to Peckham had been in effect from ancient times to "the nativitie of Christ," he advised the queen to "plant, possesse, and subdue."[47] Here Peckham used the term "plant" to suggest the establishment of a White colony in a foreign land.[48]

Like Peckham, John Dee, astrologer, alchemist and mathematician, also advised the queen on colonial ventures. He too drew on the successes of Portugal in the international system of slavery in West Africa and the Americas to frame his advice to the queen. Dee advocated the building of a strong navy in order to take possession of "foreyn regions" and to do as "other Christian Princes do now adayes make Conquests upon the heathen people."[49] But, it was the aforementioned Richard Hakluyt, the foremost proponent of colonization of his age, who best articulated England's justification for colonization that would lay the foundation for England's expansion in North America, including its participation in the growing transatlantic slave trade. In 1582, Hakluyt wrote that planting English colonies in America would be a "moste godly and Christian work" that would ultimately lead to "gayn-inge . . . the soules of millions of those wretched people" bringing "them from darknes to lighte."[50]

The writings of Peckham, Dee and Hakluyt show Christianity as an ideological link between Old World and New World colonizers in the international system of slavery. Likewise, these accounts are useful to our understanding of the development of American Whiteness as a derivative of White settlers' connecting Christian doctrine to the principles of colonialism and expansionism (the bedrock and drivers of the international system of slavery) and using both to justify Black enslavement and the theft of indigenous lands. Out of these calculations, White Virginia settlers would use this ideology to enact laws and policies adapted from the international system of slavery to organize and structure their communities around a system of White supremacy.

The ideological underpinnings of English explorers who settled in Virginia provide crucial context for understanding the depths of their Whiteness. Few accounts give us a direct statement of these leaders' perceptions of their Whiteness. Nevertheless, it is still possible to see its development from the actions and activities of those who were the most subjected to and who were the subjects of the gratuitous nature of American Whiteness: African people. One of those early Africans who provides unique insights into Black peoples understanding of American Whiteness, while also illuminating aspects of daily life in Virginia during this period, was a woman named Elizabeth Key.

Elizabeth Key was an African-Anglo woman, born in 1630 in Virginia to an enslaved African woman and a free English man. In 1655, Key sued for her freedom and that of her son in a court in Northumberland County, Virginia. After lengthy legal proceedings, on July 21, 1659, she prevailed. Key's freedom strategy rested on a claim of Englishness and Christianity, revealing crucial evidence that these terms where a common nomenclature for freedom that were understood by both English and African people in Virginia. That said, by declaring the social meaning of freedom for her and

her child in terms of Christianity and Englishness, we see the markers of
Whiteness that were already in effect in the mid-seventeenth century.

Elizabeth Key's legal suit entered the historical record at a critical moment
in the history of the burgeoning transatlantic slave trade. By 1659, when her
suit was settled, Virginia's participation in the transatlantic slave trade, as it
was for nearly all the colonies in the Americas, was on the verge of explod-
ing. Prior to her suit, just over three hundred fifty enslaved Africans were
imported to Virginia. After her suit, from 1661 to the turn of the century,
nearly six thousand enslaved Africans disembarked in Virginia. And although
we have no way of knowing the exact birthplaces of these persons, we know
that in the first half of the seventeenth century the port in Luanda located in
the Kongo/Angola region of West Central Africa exported the largest number
of slaves to the Americas, while in the second half of the century it was the
Bight of Benin on the western coast of Africa.[51]

From 1601 to 1650, the port in Luanda sent a little more than one hundred
seven thousand enslaved persons from the region to the Americas, and just
over nine thousand embarked from various ports in the Bight of Benin.[52]
During the period from 1651 to 1700, the Bight of Benin supplanted Luanda
as the largest exporter of enslaved Africans to the Americas, sending just
over one hundred twenty thousand slaves to the area compared with the thirty
thousand Luanda sent.[53] The expansion in the procurement of slaves outside
of Luanda in the latter part of the seventeenth century was a response to the
phenomenal growth in plantation slavery in the Americas. Thus, the increase
in the importation of enslaved Africans to North America, including Virginia,
resulted in a concomitant increase in slave exports out of West Africa. In
other words, while African countries were being severely depopulated as a
result of the demand for Black slaves in the Americas, Virginia was increasing the number of enslaved persons it was taking in, clearly situating Virginia
within the growing international system of slavery that included Africa, the
Americas, Western Europe and the Islamic world.[54]

It was during this time that Virginia legislators began to enact a number of
laws that ensured that African women and their children, like Key and her son,
as well as African men, would remain in bondage for life, making Elizabeth
Key's freedom suit all the more important to deciphering the markers of
American Whiteness in Virginia society.[55] Yet, long before Key's freedom
suit in 1659, as Rolfe and Pory's aforementioned letters show, the origins of
American Whiteness was set decades before these men's actions facilitated
the capture and enslavement of Africans in Virginia in 1619. An important
part of that process included the English coming to see their Whiteness as
conterminous with their regard of the term "Negro" to reference Africanness.

Thus, it should come as no surprise that Whites in Virginians would use the
word "Negro" in 1619 to describe the first two groups of *enslaved* Africans

to arrive in the colony. For example, the March 1619 census describes "32 Negroes" (seventeen women and fifteen men) "in the service of seu[er]all planters."[56] And in August of 1619, as discussed earlier in this chapter, John Rolfe famously spoke about the cargo abroad the ship the *Treasurer* as including "not any thing but 20. and odd Negroes."[57] Additionally, all the twenty-three West African people (all of whom were likely enslaved) listed in Virginia's 1624 census had "Negro" before or after their names. In fact, from this group, eight had just the term "Negro" and the person's gender next to their entry, seven had only the word "Negro" documenting their existence, three had their first name and the label "Negro" for their record, and three others had a combination of the person's first name, gender and the term "Negro."[58] The word was so ubiquitous to Whites in its association of African ancestry and with bondage that in 1659 a Virginia farmer named his cow "Negar Nose."[59]

The term "Negro" links the century long exploits of slave trading that Virginia leaders tapped into for all kinds of reasons, corrupt or otherwise, to the international system of slavery and clarifies that these men thought of themselves as naturally free and Africans as slaves. This juxtaposition of seeing persons of African descent as "Negro" and thereby subordinate to European peoples was key to understanding the development and maintenance of American Whiteness, ideas that were supported at the highest level of European and colonial government and institutions that legitimized and sanctioned this notion through their backing of slave trading ventures.

Likewise, the reports by men like the aforementioned Hawkins, Lopes, Turner and Battell reveal the extent to which the word "Negro" and "slave" were mutually constitutive terms used by Europeans to rationalize not only African enslavement but also the message of African people being of a lower order of human beings relative to Whites. Thus, the use of the word "Negro" to reference African peoples was perhaps the most potent evidence connecting Virginia to the international system of slavery, a word that has traveled across time and space deep into the middle of the twentieth century to characterize the lower social position of Blacks relative to Whites. Yet, the international system of slavery cannot be made to fully account for the totality of European thinking regarding African people, nor can slavery solely be used to define the personhood of African groups caught in this exploitive system. African people (and Native groups) had flourishing cultures, governments and social systems in their countries prior to contact with Europeans. And although we have very little to document the worldview of the thirty-two Blacks listed in the March 1619 Virginia census or the "20. and odd Negros" who arrived in Virginia in August 1619, we know that most came to the New World from out of the port of Luanda in West Central Africa, as did most of the roughly three hundred fifty African people in Virginia through 1640.[60]

An important but often misunderstood element of many West African societies during this time was slavery. Instead of the American form of slavery
that we know about, indigenous forms of slavery were a central feature in
many if not most African societies over the past millennium. In Luanda, for
example, during the period under discussion, slavery in the form of pawnage,
concubinage and chattel bondage was a regular element in the social organization of many communities and families. Yet, what distinguished African
"slavery" in the continent during this time from the enslavement of Africans
by Europeans in the New World was that the so-called slaves in African
countries, except those who were war captives, were integral parts of African
social groups and thoroughly incorporated as important members of their
societies. And although war captives were traded or sold to outsiders, and/or
used as collateral, other slaves in the society were part of the family, albeit of
a lower station than a person with biological ties to the group. As such, slave
exports from Africa initially were comprised of war captives who, over time,
became objects of war making for the purposes of acquiring slaves to sell
to Europeans. Consequently, the external demand for slaves resulted in the
emergence of slave societies in West African communities where previously
there had only been a few slaves (as we understand the term in the United
States).[61]

For example, slave exports from Africa rose gradually during the first one
hundred fifty years of the Atlantic trade, amounting to about four hundred
nine slaves from 1450 to 1600.[62] From 1601 to 1700 the slave trade was very
large, approximately one and a half million peoples.[63] The world appetite for
slaves during this period helped to push the indigenous forms of slavery in
Africa further away from a social framework in which slavery was another
form of dependency to a system in which slaves played an increasingly
important role in the economy.[64] Similarly, the demand for slaves in Virginia
as well as in some of England's other North American colonies resulted
in their transformation from a society with a few slaves to slave societies.
Colonial leaders, already aware of these indigenous forms of slavery in
African countries from their knowledge of the interworkings of the international system of slavery, increasingly exploited it to their advantage. Thus,
Virginia's demand for slaves contributed in some measure to the population
declines that ultimately weakened African countries more so than what had
been recognized by many historians of Africa and the Americas.[65] But more
importantly, it establishes that colonial leaders in Virginia utilized the tools
and techniques of exploitation taken from the international system of slavery
early in the colony's development, which allows us to see and understand the
making of American Whiteness.

The letters of Rolfe and Pory challenge the notion of Virginia exceptional-
ism—that slavery in Virginia developed independently from the international

world without influence from England or English colonies, and that slavery and racism were rare or nonexistent before the legislation of the 1660s and 1670s.[66] The letters of Rolfe and Pory confirm that the route to Virginia that these early Africans traveled was made up of a developed and still growing international network of European countries and their colonies that had traded in slaves in West Central Africa since the fifteenth century. Thus, Virginia had integrated into the international network of slavery in the very early decades of the seventeenth century rather than the later decades, and in higher numbers than what was initially believed. And this makes perfect sense, given Virginia's imperial heritage as an English colony—England was trading in slaves in the early sixteenth century, long before Virginia's settlement in 1607. Thus, the transnational governmental support used to acquire enslaved Africans dispels the myth of Virginia as an accidental enslaver. The choice these men made to join the allied nations of Europe in the international system of slavery and procure enslaved Africans to advance the progress of their colony is at the heart of American Whiteness. The assumptions involved in this clear-thinking decision provide a window into the minds of White men and how they thought of themselves as well as their thoughts about African people.

European colonizers in West Central Africa between 1600 and 1800 developed a complex network of routes, towns, ports and fortified castles that enabled the subjugation and export of a startling number of enslaved people. Similarly, from its founding in 1607, Virginia leaders organized the colony so that the plantation, the church and the judicial system overlapped to better govern the daily lives of colonial residents. One must ask in what ways was the plantation system of governance in Virginia characteristic of the slave routes and networks that existed in the international system of slavery and how, in the span of twelve years between 1607 and 1619, was the same landscape through which White Virginia servants and planters traveled (plantation, church and courthouses) experienced by African people like Key and her son? Finally, given that the slave castles of West Central Africa and the plantation systems of Virginia were both built by European indentured servants and workers as well as Africans of various degrees of freedom, all overseen by European leaders working for colonial governments to maintain dominance over large groups of people, how can we recognize the agency of Virginia's early African residents within such a regulated milieu—their resistance and their manipulation of the very landscapes designed to restrict them as a keen understanding by them of American Whiteness? Through the eyes of enslaved Africans, we learn American Whiteness from the relationship between Virginia's built environment and the percolating international system of slavery.

NOTES

1. I define the international system of slavery as the technologies of oppression and enslavement used by Europeans in the transatlantic slave trade. Among them were six key elements that overlap in various ways with other systems of domination such as colonialism and imperialism. The six key elements discussed in this dissertation as they relate to Virginia's growth and development includes: religious intolerance and persecution, territorial expansion, colonial settlement, arrogant imposition on colonial and indigenous peoples, theological justification for enslavement, and racial exclusion. Aspects of this analysis was informed by the work of Blackburn, *The Making of New World Slavery: From the Baroque to the Modern, 1492–1800*, 10–18, 33; Paul E. Lovejoy, *Transformations in Slavery: A History of Slavery in Africa, Second Edition* (Cambridge, UK: Cambridge University Press, 2000); and Walter Rodney, *How Europe Underdeveloped Africa* (Washington, D.C.: Howard University Press, 1982).

2. The March 1619 census is contained in Ferrar Papers, MS 1597A, document 159 on microfilm reel 1. It is also reprinted in William Thorndale, "The Virginia Census of 1619," *Magazine of Virginia Genealogy* 33 (1995): 168–70.

3. Many scholars have claimed that Virginia's leaders were slow to participate in the transatlantic slave trade in the first half of the seventeenth century because the colony possessed a relatively dependable supply of European immigrant labor to sustain tobacco plantations. Notable among these are: Edmund S. Morgan, *American Slavery, American Freedom* (New York: W. W. Norton & Company, 1975), 296–300; T. H. Breen and Stephen Innes, *"Myne Owne Ground": Race and Freedom on Virginia's Eastern Shore, 1640–1676* (New York: Oxford University Press, 1980), 4–5; Jordan, *White over Black: American Attitudes toward the Negro, 1550–1812*, 56, 72–73. My research shows that we should not take the small number of enslaved African imports as evidence of a lack of influence of the transatlantic slave trade or its technologies of oppression on Virginia society or its settlers.

4. The March 1619 census is contained in Ferrar Papers, MS 1597A, document 159 on microfilm reel 1. It is also reprinted in Thorndale, "The Virginia Census of 1619," 168–70. The census indicates that the European population at that date was around nine hundred twenty-eight. Other manuscripts in the Ferrar collection give census data through June 1619 that suggest the population was one thousand one hundred ninety-four.

5. "Letter of John Pory, 1619," in John Smith's *The Generall Historie of Virginia, Newe England, and the summer Isless . . .* (London, 1624).

6. There is convincing evidence to suggest that the Spanish vessel was the *San Juan Bautista,* which had three hundred-fifty enslaved "Loanda" Africans aboard, of which approximately two hundred were pirated by the English. The "20. and odd Negroes" are believed to be part of this cargo. Scholars that hold this belief include: Engel Sluiter, "New Light on the '20. And Odd Negroes' Arriving in Virginia, August 1619," *William and Mary Quarterly* 54, Third Series, no. 2 (April 1997): 395–98, and Tim Hashaw, *The Birth of Black America the First African Americans and the Pursuit of Freedom at Jamestown* (New York: Carroll & Graf Publishers, 2007), xvi. These

scholars cite evidence from "Indiferente General 2795," Archivo General de Indias (AGI), Sevilla, in support of their claim.

7. Flushing was an English seaport in the Netherlands. Beginning in the the sixteenth century it was one of the chief ports for English traffic in the Netherlands.

8. A Consortship is a temporary agreement to cooperate. In this case, it was a temporary agreement to cooperate in pirating the Spanish vessel and sharing the loot. It is believed that this vessel in consortship with the *Treasurer* was a ship called the *White Lion*. For information on the *White Lion* see Hashaw, *The Birth of Black America the First African Americans and the Pursuit of Freedom at Jamestown.*

9. In 1641, the Dutch won temporary control of Portuguese trading routes.

10. Jester, *Adventures of Purse and Person, 1607–1625*, 46.

11. Rolfe's letter to Sandys, Jan. 1619/1620, in Susan Myra Kingsbury, ed., *The Records of the Virginia Company of London*, vol. 3 (Washington, D.C.: Government Printing Office, 1906, 1933), 243.

12. According to the *Oxford Dictionary* (London: Oxford University Press, 2011), the term "his Excellency" is a mid-sixteenth century title given to certain high officials of state.

13. The merchant that Rolfe was referencing was Abraham Peirsey.

14. Yeardley was also governor from 1616 to 1617.

15. Herbert Blumer, "Race Prejudice as a Sense of Group Position," in *Race Relations: Problems and Theory*, eds. Jutsuichi Masuoka and Preston Valien (Chapel Hill: University of North Carolina Press, 1958), 219. I build upon the idea of Whiteness from Blumer's analysis of the formation of racial prejudice.

16. I draw on Frank B. Wilderson III's notions of anti-Blackness as the antithesis of European constructions of what is human in civilized societies as discussed in his texts, *Red, White, & Black: Cinemas and the Structure of U.S. Antagonisms* (Durham, NC: Duke University Press, 2010) and *Afropessimism* (Liveright, 2020).

17. Ivana Elbl, "The Volume of Early Atlantic Slave Trade, 1450–1521," *Journal of African History* 38 (1997): 75. Other sources that estimate the numbers of captured and enslaved African people who were victims of the transatlantic slave trade include: Philip D. Curtin, *The Atlantic Slave Trade: A Census* (Madison: University of Wisconsin Press, 1969) and David Eltis, *The Rise of African Slavery in the Americas* (New York: Cambridge University Press, 2000).

18. William Waller Hening, ed., *The Statutes at Large; Being a Collection of All the Laws of Virginia, from the First Session of the Legislature in the Year 1619*, 13 vols. (New York: R. & W. & G. Bartow, 1823), III: 447–62. The Virginia Slave Codes of 1705 were a series of laws enacted by the Colony of Virginia's House of Burgesses regulating activities relating to interactions between enslaved persons and European settlers. The enactment of the slave codes is considered to be the consolidation of slavery in Virginia and served as the foundation of Virginia's slave legislation. For a list of the codes see ibid., II: 481.

19. Ibid.

20. Robinson, *Black Marxism: The Making of the Black Radical Tradition.*

21. Blumer, "Race Prejudice as a Sense of Group Position," 219–20.

22. Elizabeth Donnan, *Documents Illustrative of the History of the Slave Trade to America*, vol. I (New York: Octagon Books, Inc., 1965), 8.

23. April Lee Hatfield, "The Atlantic World and the Development of Slavery in Seventeenth-Century Virginia," (University of Oregon, 1992), 10.

24. Richard Hakluyt, *Principal Navigations of the English Nation* (London: J. M. Dent and Co., 1600), XI: 23.

25. Blumer, "Race Prejudice as a Sense of Group Position," 224–25. According to Blumer, transcendent characterizations, rather than close personal interactions, inform how the masses come to define groups that are subject of racial prejudice. Moreover, it is also how the dominant group comes to think about the group about whom they are prejudiced against.

26. "A Report of the Kingdome of Congo, a Region of Affrica: gathered by Phillippo Pigafetta, out of the Discourses of Master Edwar Lopes" in Samuel Purchas, *Hakluytus Posthumus or Purchas: His Pilgrimes* (Glasgow, 1905), VI: 444–45.

27. Elbl, "The Volume of Early Atlantic Slave Trade, 1450–1521," 75.

28. Authors who take this position include: Morgan, *American Slavery, American Freedom: The Ordeal of Colonial Virginia*, G. J. Heuman and James Walvin, eds., *The Slavery Reader* (Routledge, 2003), 5.

29. "Relations of Master Thomas Turner," in Samuel Purchas, *Hakluytus Posthumus or Purchas: his Pilgrimes* (Glasgow, 1905), XVI: 291.

30. *The Strange Adventures of Andrew Battell of Leigh, in Angola and the adjoining Regions*, in Purchas, *Pilgrimes*, VI: 367–406, and reprinted in Hakluyt Society Publications, second ser., vol. VI.

31. Ibid.

32. Michael Joseph Jarvis, "In the Eye of All Trade: Maritime Revolution and the Transformation of Bermudian Society, 1618–1800" (The College of William and Mary, 1998), 19.

33. Ibid., 16. The vessel *Sea Venture* was bound for Virginia with supplies when it sank in Bermuda, an event that led to the island's settlement and colonization.

34. Nathaniel Butler, "The Historye of the Bermudaes, " ed. Sir J. H. Lefroy (London: 1882), 78, 84–85. According to Michael Jarvis, "In the Eye of All Trade," 150, there were seventy-five or more enslaved Africans that were imported to Bermuda before 1620, including a few women and their children.

35. Ibid., 147. Also see Rolfe's letter to Sandys, Jan. 1619/1620, in Susan Myra Kingsbury, ed., *The Records of the Virginia Company of London*, vol. 3 (Washington, D.C.: Government Printing Office, 1933), 243.

36. Jarvis, "In the Eye of All Trade: Maritime Revolution and the Transformation of Bermudian Society, 1618–1800," 19.

37. Edward Athen, "Ives Rich Paper," 141.

38. Orlando Patterson, *Slavery and Social Death: A Comparative Study* (Cambridge: Harvard University Press, 1982). Patterson's idea of the "slave" as a form of social death allows us to consider the ways in which Black bodies were constructed during the transatlantic slave trade, which Frank B. Wilderson III represents as "coterminous of slaveness." Frank B. Wilderson III, "Social Death and Narrative Aporia in 12 Years a Slave," *Black Camera* 7, no. 1 (Fall 2015): 139.

39. The early slave trading history of Bermuda, as well as the exchange of enslaved persons between Bermuda and Virginia, challenges the interpretation of Winthrop Jordan, who claimed that "at the start of English settlement in America, no one had in mind to establish the institution of Negro slavery." Jordan, *White over Black: American Attitudes toward the Negro, 1550–1812*, 44.

40. David Birmingham, *Trade and Conflict in Angola: The Mbundu and Their Neighbours under the Influence of the Portuguese 1483–1790* (Oxford: Clarendon Press, 1966), 32.

41. Wilderson III. Here I draw on Wilderson's analysis of Blackness as "coterminous of slaveness," 139.

42. Birmingham, *Trade and Conflict in Angola: The Mbundu and Their Neighbours under the Influence of the Portuguese 1483–1790*, 30.

43. Ibid.

44. Report on Angola drawn from the letters of Father Gouveia and Paula Dias de Novais, BNL, FG, MS. 8123 cited in Ruela Pombo, *Angola Menina* (Lisbon, 1944).

45. Hart, *Era of Colonization, 1492–1689*, 1586.

46. James Baldwin, "The White Problem," in *One Hundred Years of Emancipation*, ed. Robert A. Goodwin (University of Chicago: The Public Affairs Conference Center, 1964). I draw on Baldwin and his ruminations in 1964 about the rationalization that White men came up with to ease their Christian conscience about enslaving African people.

47. David B. Quinn, *Explorers and Colonies: America, 1500–1625* (London: Hambledon Press, 1990), 207–23.

48. The term "plant" in this context was a program of social control in which colonizers attempted to gain control of land from indigenous populations. In this case, it was English leaders gaining control of land occupied by Native Americans. Plantations were the actual settlements where European immigrant labor was co-opted to assist in the colonization processes. For a history of this concept, see Theodore W. Allen, *The Invention of the White Race: Racial Oppression and Social Control*, 2 vols., vol. I (New York: Verso, 1994), 58–60, 65–70.

49. Peter J. French, *John Dee: The World of an Elizabethan Magus* (London: Routledge, 1972), 178–99.

50. Richard Hakluyt, *Divers Voyages Touching the Discovery of America* (London: Thomas Dawson, 1582), 8.

51. David Eltis, "A Brief Overview of the Trans-Atlantic Slave Trade," Voyages: The Trans-Atlantic Slave Trade Data Base, http://www.slavevoyages.org/last/assessment/essay-intro-01.faces (Accessed April 27, 2008). The database shows that between 1626 and 1660, three hundred fifty-five enslaved Africans had disembarked in Virginia's ports. Between 1626 and 1660, nearly fifty thousand enslaved Africans embarked from the Luanda port in West Central Africa, compared to just over nine thousand persons who embarked from ports in the Bight of Benin, the next largest region of slave embarkations to the Americas during this period.

52. Ibid.

53. Ibid. From 1651 to 1700, one hundred twenty thousand seven hundred persons left the Bight of Benin for the Americas, while thirty thousand seven hundred nineteen left Luanda.

54. Lovejoy, *Transformations in Slavery: A History of Slavery in Africa, Second Edition*, 21.

55. Virginia slave laws of the 1660s and 1670s include:

1662: the child of a slave takes on the status of the mother

1667: baptism does not bring freedom to Blacks

1669: allows the casual killing of slaves

1670: servants for life the deemed as the normal condition of Blacks

1670: forbade Blacks and Native Americans, though baptized, to own Christian slaves

See Hening, *The Statutes at Large*, II: 170, 260, 266, 270.

56. The March 1619 census is contained in Ferrar Papers, MS 1597A, document 159 on microfilm reel 1. It is also reprinted in Thorndale, "The Virginia Census of 1619," 168–70. The census indicates that the European population at that date was around nine hundred twenty-eight. Other manuscripts in the Ferrar collection give census data through June 1619 that suggest the population was one thousand one hundred ninety-four.

57. Rolfe's letter to Sandys, Jan. 1619/1620, in Susan Myra Kingsbury, ed., *The Records of the Virginia Company of London*, vol. 3 (Washington, D.C.: Government Printing Office, 1933), 243.

58. Jester, *Adventures of Purse and Person, 1607–1625*, 22, 27, 29, 34, 46, 49, 62. For an examination of the significance of the word "Negro" as a label of difference see: Winthrop Jordan, *White over Black: American Attitudes toward the Negro, 1550–1812*, chapter 2; Moore, *The Name "Negro" Its Origin and Evil Use*, 33–55; and Bibby, "The Power of Words."

59. "Charles City County Court Order Book, 1658–1661," 177.

60. David Eltis, "A Brief Overview of the Trans-Atlantic Slave Trade," Voyages: The Trans-Atlantic Slave Trade Data Base, http://www.slavevoyages.org/last/assessment/essay-intro-01.faces (Accessed April 27, 2008).

61. According to M. I. Finley, "Slavery," *International Encyclopedia of the Social Sciences* 14 (1968): 310, slavery is transformed as an institution when slaves play an essential role in the economy.

62. Elbl, "The Volume of Early Atlantic Slave Trade, 1450–1521," 31–75.

63. Ibid.

64. Lovejoy, *Transformations in Slavery: A History of Slavery in Africa, Second Edition*, 19.

65. Scholars such as ibid., and Patrick Manning "The Impact of Slave Trade Exports on the Population of the Western Coast of Africa, 1700–1850," In Serge Daget, ed., *De la Traite a l'esclavage*, 2 vols (Paris, Societe francaise d'histoire d'Outre-Mer), II: 111–34, conclude that the external demand by Europeans for slaves that manifested in the transatlantic slave trade significantly transformed African societies.

66. Hening, *The Statutes at Large; Being a Collection of All the Laws of Virginia, from the First Session of the Legislature in the Year 1619*, II: 170, 260, 66, 70. Virginia slave laws of the 1660s and 1670s include:

1662: the child of a slave takes on the status of the mother

1667: baptism does not bring freedom to Blacks

1669: allows the casual killing of slaves

1670: servants for life the deemed as the normal condition of Blacks

1670: forbade Blacks and Native Americans, though baptized, to own Christian slaves

Many scholars conclude that race did not fully emerge until the latter decades of the seventeenth century after Bacon's Rebellion. Notable in this claim are Breen and Innes, "*Myne Owne Ground": Race and Freedom on Virginia's Eastern Shore, 1640–1676*; Kathleen M. Brown, *Good Wives, Nasty Wenches, and Anxious Patriarchs: Gender, Race, and Power in Colonial Virginia* (Chapel Hill: University of North Carolina Press, 1996); and Edmund S. Morgan, *American Slavery, American Freedom* (New York: W. W. Norton and Company, Inc., 1975).

Chapter 2

Duty Boys, Company Tenants, Slaveholding Ladies and Wealthy Planters

How the International System of Slavery Made European Emigrants White, 1619–1650

If the development of American Whiteness was inevitable from the activities in the sixteenth century that connected the English African Company and aspiring slave traders to the international system of slavery, then almost every European person who immigrated to or was born in Virginia in the seventeenth century participated directly or indirectly in making American Whiteness take hold by internalizing the racial precepts (i.e., anti-Blackness, White racial hegemony, etc.) passed down from each one of these predecessors that made Blackness synonymous with slavery and Whiteness synonymous with freedom.

The manifestation of this North American version of White supremacy began *not* in 1619 with the arrival of the first groups of enslaved Africans in Virginia, but in 1607 with the arrival of the first groups of European planters, investors and indentured servants and others who began the brutal process of colonizing Virginia.[1] Besides the massacre and removal of Native Americans as well as the outright theft of their lands, the making of American Whiteness gained its regional coherence with wealthy planters leveraging poor and indentured Europeans to consent to their leadership and adhere to the social structures they established. In return, poorer European immigrants gained the possibility of social mobility and received favored economic, political and social status over indigenous and African peoples, which were/are the structural expressions of American Whiteness.

Thus, at the precise moment that poor Europeans heeded the call to help planters and investors in the colonization of Virginia, the racial precepts inherited from the international system of slavery took on a new paradigm and shifted the structure of social relations from class to race with the alignment of the interests of Europeans to the expectations and quid pro quo inherent in the privileged social position Whites, especially poor Whites, were given over non-Whites, in Virginia and the New World, regardless of wealth, for centuries to come. So, instead of the usual caste like dynamics that governed relations between poor and wealthier people in European societies, in the New World, when poor and indentured Europeans agreed to relinquish their self-determination to that of wealthy planters, investors and representatives of Virginia society, the administration of European colonialism and all its attendant features was restructured to include a duty to poor Whites.[2] And at once, poor Whites became "junior partners" in the making of American Whiteness, a role that was key to the entrenchment and spread of White supremacy throughout the New World.[3]

For poor Europeans, the choice to tie their fate to their wealthier, well-traveled countrymen was an easy one. Faced with all sorts of uncertainties, up to and including death after immigrating to the New World, poorer Europeans were wholly dependent on European planters and investors not only for their livelihoods but for their sheer survival. As a result, desperate European men and women would acquiesce not only to the arduous work requirements necessary for colonization but also to the rules, values and standards established for Virginia, even if it did not necessarily result in their gaining the level of wealth and standing enjoyed by the colony's elite. For this concession, Virginia leaders instituted legal restrictions that limited the length of their indenture, which ensured that the social position of poorer Europeans would never be as low as a slave. This policy meant that at best poor Europeans would have opportunities for landownership and good jobs and at worst a social position above that of enslaved Africans. Moreover, these compromises established the fundamental relations between Whites, regardless of standing, that paved the way for their shared identification with Whiteness.[4] And this shared identification with the expectations of Whiteness was the object around which their abiding duty to each other was secured. Therefore, willingly submitting to indentured servitude for a specified period of time did not hinder the possibilities for prosperity or Whiteness for Europeans. On the contrary, temporary servitude was the "price of the ticket" that ensured poorer Europeans social mobility and other benefits in the New World that came with the conferral of Whiteness.[5]

How exactly did European servants achieve the economic security and the social position they so desperately desired with an embrace of American Whiteness? The most successful in Virginia did so by emulating their masters in a belief in propriety as Whites over the homeland of Indigenous peoples and by assuming their superiority over African people. In doing so, they became permanent constituents of the elite and coconspirators in the creation of American Whiteness by collaborating with Virginia leaders in the theft of Native people's lands and in the expansion of the international system of slavery.

Historically, European countries that have participated in the build-up of the international system of slavery have always relied on the support of imported European laborers to colonize and conquer indigenous lands and peoples. Much about this history will seem familiar to us, yet it also serves as a useful model for understanding the role White laborers' willing and sometimes reluctant consent to exploitation had in reshaping not only the international system of slavery but also the character of Whiteness and anti-Blackness in Virginia and throughout the New World before and after the arrival of enslaved Africans.[6]

For example, we know that European nations regularly used their lower-class countrymen to perform all kinds of laborious tasks to reduce the costs associated with the colonization of Africa and the Americas. In fact, since the fifteenth century, including during the transatlantic slave trade and European settlement in the New World, countries like Portugal and England sent their volunteer and reluctant "undesirables" to its colonies to build the slave castles, plantations, churches and courthouses that facilitated their hegemony, which also became the machinery of White supremacy through which laws were enacted, subjection and enslavement justified, and indigenous lands conquered. It was under this rubric that the Portuguese shipped Jewish peoples and criminals in the early sixteenth century to build its colony of São Tomé, an island in the Gulf of Guinea in West Africa, and likewise in the early seventeenth century it was the circumstances under which England dispatched its criminals, orphans and vagabonds to help in their colonization of Virginia.[7]

Similar hegemonic motivations moved European colonizers of Africa and the Americas to use conscripted and enlisted laborers from their countries to work alongside enslaved Africans in the production of cash crops to be sold in overseas markets. In sixteenth-century São Tomé and early seventeenth-century Bermuda, for instance, poor European laborers and enslaved Africans were respectively enlisted to produce sugar cane and tobacco to advance the desires of the wealthy elites to be major players in international trade markets.

European laborers were also brought into colonial territories by the elite to perform a number of nonagricultural duties essential to preserving their colonial power. For instance, in 1571 the Portuguese transported eighteen masons and builders, a physician and a barber to occupy and fortify São

Tomé.[8] Similarly, in 1607, England dispatched one preacher, one surgeon, six carpenters, one blacksmith, one sailor, one barber, one mason and two brick-layers to help inculcate its rule in Virginia.[9] Sometimes these persons were also used to carry out urgent military duties, such as when Virginia's first one hundred seventy-two European inhabitants were ordered to secure territory they occupied by building fortified communities in areas near the woods to hold off Native Americans who were fighting to defend their lands against European colonization.[10] At other times, European emigrants were routed to colonies by European authorities specifically to engage in military combat, like when six hundred Portuguese soldiers were sent to São Tomé in 1560 to help conquer kingdoms in the West African nation of Angola.[11]

Such colonial ventures (São Tomé, Virginia and Bermuda) show that throughout the early history of European colonization of Africa and North America, from the sixteenth century to the seventeenth century, very little had changed in the circumstances surrounding the use of White labor, willing or otherwise, to support European colonization ventures. With settlement in the New World, what did change was a paradigmatic shift in the outlook of poor Europeans that made them more willing to endure the exploitation of their labor and submit to the leadership of wealthy planters. Specifically, it was the anticipation of automatic citizenship, the value of which included material and social advantages and standing over African and indigenous peoples.[12] This turn represented an important alteration to the relational dynamics between poor and wealthier Europeans that gave new life and meaning to the racial aphorisms of European colonialism: it made White supremacy a mainstream element in the creation of civil society.[13]

Said another way, the agreement by poor Whites to temporarily cede their labor and autonomy to New World colonization projects in the hopes that it led to increased opportunities as citizens that distinguished them from indigenous and African people became constitutive of the orderly mak-ing of a society structured around the expectations in Whiteness. And the privileges transferred to poorer Whites for their acquiescence thus provides a straight line to their identification with Whiteness and anti-Blackness, beliefs that wealthy planters with ties to the international system of slavery via the English African Company had already adopted and were using to colonize Virginia.

Therefore, willingly accepting a subordinate place on the rung of Whiteness was a clear-eyed, pragmatic choice for poor Europeans who were migrating to a New World being built on White supremacy. Despite all this, for poorer Europeans, the fraternity of Whiteness was still fraught with antagonisms between them and the planter elite who exercised total control over them and who demanded unrequited obedience from their unlettered countrymen in exchange for automatic citizenship, social mobility and social position over African people, in particular.[14]

For example, the antagonism was fueled by the fact that Virginia planters strictly regulated the labor of European workers, requiring them to adhere to rigid work rules or face whippings and/or incarceration. In fact, before the arrival of the "32 Negroes" in March 1619, it was European indentured servants who were synonymous with debasement. The treatment and work conditions of European servants during this time were often so bad that only enslaved Africans would supplant their low standing. A window into this period that illustrates the debasing trade-offs made by poor Europeans in exchange for citizenship is seen through the lives of the indentured laborers recruited to Virginia under the Sandys program. This program exemplifies the lowliness of these workers before and shortly after the arrival of African peoples but also it is key to understanding the inherent tensions contained in the concession European indentured servants made with their wealthy bosses in exchange for the racial and social benefits of citizenship that were/are imbued in American Whiteness.

The Sandys program was designed and implemented in 1619 for the recruitment of temporary European laborers to work in England's North American colonies. Named after its architect, Sir Edwin Sandys, mentioned earlier as a founder of the Virginia Company and a son of the Archbishop of York, the Sandys program delivered much-needed labor to Virginia. Eager planters and investors looked to the Sandys program for European workers to "cleere grounds, fell trees, set corne, square timber and plant vines and other fruits brought out of England" in order to transform Virginia's uncultivated lands into crop producing farms and plantations.[15]

The program was only in existence for three short years, 1619–1622, but during that time Sandys drafted around three thousand five hundred men from England to work the fertile lands of Virginia.[16] This period also marked the arrival of enslaved Africans, the "32 Negroes" in March 1619 and the "20. and odd Negroes" in August of that year, who supplanted Sandys recruits as the lowest class of laborers and persons in Virginia society, which ironically only intensified the antagonisms between European indentured servants and wealthy planters. Specifically, when enslaved Africans began arriving in larger numbers, Blackness and enslavement became the living object lesson around which European indentured servants understood the precariousness of their rank and their dependency on wealthier Whites, which therein forced them to anxiously cleave even more tightly to the foremost expectation of Whiteness: to be above Blacks and above Black slaves. With this in mind, the Sandys program is an important framework to view the trajectory of Whiteness for poor Europeans in Virginia but also to exemplify the personal price they paid, and continue to pay today in America, for aligning their interests to wealthier Europeans during this period in exchange for social position over African and indigenous people.

For instance, the two classes of European indentured servants that arose out of the Sandys program were the so-called tenant laborers and duty boys. Tenant laborers and duty boys both were required to work a significant number of years before gaining their freedom; for tenants it was seven years, and for duty boys it was fourteen. Tenant laborers were the highest ranked servants in the Sandys program. They were enticed to the colony by the prospect of work that was akin to that of a sharecropper. The plan was that once these men were recruited by Sandys to Virginia, they would then become the property of the Virginia Company who, after paying for their transportation to the colony, would assign tenant laborers to work for planters, investors and other high-ranking persons such as members of the Virginia General Assembly for a period of seven years. In exchange they were required to give half their earnings during their term of service to the Virginia Company.[17] Once their obligation was completed, tenant laborers would receive fifty acres of land and some form of monetary compensation called freedom dues.[18]

Despite being the highest ranked laborers in the Sandys program, tenant laborers were still subject to immense exploitation. In fact, these men were sometimes treated quite harshly. Some complained of being treated like slaves.[19] And, they were often poorly fed, consuming a diet that typically consisted of corn and water.[20] Investors like Edward Bennett, who by 1625 was one of the top fifteen men in Virginia who owned ten or more servants and enslaved persons, was an example of the type of planter who exploited tenant laborers. For example, planters and investors like Bennett regularly imposed their authority on tenant laborers by hiring them out to privately owned plantations for profit.[21] In one instance, fifty of the one hundred "lusty" tenant laborers who arrived in Virginia in 1619 to clear, fence, plant and build on investors' lands were hired out by their owners to other plantations.[22] George Sandys (father of aforementioned Edwin Sandys) hired out two of his tenant laborers, David Mansfield and John Claxon, to work on a privately owned plantation.[23] We have no way of knowing more precisely the extent to which Mansfield, Claxon and other workers were hired out, but we do know that once under the supervision of the employer, tenant laborers were so "unmercifully used that it [was] the greatest cause of [their] discontent."[24]

If tenant laborers were the highest ranked servants that came out of the Sandys program, then duty boys were the lowest. The term "duty boy" got its moniker from the name of the ship (the *Duty*) that transported a number of European workers into Virginia. The muster of 1624 shows twelve European male servants were transported to Virginia on the *Duty*, suggesting that these twelve men were likely indentured as duty boys.[25] Instead of the seven-year maximum work requirement that applied to tenant laborers, the term of service for duty boys was fourteen years. And if a duty boy committed a crime at any time during the first seven years of service, then an additional seven years was added to his term, which meant their indenture often exceeded the typical fourteen years. Even so, after their fourteen-year period of labor, duty boys, like tenants, still received fifty acres of land to jump-start their life of independence.

It is tempting to interpret the harsh working conditions of tenant laborers and duty boys as evidence that there were no appreciable differences between bonded Africans and Europeans, and therefore no evidence of fully formed racial categories of Blackness and Whiteness during this time as some scholars have claimed.[26] Indeed, comparing working conditions at first glance seem to be a good starting point for examining the presence (or lack thereof) of racial formations and social distinctions between Black and White people during this time. However, the amount of government mandated time spent in servitude provides a more useful measure for analyzing the differences between European and African people who were in some form of bondage. Specifically, the fact that from the beginning European people's servitude was temporary and African people's was indefinite proves there were real racial and social distinctions between the Africans and Europeans in place during New World settlement. And although not all Africans during this time were "slaves," no slaves were European, a fact which suggests incipient White racial solidarity.[27] Moreover, it shows that the fixed amount of time spent in servitude by Europeans was a seventeenth-century expression of White racial sensibilities about freedom and belonging if not actual evidence of a White racial identity. The trial of John Punch was exemplar of this sensibility.

John Punch, an African man, and his two European friends, "Victor, a Dutchman, and James Gregory, a Scotchman," were all on trial for running away to Maryland from their Virginia master, Hugh Gwyn. The men were sentenced by the Virginia General Court on July 9, 1640, after Gwyn brought the men back to the colony for punishment. Their penalty was detailed in a lengthy opinion that stated:

> The court doth therefore order that the said three servants shall receive the punishment of whipping and to have thirty stripes apiece. . . . Victor and James Gregory shall first serve out their times with their masters according to their Indentures, and one whole year apiece after the time of their service is Expired By their said Indentures in recompence of his Loss sustained by their absence, and after that service to their said Master is Expired to serve the colony for three whole years apiece, and that the third being a negro named John Punch shall serve his said master or his assigns for the time of his natural life here or elsewhere.[28]

The court's ruling was illustrative of a society influenced by the principles of the international system of slavery, one in which Victor and Gregory as Europeans, who, although in bondage, were ranked above Punch, an African. And, despite all being referred to as servants in the ruling, Victor and Gregory's punishment, even for the same crime, was ordered to be no more severe than a whipping and an increase in their fixed term of service, while for Punch it was lifetime servitude. So, given these racial distinctions in sentencing, the lifetime servitude that was prescribed only for Punch clearly shows a different social position between him and the two White men that rested on standing notions of who was subject to slavery (Punch) and who was not. Thus, the details of this case show that the time spent in servitude was indeed a proxy for Whiteness and citizenship more than working conditions were and, as such, demonstrates the favored social position even poor Whites already had over Africans in Virginia as early as 1640.

By virtue of their European ancestry and common culture and language, tenant laborers and duty boys were imbued with certain freedoms by the planter elite that were not given nor assumed for so-called "Negroes" like John Punch. Thus, as the racial moniker "Negro" suggests, African people had no path into honorary Whiteness or incorporation into Virginia society like European indentured servants had, being that they, by virtue of their African ancestry, were imported into the colony initially as permanent laborers by the same planter elite who oversaw the training and incorporation of poor Europeans as citizens into Virginia society. With this in mind, it is useful to think about the servitude of tenant laborers and duty boys like Victor and James Gregory as the social equivalent of an apprenticeship into the expectations of Whiteness, given that unlike bonded Africans, most European indentured servants had contracts stipulating their length of service and, in some cases, the type of work they performed before moving onto a life of freedom with land and a stipend given to them by the Virginia government. So although tenant laborers and duty boys could be physically punished and treated, in some cases, as badly as the Africans, European ancestry meant that they still had some rights and guaranteed prospects for freedom and incorporation into civil society even while in bondage that were understood as not applicable to African people.

Inside and outside the courtroom, Punch, Victor and Gregory were most likely aware of these racial and social distinctions. By running away, Punch evidences his understanding of the stark realities of this dichotomy that included written and unwritten codes and customs designed to reinforce his subordinate and outsider status within the social structure of the plantation, which, as early as 1640, had ranked people in Virginia according to their position in the international system of slavery: "White over Black."

Nonetheless, by volunteering their labor and reaping the benefits from the strictures of race already in place in a New World they helped create, European emigrants like Victor and Gregory participated in the making of American Whiteness. And even if they may have assigned different meanings to their reasons for immigration, they still understood temporarily ceding their labor to planters and investors as the price of Whiteness, one that should be read as a statement of their allegiance to planters and a testament of their expectations from a colonial project that encompassed all sorts of religious and racial justifications for settlement, enslavement and subjugation of indigenous and African peoples. It was for these reasons and others that White servants, including tenant laborers and duty boys, embraced Whiteness and in doing so were conferred automatic citizenship and other freedoms that at once ranked them higher than Black and indigenous people in Virginia.

Yet, even as poor Europeans submitted to labor exploitation and other demands in exchange for citizenship, for wealthy planters driven by the spirit of colonialism that infused the activities of early seventeenth-century Virginians, the Sandys program was as crucial to their Whiteness conferred by mastery over humans as the Whiteness conferred by acquiescence was to the poor. To this end, wealthy Virginians would launch a full-scale lobbying campaign on behalf of Sandys to solicit England's cities and counties for its poor and indigent to man Virginia's labor force.[29]

Intense lobbying efforts made by Virginia leaders who supported the Sandys program sought to convince English officials to supply the labor needed for the development of its first North American colony using the indigent and idle, arguing that ridding the country of this group was an economic as well as a public good that would attract future investors and speed up the country's colonization plans. And knowing England's rigid social pecking order, Virginia leaders presented English officials with a plan that advocated the short-term and long-term advantages of using poor people to do the manual work necessary for colonization, making the case that disposing its outcasts to the Sandys program was a prudent fiscal policy that would absolve the English government of its obligation to aid the poor while also providing Virginia planters and investors with a cheap yet powerless labor pool in which to advance its colonization plans and of course their personal profits.

Seeing the social and economic benefits of this plan, England gladly ceded many of its vagrants to Sandys, thereby providing Virginia planters and of course England with some of the human resources needed to achieve its early settlement goals until enslaved Africans began arriving in larger numbers. One gift to Sandys by the city of London, for example, added one hundred destitute "boys" to its pool of laborers available to work for Virginia planters.[30] Such maneuvering over the lives and livelihoods of poor Europeans by the English government and wealthy Virginia planters further fueled the antagonistic relationship between them even as the poor begrudgingly accepted the benefits of citizenship as the reward for temporarily ceding their self-determination in support of the colony.

Meanwhile, by 1621, the Sandys program had expanded its labor business to England's second North American colony, Bermuda, to help speed its colonization. Concomitantly, this expansion presciently coincided with an increase in Bermuda's population of enslaved Africans. By 1620, there were at least seventy-five enslaved persons in Bermuda.[31] This fact, combined with Bermuda's rapidly growing tobacco and sugarcane production (until 1624, Bermuda's tobacco production consistently surpassed Virginia's), put increased pressure on ambitious Virginia planters to match the agricultural output of its sister colony, which positioned Sandys to meet this demand with indentured European laborers from England.[32] In one instance, forty-four enthusiastic planters, among them the aforementioned Edward Bennett, signed up for Sandys services.

Bennett was the ideal type of planter for the Sandys program's labor business.[33] He was a wealthy merchant from London anxious to take advantage of the opportunity to turn land and labor (indentured or enslaved) into a profit.[34] And the benefits offered by the Virginia Company for hiring European laborers steered striving planters eager to best Bermuda's agricultural production directly to the Sandys program to service their labor needs. A standard example was the Virginia Company's stock purchase program, which provided planters like Bennett one hundred acres of land for every share of stock they bought plus an additional fifty acres for every European laborer they hired to work their lands.[35]

Besides land, planters like Bennett also received something equally as tangible as hiring European laborers: the stature from being a master of men. In the early seventeenth century and through much of the nineteenth century, being a master of men was the penultimate measure of a White man's stature and patriarchy. And the European laborers provided by the Sandys program in many ways underwrote the realization of this kind of stature that was often expressed in such things as plantations that bore the family name, like the aforementioned Flowerdew Hundred plantation, which was patented in 1618 by Governor George Yeardley after his father-in-law, Anthony Flowerdrew.[36] Immortalizing a plantation in one's family name demonstrated a planter's personal commitment to Virginia's success, which would ultimately improve the speed of land development and the resulting benefits therein. But equally and often more important, erecting a plantation in one's name reinforced a man's public persona as a master, which naturally drew these men to the mushrooming transatlantic slave trade. And wittingly or unwittingly, the land grants offered by the Virginia Company ironically made the purchase of enslaved Africans more viable for Virginia planters bent on affirming their stature and, by extension, their Whiteness, through owning human beings.

A case in point was Bennett, who by 1625 had added two enslaved Africans to his stable of ten European servants. The African persons were described in his records as simply "Antonio a Negro" and "Mary a Negro woman."[37] As it turns out, "Antonio" and "Mary," who I discuss in more detail in chapter 3, were the famous couple Anthony and Mary Johnson, who eventually became property owners and who also owned an African "slave" and several servants.[38] As master and mistress, the Johnsons' social position, similar to Bennett but on a much smaller scale, has been widely touted by scholars of the early seventeenth century as proof of the absence of the racial formations of Whiteness and Blackness in Virginia.[39] But more than being an example of a color-blind Virginia, the Johnsons' standing was an anathema to felt expressions of Whiteness via mastery that increasingly portended growing anti-Blackness in the region that shaped interracial and intra-racial relations in Virginia and the New World for decades to come.

Anti-Blackness in Virginia grew exponentially after 1619 with the purchase of enslaved Africans like the Johnsons, who, during the growth of the international system of slavery, worked alongside European indentured servants like those brought in by Sandys and subsidized by the Virginia Company. Thus while planters like Bennett manipulated two of North America's most utilized bondage systems (African slavery and European indenture servitude), for personal gain and prestige, their actions also heightened the insecurity of poor and indentured Europeans who were nervous about the prospects of their social position in the colony under the leadership of men increasingly active in the slave trade. The move toward enslaved labor thereby intensified the vulnerability of poor Whites to wealthy planters, which furthered the antagonistic relationship between them and concomitantly increased their disdain for Black people as the object of their insecurity.

Despite the inherent tension between free and enslaved labor that scholars debate and the Johnsons embodied, including what their freedom meant to the expectations of European indentured servants, the Sandys program nonetheless (likely as a matter of its own self-interest) endorsed the use of indentured European servants for not only their labor, but also as purveyors and progenitors of English culture, something that free or bonded Africans like the Johnsons were obviously unable to do. Particularly, Sandys officials backed many planters like Bennett using European indentured servants to assist the colony in subduing Native people by helping to "educat[e] their children [and] teaching them English culture and other skills and [by] acquainting them with the more sophisticated aspects of Christianity and civility," labels that in the early seventeenth century were universal descriptors connoting Whiteness.[40] Thus, it was the real and symbolic value that European indentured servants, even in their temporary servitude, held for advancing and sustaining the creation of a White society and citizenry that compelled Sandys to promote tenant laborers and duty boys to planters as a special type of servant that was crucial to the making of a White civil society in Virginia. So, in doing the literal and figurative "work toward Whiteness," the European servants who built the churches, homes, courthouses and plantations that defined the racial and social relations between them and Native and African groups were also building an idealized social and political identity for themselves and all poor Europeans as White.[41]

That said, the value of European indentured servants to the creation of a White civil society should not distract us from the fact that land and unfree laborers of all stripes were what Virginia planters in the seventeenth century really wanted. And men like Bennett understood the economic power and leverage they had over European indentured servants and the local government to shape the direction of the colony, which was one reason why so many of these men cleverly seized upon land grants offered by the Virginia Company for hiring White laborers. The records do not indicate how much land Bennett, for example, received for hiring White laborers. However, from his indentured servant holdings alone, Bennett would have received five hundred acres (fifty acres per person) from the Virginia Company.[42] One indication of the vastness of his land, servant and slave holdings that came from his taking advantage of these land grants was the fact that he had to dispatch his nephews Robert and Richard Bennett to Virginia to help manage all the property and servants that he acquired as a shareholder of the Virginia Company and patron of the Sandys program.

This arrangement between Bennett and his nephews exemplifies what the successful consummation of the master/junior partner relationship looked like among classes of Whites, one that began in the international system of slavery and culminated in the colonization of Virginia and the creation of a White civil society.[43]

Other programs offered by the Virginia Company that planters took advantage of that increased their wealth and stature included programs that subsidized the room and board of European servants under their charge.[44] In exchange, the Virginia Company pushed planters to diversify their mix of commodities with crops other than tobacco such as silk grass, pitch, tar and lumber.[45] Planters generally scoffed at such heavy-handed invasions into their business decisions, so, to appease them, the Virginia Company allowed planters to keep a share of the profits made by European servant labor even though Virginia planters were clearly moving toward importing more enslaved Africans into the colony, whose expertise in growing and curing tobacco and tropical crops such as sugar cane had proved profitable for their counterparts in Bermuda.[46] For example, by 1625, six of the largest planters, including Bennett, George Yeardley and Abraham Peirsey, all had enslaved Africans working on their plantations, likely because their skill at tobacco cultivation was perceived as a key to Bermuda's temporary rein in agricultural production.[47]

Despite all the economic incentives offered by the Virginia Company, the indeterminate lengths of service mandated for Blacks could not be over-looked by wealth-seeking planters who, by the mid-seventeenth century, began exploiting the labor of the roughly three hundred Africans in Virginia in more diverse ways (as property, as commodities and as collateral), which not so ironically opened up more opportunities for newly freed European servants to distinguish themselves as junior partners to the planter elite. Yet, these opportunities were not automatic and required more than just being freed from indentured servitude; they required such things as mastering the language and countenance of Whiteness.

Embodying the demeanor of Whiteness included embracing its vernacular that consisted of pejorative metaphors such as "negro" and "savage" that connoted an acceptance of European people's superior humanity and social position relative to Africans and indigenous peoples. The use of the terms "negro" and "savage" in early seventeenth-century Virginia were holdovers from the international system of slavery, propagated by the Virginia Company in order to establish real and symbolic distinctions in society of the dominant social position of Europeans that reflected personal as well as the widely accepted assumptions about freedom and liberty that were seen as the propriety of Whites regardless of class. One important conception of Whiteness carried in the epithets that up-and-coming junior partners learned to embrace was the concept of White racial purity, which was translated in everyday life to mean that European people of all ranks should have no openly intimate relations with African or Native peoples.

As it was with Native Americans, Virginia leaders particularly frowned upon intimate relations between poor European men and African women because it disrupted the social cohesion that strict boundaries on sexual contact demanded for the creation and maintenance of a White civil society. The colony's ideology about interracial sex had its roots in the religious justifications for the enslavement of African people and the colonization of Africa that date back to the fifteenth century, made by European countries that had rationalized it was sanctioned by God.

Initially these rationalizations took the form of commentary about Black people's physiques, like what was found in Richard Hakluyt's sixteenth-century collection of transatlantic travel narratives, *Principal Navigations* (mentioned in chapter 1), about Black women's bodies. In this collection, Hakluyt published several essays with racialized language that suggested that the African female body was abnormal and therefore by implication was suitable for enslavement compared to the prevailing beliefs about White women.[48]

These ideas continued to flourish in the seventeenth century in the writings of authors like Richard Ligon, who expanded upon White men's imaginations about Black women's bodies with lewd tales about Black women in places like the Caribbean having outsized breasts. His stories included tall tales of Black women with "breasts [that] hang down below their Navels, so that when they stoop at their common work of weeding, they hang almost to the ground, that at a distance you would think they had six legs."[49]

This notion of the abnormal and animalistic Black female body that stirred in the minds of White men during this era and for more than a century after prefigured all sorts of laws, policies and customs then and into the twentieth century that sought to control, debase and literally capitalize on Black women's physical and reproductive capacities by any means necessary, including rape.[50] This idea was also used to justify restrictions on intimate relations between so-called "Christian" (European) men and "heathen" (African) women in order to maintain the racial pecking order of White over Black.

In Virginia, these sexualized writings and images about the Black female body likewise stood as a framework for wealthy planters to teach their lower-class junior partners that Black people were both alien and subordinate to European people and, for fear of denuding the White race, not institutionally recognized as virtuous sexual partners. Aspects of all these assumptions (racial, religious and sexual) intersected in the Hugh Davis trial.

Hugh Davis was a European indentured servant who was found to have had sex with an African woman. On September 17, 1630, the General Court punished Davis for this offense, ruling: "Hugh Davis to be soundly whipped, before the assembly of Negroes and others for abusing himself to the dishonor of God and shame of Christians, by defiling his body in lying with a negro, which fault he is to acknowledge next Sabbath day."[51]

While the name of Davis's sexual partner was not mentioned and her status or religion is unclear, we learn several things about the colony's racial and religious views from this verdict. First, we learn from this decision who *was* White, as the opinion defined the behavior expected of Davis as a "Christian." Just as important, we also learn who was *not* White. The judgment that Davis be "soundly whipped" before an assembly of "Negroes and others" discloses a common understanding of the meaning of the racial identifications of the persons in the colony who were to witness his punishment. Moreover, the judgement shows that court members had an established image or conception of the meaning of its own racial group as White and Christian but not "Negro."[52] So, when the court convened a crowd of "Negroes and others" to observe Davis's beating for "lying with a negro," the court was clearly distinguishing itself and Davis as White, thereby suggesting it was unchristian for Whites to have sex with Blacks.[53]

And yet White men did have sex (consensually or by force) with Black women. Nonetheless, the prevailing idea of the abnormal and animalistic Black female body still found utility in Virginia for advancing policies that officials engineered to bring about the perpetual enslavement of Black people, policies that furthered the racial and social distinctions between Blacks and Whites regardless of status or gender. But specific to the issue of race and gender and the steady enslavement of Black people, colonial leaders used the animalistic trope about Black women to propagate assumptions about the differences between European and African women that anticipate the 1643 slave law, which taxed the labor of Black women the same as it did for men while exempting White women from this mandate.[54] This legislation appeared during a time when Virginia leaders were clarifying the social position of Black women as an important commodity that increased one's status and wealth, a process that prefigured the 1662 slave law that unambiguously codified racial slavery around Black women's reproduction. The 1662 act states: "Whereas some doubts have arisen whether children got by any Englishman upon a Negro woman shall be slave or free . . . all children born in this colony shall be bond or free only according to the condition of the mother."[55]

The law's redefinition of a centuries-old English custom of establishing paternity by the child's father with this new rule that only applied to the progeny of Black women clearly shows that the racial categories of Whiteness and Blackness that were built around Black women's labor and laboring capacities had firmly taken hold in Virginia by 1662. This law's prehistory occurs after the surge of growth in the colony's initial participation in the burgeoning transatlantic slave trade nearly two decades prior. Of note was the period between 1635 and 1656 when Virginia imported just over two hundred African persons into the region, with untold numbers of births that likely occurred during this span that forever altered the social distance between European and African people by race and gender after this time.[56] Thus, when examined in tandem with the 1643 slave law and the exponential increase in the colony's enslaved population as a result of the 1662 law, the two measures expand our understanding of the relationship between Black women's enslaved and reproductive bodies and Whiteness. Likewise, the 1643 and 1662 laws raise interesting questions about White maleness and the role of Black women and men in this construction.

As mentioned earlier in this chapter, by mid-seventeenth century Virginia planters began using enslaved people in increasingly diverse ways, including as collateral and as commodities. One example that was prominent in the 1640s and 1650s that coincided with the swell of enslaved Black people into the region either by birth or importation was the practice of White men gifting enslaved Black females to needy family and friends. The gifting of enslaved females marked an emerging sense of White racial and class consciousness during these decades that, depending on the context, could be done to flaunt status or masculinity or for other symbolic reasons. Either way, what was clear was that gifting practices were as much a way of talking about Whiteness and maleness and its attendant class distinctions among planters as they were about distinctions between bonded European and Africans that scholars try to use to disprove White racism during this period.[57]

Take, for instance, the scenario of a middling planter who was tight with a larger one. Receiving an enslaved female as a gift might express one's masculinity among the planter class or signify one's improved standing in the community. A case in point was that of Francis Pott. On April 10, 1646, he *gave* Stephen Charlton "one Negro woman called Marchant and one boy Negro (likely her son) called Will for peaceable enjoyment."[58] If Pott's gift was to help Charlton get started as a slaveholder, then the gift signified prestige and masculinity for both men. If Pott was trying to help Charlton in a time of financial distress, then the gifting of Black females was a way to ease the burden, which still could be read as a statement about Pott's and Charlton's masculine stature as participants in the international system of slavery. One year after receiving the enslaved woman, we see Charlton's machismo expressed in his newfound stature as a slaveholder when he went on to gift a two-year-old "Negro childe," Grace-Susanna, to his widowed sister, also named Grace, to "enjoy until she be of the age of thirty years."[59] We have no way of knowing for sure how Charlton came to possess Grace-Susanna or why he gifted her to his sister. Perhaps Charlton had gifted the young girl to help his sister with the uncertainties of daily life and/or to flaunt his standing as a slaveholder and patriarch like Pott did with him. Nonetheless, the gifting of Black women was indisputable evidence of White men's embrace of their masculinity through racial formations about Blackness as property and Whiteness as property holder.

Along these lines, an English mariner named Thomas Jacob was probably motivated by a similar set of race-based masculine formations as Charlton when, in 1642, he gifted a "Negro" woman, Susanna, to a newly widowed Bridget Severne and her son John to be used by "their heirs freely and for ever."[60] We do not know why Jacob gifted Susanna to Serverne. It could be that Jacob was trying to impress the widow as a potential suitor. Even so, the gifting of the enslaved woman represented Jacob's membership in the upper ranks of Whiteness that was secured in the commodification of the Black female body. And this racialized human commodity was thusly assigned to Severne and her son by Jacob as his gift of patriarchal protection against life's unexpected events.

To be sure, the gifting of enslaved African women as Pott, Charlton and Jacob did told ambitious Whites (servants, former servants and middling planters) that "African women's bodies were the vessels for crafting real and imagined legacies" for themselves and their families.[61] A key factor to warrant this belief was the fact that an enslaved African woman's "increases," or the children she bore, unlike indentured White women, were subject to permanent bondage, which was why most White men purchased a Black female as their first slave.[62] Thus, Black "women's work and [Black] women's bodies were inseparable from the landscape" of slavery, including the transformation of White men and women into masters and mistresses and colonial Virginia into a White civil society.[63]

By making an enslaved female the first purchase, an aspiring planter or former indentured servant successfully incorporated the trappings of Whiteness via the international system of slavery into his identity. In this fashion, when English emigrant John Custis bought an enslaved girl named Doll in 1653, he was buying his way into the master class. Custis bought Doll from Argoll Yeardley—his brother-in-law and son of the former Virginia governor, George Yeardley. Yeardley sold his "Negro girl" to Custis for him to "have her and her increase to be in full satisfaction of him and his heirs."[64]

In 1653, Custis was a new immigrant and was newly married. Purchasing Doll was a way of establishing financial security for his family as well as for establishing a name for himself in the community. Possibly too, he decided to purchase an enslaved female so that her increase could belong to him, thereby multiplying the value of his initial investment. Either way, Doll represented Custis's passage from the status of non-slaveholder to slaveholder and his wife into a slaveholding lady, allowing them to join his brother-in-law Yeardley and his family in the upper classes of Northampton County, Virginia, society. And his ascent to the upper classes was rapid. Two years after purchasing Doll, Custis was elected to the bench as member of the Northampton County Court.[65] A few years later, after he acquired more enslaved Africans, he repeated the practice of his predecessors—lifting poor White men out of poverty and into the slaveholding class through the body of a Black woman—when he sold Doll to a former European indentured servant named William Gascoigne.

The life of Doll and the previously mentioned Black women and children who were gifted by slaveholders to their family and friends enables us to focus on the daily practices of Virginia planters that connected them to the growing transatlantic slave trade. Moreover, the life of Doll and the other Black women and girls illustrates the variations in planters' perspectives regarding Black female labor. In selling Doll to Custis, for example, Yeardley was able to use his wealth generated by slave labor to jump start the life of his emigrant brother-in-law and his sister. Along the same lines, Custis, with the purchase of Doll, signaled to the community his intent on being part of Virginia's master class. He showed the community that his ambitions had finally come to fruition after he sold Doll to Gascoigne. For Gascoigne, Doll was proof of the potential of upward mobility for former European indentured servants like him who constituted a large block of potential junior partners crucial to the making of American Whiteness as three-fourths of Europeans living in Virginia during the seventeenth century arrived as indentured servants.[66]

The importance of enslaved females and the developing transatlantic slave trade to the advancement of European emigrants, male and female, explains why girls like Grace-Susanna and Doll would command a higher price on the open market than European servants, male or female.[67] Generally, an enslaved African female in the 1640s would cost around twenty-five hundred pounds of tobacco.[68] In contrast, the cost of European female and male indentured servants during this same period averaged around thirteen hundred and eighteen hundred pounds of tobacco respectively.[69] The higher valuation for enslaved African females reflected the planters' interest in substituting enslaved African females for uses beyond agriculture, like gifting, which may account for the parity in the ratio of enslaved females and males in the New World through 1660.[70]

The diverse use of enslaved female labor in the English colonies might have even affected the intercolonial trade in African women, given that the vast majority of enslaved persons in the seventeenth century were imported rather than born in Virginia. In fact, through the 1670s, most Blacks arrived in Virginia after a layover in another English colony.[71] Therefore, the variations in the uses and expectations for African women in Virginia may have been influenced by other colonies, like Bermuda, which were more active in the transatlantic slave trade.

Black female labor was an important boundary-crossing commodity that connected European peoples in Bermuda and Virginia. Examples of such intercolonial connections around Black women can be observed in the transactions of several planters. Take the Bermudian planter Thomas Durham, who requested three enslaved Black men and one Black woman from Nathaniel Rich in 1620 to work his land.[72] We have no way of knowing where Rich got his slaves, but it was possible that he was assisted by his brother, Robert, mentioned in chapter 1, who was a Virginia Company shareholder and a planter in both colonies. A similar scenario as that of Nathaniel Rich occurred in 1621, when Daniel Elfrith, who had captained slave ships into both colonies, attempted to broker a deal between Rich and another planter that would have landed Rich two more enslaved Black women.[73] In all, the cases reveal the extent to which ideas about Black female labor influenced English colonies via the evolving international system of slavery.

Although we have very little to document the lives of enslaved girls like Doll and Grace-Susanna (or the women in Bermuda), we know that their mothers were likely African-born, as were most of the roughly three hundred fifty African peoples in Virginia through 1660.[74] If we are to understand the personhood of African girls and women during the initial years of slavery and how they dealt with their oppression while still building community under this system, we must begin by studying the lives of women in the Angola region of West Central Africa. Again, I turn to the excellent research of Joseph Miller on the Mbundu peoples of Angola in the sixteenth and seventeenth century, which allows us to make more confident generalizations about African females in early Virginia since the seaport in Luanda, Angola, was the place where they, and most other Blacks in the New World during this time, departed from.

What can we learn from women in Mbundu societies that may help us understand Black women in the New World? What skills did they possess that show how Black women in Virginia may have mitigated their oppression? How did Mbundu women train their daughters to alleviate threats to their autonomy? Although we do not know the exact birthplaces of the African women in Virginia or their ethnic group, Miller's study provides us with knowledge about overlapping and regional cultures common to kingdoms in Angola that allow us to better answer such questions.

According to Miller, Mbundu societies were matrilineal, with descent and inheritance reckoned through women but with most forms of authority in the hands of men.[75] Under this structure, girls were usually born in their father's village where they remained until marriage, and then went to live with the kinsfolk of their husbands. As a result, most Mbundu women never lived in their maternal lineage village until they reached old age. This constant movement between lineages meant that most Mbundu women would raise their children in their husband's lineage group rather than with their mothers. Lacking a reliable chronicler of the perceptions of West African women about their working conditions in Virginia, we are left to speculate about whether they used their indigenous knowledge of lineage systems toward mitigating the upheavals of internal slave trading that took place in the colony.

For instance, the women on the plantation where Grace-Susanna and Doll were sold might have appointed a woman to care for the girls while they were separated from their mothers. If so, this woman would be each girl's surrogate mother for the entire time they were on the plantation. It would be unlikely that the girl's European owners were aware of such arrangements because these relationships were common to matrilineal societies in West Africa, where girls and women established a variety of kinship relations with other women who moved in and out of their group as a result of marriage or divorce or because of their status as a concubine, pawn or slave. It is from this context that we imagine that Grace-Susanna and Doll's surrogate mother raised her new "daughters" like any mother would, teaching them about agricultural production techniques, such as how to grow and tend to crops, and training them in domestic skills——how to cook and make food stretch and how to sew and mend their clothing to make it last, as well as other methods essential to their survival.

As Grace-Susanna and Doll got older, they would learn from the women in their community how to navigate the Black and White landscapes of the plantation communities, learning who to trust and not to trust. They would also likely be taught the language and customs of the various ethnicities of Africans on the plantation and how to code-switch between them as needed. These skills were probably what Grace-Susanna and Doll mastered from the women on the plantations where they resided, and it was possibly what the eight-year-old "negro girle" on the plantation of William Burdett also learned.

Burdett was a former indentured servant who, before he died in 1643, had achieved a certain amount of upward social mobility. He had amassed at least one thousand five hundred acres of land, had at least nine confirmed servants and/or slaves and had been appointed as a Burgess to represent Accomack County in the General Assembly.[76] An inventory of his estate listed "one negro girle about 8 years old [valuing] at 2000 pounds of tobacco," which was twice the value of any one of his White servants.[77] Probably unbeknownst to Burdett, the women in the Black landscape surrounding his plantation saw to it that the young girl had a surrogate mother to train her in agricultural techniques and other survival skills while she lived on his plantation. This scenario would likely repeat itself once the girl was sold during the liquidation of Burdett's estate.

The reality of life under the 1643 slave law meant that once Doll, Grace-Susanna and the eight-year-old girl were of age, almost no amount of work was viewed as too strenuous for her given that the law taxed African women's labor as equal to that of any man.[78] As such, slave masters of the 1640s, just as those from earlier decades, surely endeavored to "wrench as much labor as possible from [Black females] without injuring her capacity to bear children."[79] To this end, female African children like Grace-Susanna, Doll and others held particular historical significance to the class mobility of European men, be it a former indentured servant like Burdett, a poor European emigrant like John Custis, or relatively wealthy men like Francis Pott, Stephen Charlton or Argoll Yeardley. Especially when considering the looming 1662 slave law that made enslaved Black women's children slaves also.

That said, even though most European men who could afford to purchase an enslaved African did so, those less wealthy, including many former servants, obtained the trappings of Whiteness by purchasing European indentured laborers instead. As stated, the increasing importance of enslaved women (and men) to European class mobility meant that bonded Blacks in Virginia cost two to three times as much as any class of European servant. As a result, many former tenant laborers and duty boys could only afford to enter the ranks of mastery by purchasing a European indentured servant.

This was the case for former tenant laborers Richard Berkeley and John Smyth, who in 1626 requested two duty boys apiece "for their owne pryvate benefit and imploymentes."[80] These men joined a fraternity that included two other former tenant laborers in the area, Francis Fowler and Thomas Dunthorne, who in the same period also owned European servants. So, despite the fact that a master of a European indentured servant held a lower social standing than an owner of an enslaved African person, it nonetheless allowed the European emigrants who purchased one to write themselves into the upper classes of Virginia society, just as planters and investors had done before the arrival of enslaved Africans in 1619.

It is important to remember that being masters of European indentured servants has historical significance to our understanding of the development of American Whiteness in that before the arrival of enslaved Africans in 1619, European class mobility was contingent upon large landholdings and mastery over White servants who did the work of colonization. Over time, it was many of these former European servants, like those previously mentioned, who went on to purchase White indentured laborers for themselves. And when they did, they immediately moved up in class to a rank just below the slaveholding planter elite, which made the social position of the individuals in this group most dependent and beholden to the colony's racial agenda of White over Black. Thus, for this aspiring group of European emigrants, White servants represented the nearest symbol of status to owning a slave, which was the pinnacle of mastery and prestige. Moreover, it was the fastest and cheapest way to upward mobility. So it was not surprising that these wannabes stole White servants, lured them and even fought over them in order to climb the social ladder of Whiteness.[81] To this end the achievement of the title of master, however they came by it, allowed these European men to distance themselves socially from other former European servants in seventeenth-century Virginia who had no European servants or enslaved Africans under their authority.

It was within this historical context that many former European servants moved up the intra-racial class rankings to embody Whiteness as junior partners and colleagues of the slaveholding elite. That said, White men were not the only group who benefited from the social transformation that arose from the colonization of Virginia and the growing transatlantic slave trade. Many White women (wives, mothers and sisters) embodied Whiteness as mistresses to their husband's servants and slaves.

The history of American Whiteness for White women arose out of the influx of European men who immigrated to Virginia (eight to ten thousand a month by the mid-seventeenth century) to do the hard labor of colonization required for the building of White civil society. One of the keys to this venture's success was preventing White men from developing intimate relations with Native or African women, which put pressure on the Virginia Company to avidly recruit White women into the colony to marry these men.[82] In 1620, Virginia Company officials sponsored the immigration of ninety unmarried Englishwomen to the colony with the hopes that they would marry and procreate with European male settlers. In 1621, they again solicited subscriptions for single girls and widows to immigrate to Virginia, which led to fifty-seven White women settling in the colony.[83]

Once in the colony, Virginia Company officials expected that the women "at their first landing be housed, lodged, and provided for of diet till they be married. And in case they cannot be presently married we desire they may be put to several householders that have wives till they can be provided husbands."[84] So although the vast majority of White women who immigrated to the region in the early seventeenth century came as indentured servants, the expectation was that the bulk of their labor would be of a domestic nature in support of the civic agenda of White men.

Virginia Company leaders insisted that the colony "can never flourish till families be planted."[85] To this end, White women's labor was deliberately exempted from taxation to achieve the type of family-centered society that officials envisioned for Virginia. No matter that White men outnumbered White women four or five to one, the importation of White women into the colony was the linchpin to the development of a White civil society and the nuclear family, which had the concomitant benefit of decreasing the likelihood that men like Hugh Davis would marry or form intimate ties with Native and Black women.[86] It was under these circumstances, as domestic partners to White male workers, that European women heeded the call of the Virginia Company and did their part in effectuating the racial colonization of Virginia.

The willingness of White women to serve in this domestic and political capacity to advance the pace of Virginia's colonization made them, like their male counterparts, constituents in developing a White civil society via the international system of slavery. By voluntarily supplying the colony with the domestic labor needed to form the families that would "fix people to the soil" and prevent copulation with African and indigenous women until the White population increased naturally, European women became accomplices in the culture of colonialism at home and abroad that became the staple of White womanhood, which tied their fate to the political and economic agenda of White men for decades and even centuries to come.[87] And like their male comrades, White women's intense dependence on planters and investors ensured their full immersion in the racial practices that pervaded an advancing international system of slavery. As a result, White women would claim a sense of Whiteness on par with that of their mates. And nowhere was White women's claim of Whiteness as fulsomely expressed as much as it was with slaveholding women.

Slaveholding created a new domestic identity for White women as slave mistresses. Take the case of Mrs. Yeardley. Once her husband George had acquired eight enslaved persons in 1619 from aboard the *Treasurer*, she was instantly set apart from the approximately two hundred White women living in Virginia between 1620 and 1622 whose husbands only owned European indentured servants.[88] As a slave mistress, Mrs. Yeardley's duties included managing the eight nameless "Negroes" (three women and five men) who were listed in the 1624 census as part of their household. Perhaps the three enslaved women helped Mrs. Yeardley raise her two sons, Argoll and Francis, born in 1621 and 1624 respectively, and maybe the five enslaved men did the routine tasks that were needed to maintain their two plantations: Flowerdew Hundred and the one on Hogs Island. Possibly too, maybe the five men were assisted by the three other African persons, Anthony, John and William, known to have resided on the Flowerdew plantation in 1624.[89] Either way, owning enslaved Africans gave women like Mrs. Yeardley a distinctly elevated class position at a time when very little separated the lives of White people in the upper classes.

Such distinctions probably encouraged a degree of class envy among the Europeans who would have been in the same prestigious social position as the Yeardleys if they also owned African people or even a European indentured servant or two. The simple fact was that Whites who only owned European servants were ranked in a lower social position than those who owned African people, and those Whites with no servants or slaves at all were ranked lower still. Thus, as a slaveholding lady, White women like Mrs. Yeardley were freed from the worry of having to go to work in the fields like other White women might have had to do. The lifting of this anxiety allowed her to focus on making a household that was suitable for a governor and master.[90]

Mary Tucker, the wife of William Tucker, one of the fifteen prominent masters in the colony referred to in chapter 1, was also a slaveholding lady. In her case, she was the mistress over an entire enslaved African family. They were recorded in the 1625 muster of the Tucker household as "Antoney Negro: Isabell Negro: and William theire Child Baptised."[91] The records do not indicate which of them they acquired first, Antoney or Isabell. No matter the order, ownership of an enslaved family made the Tucker legacy all the more secure, since a bonded nuclear family would likely reproduce itself faster. For this reason, Tucker might have acquired Antoney first and then later purchased Isabell to be his wife. Alternatively, perhaps Isabell was initially bought by Tucker to be a nurse to their infant daughter Elizabeth or a maid for his wife, Mary. Nonetheless, the history of slaveholding in the 1620s suggests that enslavement was about more than economics; it also created an emerging aesthetic of class and gender etiquette for Whites that, by the 1640s, turned men into stately masters and women into refined mistresses.

It is tempting interpret the domestic role of White women and the tax-exempt status of White female laborers as part of what historian Kathleen Brown labels "English gender conventions" rather than racial ones. Indeed, in England, as Brown explains, field work was not the primary responsibility of most English women.[92] The majority, she posits, spent their time maintaining households. Once in Virginia, colonial leaders did not spend a great deal of time scrutinizing their assumptions about European women as domestic laborers. However, because of the transatlantic slave trade planters in the early decades of the seventeenth century did find themselves examining their beliefs about Black women and their labor. The consequence of their conclusions gave rise to the 1643 law that exempted White women and their labor from taxation and likewise left the status of indentured White women's children as determined by the child's father in contradistinction to enslaved Black women's children, whose status was determined by their mother, a custom that was legitimized with the 1662 slave law. Without a doubt, the transatlantic slave trade was key to the making of American Whiteness through all sorts of assumptions about White women's and men's labor and freedom relative to Black women and men.

That said, during the 1620s, White women and men in Virginia were still learning how to be mistresses and masters within a growing international system of slavery, and doing so had real consequences for how European people embodied Whiteness and envisioned their new identity as slaveholders.[93] By the 1640s, the status of owning slaves had trickled down from the early entrants into slaveholding like the Yeardleys, the Tuckerses and Abraham Peirsey to newcomers like Stephen Charlton and Richard Vaughan, who likewise participated in the transatlantic slave trade and experienced its transformative effects within their families for decades to come.

For example, owning a slave reformulated the organization of domestic life for White people and their children, who were schooled by their parents in the principles of hierarchy rooted in the evolving transatlantic system of slavery. We see this when Richard Vaughan bequeathed his "Negro Susan" (Grace-Susanna mentioned earlier in this chapter) and his "Negro Jane" (her sister) to his seventeen-year-old stepson John Waltham on April 22, 1656, thereby setting the stage for John to transition from being a former playmate of Grace-Susanna and Jane to being their master.[94] By bequeathing enslaved "Negros" to his son, Vaughan lovingly nudged John into his identification with Whiteness both as a patriarch and a slaveholder via the growing transatlantic slave trade.

Although John Waltham was seventeen when he became master over Grace-Susanna and Jane, his stepfather Vaughan actually began the process of grooming him in some of the tenets of slaveholding much earlier. The process started in 1649, when John turned eight and Vaughan deeded him four hundred fifty acres of land near their home in Northampton County, Virginia.[95] The proximity of the land to the family's estate allowed Vaughan to carefully manage John's development as a soon-to-be planter and slaveholder. One could imagine that Vaughan taught young John about the ups and downs of planting and all that it entailed, such as buying and selling slaves in anticipation of trends, financial hardships and other unexpected pitfalls.[96] The special instructions Vaughan likely issued to John—advice on navigating the international system of slavery, both internally and externally, and its function as a source of a family's financial security and social standing—all made slaveholding a part of the project of preparing John for membership in the upper class.

Much of their father-son relationship probably also entailed Vaughan teaching his stepson how to exert his authority over his household, which in the early seventeenth century included his wife, children, servants and enslaved persons. Even for seventeen-year-old Waltham, being a slave master meant that he legally had unfettered sexual access to his female laborers. It also meant that he held control over other men's sexual access to the women in his household and that he had the legal right to discipline his family members and laborers as he saw fit, including killing them, as the law allowed a master to do to enslaved Africans if done during the course of punishment.[97] To this end, growing up in a household in 1647 with enslaved African women such as Grace-Susanna and Jane and then becoming their master in 1656, John experienced firsthand the powerful legacy of Whiteness through the institution of slavery and patriarchy, or what Cheryl Harris calls "racial patriarchy," that is, the ideology of White supremacy and White male control over women's (Black and White) reproduction and sexuality.[98] Patriarch would be a status that his son, John Waltham III, would eventually inherit from him in the form of enslaved property after his death. Perhaps this is why slavery, an institution that represented the transnational nature of wealth in the early seventeenth century, became such a powerful symbol of White people's freedom toward the end of the seventeenth century.

Understanding the emergence of slaveholding as a transformative activity and expression of one's wealth and Whiteness brings us back to the relationship that European emigrants in Virginia had with an expansive international system of slavery, which facilitated the proliferation of enslavement and colonization around the world. This history's various subtexts spanned nearly a century, from English emigrants' participation in the colonization of São Tomé in the sixteenth century, which supported Portugal's attempt at conquering Angola kingdoms, to their role in building the institutions that helped subdue Virginia's Native peoples after 1607 and that paved the way for the enslavement of Africans in the colony a little more than a decade later.

By the 1640s, guarantees against permanent bondage combined with the hope for landownership and good jobs contributed to an emerging concept of Whiteness that was defined by elites and adopted by lower-class Europeans around distinct ideas about freedom, gender and race. By this measure, owning enslaved Africans was a means for rewriting their future, just as the generation before them had done more than twenty years earlier. I call this the "trickle-down effect of Whiteness," which developed via participation in the rapid growth of the transatlantic slave trade, allowing Europeans of all classes to identify their social position in opposition to Africans, a practice which continued well into the twentieth century United States with slave codes and Jim Crow laws and customs.[99]

Reconstructing the major transformations in European identity after the arrival of African peoples in 1619 creates new perspectives from which to analyze White racial formations that predate Bacon's Rebellion. Whereas most studies point to the rebellion led by Nathaniel Bacon in 1676 as representative of racial solidarity between Africans and poor Whites, I argue that it actually demonstrates the existence of racial solidarity among Whites as expressed by the outrage of the poor White men who followed Bacon over not receiving land like the elite White men.[100] In other words, the White followers of Bacon saw themselves as White too, hence their outrage at not receiving their share of Native land. And like it was with Native American land, the enslavement of Africans and their potential for permanent bondage since their arrival in 1619 likewise provided the basis for a racial identification of Whiteness among Europeans who were under no such restrictions. Thus, there were two core assumptions upon which European identity rested in the early decades of the seventeenth century: that Whites ranked higher than Blacks regardless of class, and that owning even one slave symbolized belonging to the upper ranks of the dominant group of Whites. As slaveholding became a viable option for former indentured servants, who because of their contracts could not expect to purchase a slave of their own until their mid-twenties, most jumped at the chance to hold this symbol of wealth, self-sufficiency and White racial identity as soon as their finances allowed, all of which predates Bacon's Rebellion.

This point was exemplified in 1647 by Stephen Charlton when he gifted two-year-old Grace-Susanna to his widowed sister and later to her and her new husband Richard Vaughan until they could establish their own family of enslaved persons. In doing so, Charlton was embracing the legacy of

Whiteness through a thriving transatlantic slave trade that men like William Tucker had participated in more than twenty years earlier. In turn, when Richard Vaughan purchased Grace-Susanna's mother, Galatia, by way of the same system, the acquisition showed that aspiring planters fully and routinely embraced African slavery and concomitantly Whiteness as a means of securing their family's financial future.

Historians disagree about the role that the demand for slaves had on the growth and development of the transatlantic trade.[101] But there is little disagreement that the growth of the international system of slavery resulted in social and economic transformations in both West Central Africa and in Virginia. African kingdoms like Angola and Benin were weakened as a result of the depletion of their most valuable resource: human beings. These African women and men were the commodities by which colonies like Virginia and Bermuda were strengthened. Quite simply, Africa's loss was England's and Europe's gain. Changing forms and expectations about slave labor, new uses for enslaved women and the resulting class distinctions among Whites that enslavement engendered all supported a transformation of Virginia into a White civil society through a diffusion of slaveholding up and down the social ladder for Whites. And in an effort to move up in class through slaveholding, most planters adopted the Black exploitation practices and principles of the international system of slavery that pervaded all aspects of life in Virginia.

What were the transnational institutions of slavery in early seventeenth-century Virginia and what did they look like? How did Blacks and Whites navigate and manipulate this landscape? How did both interpret it? The next chapter looks into the institutional geography of Virginia's White landscape, showing the influence of the international system of slavery on its spatial design.

NOTES

1. Records indicate that the first Africans arrived in the Americas in 1526. Henry Louis Gates PBS Series on African American History.

2. Isabel Wilkerson, *Caste: The Origins of Our Discontents* (New York: Random House, 2020). Wilkerson describes the immutability of caste in many societies including Nazi Germany and India.

3. Frank B. Wilderson III, *Afropessimism* (New York, NY: Liveright Publishing Corporation, 2020), 203. According to Wilderson "junior partners" are people who are human but not White heterosexual males and who are targets of White supremacy and patriarchy, respectively, and, simultaneously, the agents and beneficiaries of anti-Blackness. I borrow this term and recast poor and working-class Whites to discuss the ways in which they were simultaneously the agents and beneficiaries

of anti-Blackness during the early decades of the seventeenth century even as they suffered growing pains in the relational dynamics with wealthy Whites as a result of their status.

4. Matthew Pratt Guterl, "A Note on the Word 'White,'" *American Quarterly* 56, no. 2 (June 2004): 439–47. One of the ways Guterl defines Whiteness is as an "inchoate conglomeration of factors that give group advantage to White people, often without showing it explicitly, but also including old-fashion, in-your-face racism, and color-blind things." I draw on his analysis when discussing the ways in which European immigrants held advantages over African persons in early seventeenth-century Virginia in areas such as good jobs and barriers against permanent bondage.

5. James Baldwin, *The Price of the Ticket: Collected Nonfiction, 1948–1985* (New York: St. Martin's, 1985).

6. For an extensive discussion on evolution of the White laboring class in seventeenth-century Virginia see Allen, *The Invention of the White Race: The Origin of Racial Oppression in Anglo-America*, II. His thesis is laid out concisely on pages 240–41 in volume II. I draw on Allen's historical analysis of English attempts to colonize Ireland from the fifteenth through the eighteenth centuries to support my analysis of the attempts at colonization in West Central Africa in the sixteenth century and Virginia in the seventeenth century. Also see Allen's volume I, 52–70.

7. Birmingham, *Trade and Conflict in Angola: The Mbundu and Their Neighbours under the Influence of the Portuguese 1483–1790*, 25; James Horn, *A Land as God Made It: Jamestown and the Birth of America* (New York: Basic Books, 2005), 244–45.

8. Ibid., 46.

9. Philip L. Barbour, ed., *The Complete Works of Captain John Smith, 1580–1631* vol. I (Chapel Hill: University of North Carolina Press, 1986), 20–21.

10. *The Jamestown Voyages under the First Charter, 1606–1609*, 2 vols., vol. I, II (1969), 24.

11. Birmingham, *Trade and Conflict in Angola: The Mbundu and Their Neighbours under the Influence of the Portuguese 1483–1790*, 45. São Tomé, first occupied by the Portuguese in the late fifteenth century, is less than five hundred nautical miles from Angola.

12. Dictionary.com defines citizenship as "the state of being vested with rights and privileges and duties of a citizen." It is the rights and privileges vested upon European indentured servants by virtue of their Whiteness that I call them citizens and discuss the parameters of their citizenship relative to African and indigenous peoples.

13. According to Wilderson in *Afropessimism*, civil society is defined as political organizing, office work, divisions of labor and writing. I expand on this idea to include the politics of race in the structuring of civil society.

14. I draw on the work of Wilderson III in *Afropessimism* on the relational antagonisms that exist in society of which the worker/boss is one in which the worker is disciplined with violence when they refuse to adhere to the rules that govern civil society. Here, I extend this framework to show that under the conditions of survival in New World settlement, the terms of agreement in Virginia civil society also worked to make American Whiteness.

15. A. G. Bradley, ed., *Travels and Works of Captain John Smith President of Virginia, and Admiral of New England, 1580–1631* (Edinburgh: John Grant, 1910), II: 502.

16. Alexander Brown, *The Genesis of the United States*, vol. II (Boston: Houghton, Mifflin, & Co., 1891), 782.

17. Susan M. Kingsbury, ed., *The Records of the Virginia Company of London: The Court Book, from the Manuscript in the Library of Congress*, 4 vols. (Washington, D.C.: Government Printing Office, 1906), III: 99–100. The tenant laborers were left with very little money after giving over half to the Virginia Company and some to the planter.

18. Ibid.

19. "The Tragicall Relations of the Virginia Assembly 1624," in *The English Literatures of America, 1500–1800*, eds. Myra Jehlen and Michael Werner (1996).

20. Kingsbury, *The Records of the Virginia Company of London: The Court Book, from the Manuscript in the Library of Congress*, IV: 175.

21. Ibid., 87–88. The wealth generated from tobacco produced by enslaved laborers, who were brought to the island duty-free, made Bermuda England's most prosperous colony prior to 1625.

22. Kingsbury, *The Records of the Virginia Company of London: The Court Book, from the Manuscript in the Library of Congress*, III: 479, 489.

23. Jester, *Adventures of Purse and Person, 1607–1625*, 39.

24. Kingsbury, *The Records of the Virginia Company of London: The Court Book, from the Manuscript in the Library of Congress*, III: 489.

25. Jester, *Adventures of Purse and Person, 1607–1625*, 8, 15, 27–29, 38, 40, 42, 66.

26. Morgan, *American Slavery, American Freedom*, 155, 318 and Breen and Innes, *Myne Owne Ground*, 111, 112, suggest that free Blacks were treated the same as Whites.

27. Cheryl I. Harris, "Whiteness as Property," *Harvard Law Review* 106, no. 8 (1993): 1717. I put "slave" in quotes to denote indefinite servitude whereby freedom is only got by manumission or self-purchase. In Virginia, since 1619, this was the circumstances under which bonded Blacks labored. This was not the circumstance for bonded European laborers.

28. "Decisions of the General Court," *Virginia Magazine of History and Biography*, January 1898, 236.

29. Kingsbury, ed., *Records of the Virginia Company of London: The Court Book, from the Manuscript in the Library of Congress*, I: 411–12, 479–80, 489.

30. Ibid., I: 304–7.

31. Jarvis, "In the Eye of All Trade: Maritime Revolution and the Transformation of Bermudian Society, 1618–1800," 149.

32. Ibid., 87.

33. Wesley Frank Craven, *Dissolution of the Virginia Company: The Failure of a Colonial Experiment* (Gloucester: Peter Smith, 1964), 59.

34. Kingsbury, *The Records of the Virginia Company of London: The Court Book, from the Manuscript in the Library of Congress*, I: 21. New Adventurers arrived in

the colony after Sir Thomas Dale's 1616 departure. Also, New Adventurers received fifty acres of land after seven years of residency, instead of one hundred acres after three years like Old Adventurers.

35. "Abstracts of Virginia Land Patents," *Virginia Magazine of History and Biography*, III (1896): 53–56; Morgan, *American Slavery, American Freedom*, 94. Investors got one share of stock in the Virginia Company for each share purchased.

36. Martha W. McCartney, *Virginia Immigrants and Adventurers 1607–1635: A Biographical Dictionary* (Baltimore: Genealogical Publishing Co., Inc., 2007), 87, 423, 749. For a listing of Yeardley's servant and enslaved population see Jester, 22, 27, 29, 46.

37. Jester, *Adventures of Purse and Person, 1607–1625*, 46. Evidence suggested that "Antonio" was Anthony Johnson, the enslaved African man who owned a slave and several servants. Johnson eventually married Mary.

38. I put the term "slave" in quotes to denote the different understanding of the meaning of this status to African and European people during this period and throughout the history of the transatlantic slave trade. For more information see G. Ugo Nwokeji, *The Slave Trade and Culture in the Bight of Biafra: An African Society in the Atlantic World* (New York: Cambridge University Press 2010) and Walter Rodney, *How Europe Underdeveloped Africa* (Washington, D.C.: Howard University Press), 1982.

39. Notable scholars who take this position include: Oscar and Mary Handlin, "Origins of the Southern Labor System," *William and Mary Quarterly* VII, no. Third Series (1950); George M. Fredrickson, *The Black Image in the White Mind: The Debate on Afro-American Character and Destiny, 1817–1914* (New York: Harper & Row, 1971); Morgan, *American Slavery, American Freedom: The Ordeal of Colonial Virginia*; Breen, *"Myne Owne Ground": Race and Freedom on Virginia's Eastern Shore, 1640–1676.*

40. Kingsbury, *The Records of the Virginia Company of London: The Court Book, from the Manuscript in the Library of Congress*, III: 102–15. Morgan, *American Slavery, American Freedom*, 97–98.

41. Guterl, "A Note on the Word 'White,'" 439–44. Such institutions were part of what Guterl calls the "inchoate conglomeration of factors that give group advantage to White people." David R. Roediger, *Working toward Whiteness: How America's Immigrants Became White: The Strange Journey from Ellis Island to the Suburbs* (New York, NY: Basic Books, 2005). Here I build on Roediger's work to consider how New World Europeans became White.

42. Ibid. Kingsbury, I: 21.

43. Morgan, *American Slavery, American Freedom*, 119. Richard Bennett (Edward Bennett's nephew) was the governor of Virginia from April 30, 1652, to March 2, 1655.

44. Kingsbury, ed., *The Records of the Virginia Company of London: The Court Book, from the Manuscript in the Library of Congress*, III: 275–80, 473, 489.

45. Ibid. In 1621 the Virginia Company failed in the attempt restrict tobacco growth to no more than one hundred tobacco plants per year. Jarvis, "In the Eye of All Trade:

Maritime Revolution and the Transformation of Bermudian Society, 1618–1800,"
144, 152–55.

46. Kingsbury, ed., *The Records of the Virginia Company of London: The Court Book, from the Manuscript in the Library of Congress*, III: 99–100.

47. For a listing of Bennett's, Yeardley's and Peirsey's enslaved population see: Jester, *Adventures of Purse and Person, 1607–1625*, 22, 27, 29, 46. Through 1624 Bermuda exceed Virginia's tobacco output. By 1625, Virginia had surpassed Bermuda, producing 79,875 pounds of tobacco compared to Bermuda's 70,000 pounds. Javis, "In the Eye of All Trade: Maritime Revolution and the Transformation of Bermudian Society, 1618–1800," 769. For more information on tobacco production in Virginia and Bermuda, see Russell R. Menard, "The Tobacco Industry in the Chesapeake Colonies, 1617–1730: An Interpretation," *Research in Economic History* 5 (1980): 109–77, and Lord Sackvill's "Papers Concerning Virginia, 1613–1631," *American Historical Review* 26 (1921): 496–516.

48. In *Principal Navigations and Voyages*, edited by Richard Hakluyt (London, 1598–1600).

49. Richard Ligon, *A True and Exact History of the Island of Barbados* (London 1657), 51. See also Jennifer L. Morgan, *Laboring Women: Reproduction and Gender in New World Slavery* (Philadelphia: University of Pennsylvania Press, 2004), 14.

50. Pamela Scully, "Rape, Race, and Colonial Culture: The Sexual Politics of Identity in the Nineteenth Century Cape Colony, South Africa," *The American Historical Review* 100, no. 2 (Apr. 1995): 337. Scully argues that "colonialism created the conditions that authorized the pervasive rape of black women by white men."

51. Hening, ed., *The Statutes at Large; Being a collection of All the Laws of Virginia, from the First Session of the Legislature in the Year 1619*, I: 146.

52. Blumer, "Race Prejudice as a Sense of Group Position," 218.

53. Pratt, "A Note on the Word 'White,'" 439. According to Pratt, the courts were one of the institutions that gave group advantage to White people.

54. Hening, ed., *The Statutes at Large; Being a Collection of All the Laws of Virginia, from the First Session of the Legislature in the Year 1619*, I: 243. The 1643 statute reads in part as follows: "Be it also enacted and confirmed there be tenn pounds of tob'o. per poll & a bushell of corne per poll paid to the ministers within the severall parishes of the collony for all tithable persons, that is to say, as well for all youths of sixteen years of age as vpwards, as also for all negro women at the age of sixteen years."

55. Ibid., II: 26.

56. "Virginia Land Patents, 1623–1660."

57. Theodore W. Allen, *The Invention of the White Race: Racial Oppression and Social Control*, 2 vols., vol. I (New York: Verso, 1994). Those scholars include: Douglas J. Deal, *Race and Class in Colonial Virginia: Indians, Englishmen, and Africans on the Eastern Shore During the Seventeenth Century* (New York: Garland Publishing, Inc., 1993); Oscar and Mary Handlin, "Origins of the Southern Labor System," *William and Mary Quarterly* VII, no. 3rd Series (1950): 199–222; and Edmund S. Morgan, *American Freedom* (New York: W. W. Norton and Company, Inc., 1975).

58. "Northampton County Virginia, Orders, Deeds & Wills 1651–1654 Book 4," 28.

59. "Northampton County Virginia Record Book: Orders, Deeds, Wills, Ect., 1645–1651 Book 3," 289. The transaction was made on March 19, 1647.

60. "County Court Records of Accomack-Northampton, Virginia 1640–1645," folio 79, 80.

61. Morgan, *Laboring Women: Reproduction and Gender in New World Slavery*, 83.

62. "Reasons of ye Planters of Barbados about Nonpayment of Custom," in Thomas Povey, *Booke of Entrie of Forreigne Letters, 1655–1660*. This text had Barbadian slaveowners referring to female slaves of childbearing years as "increasers." Although it was not until 1662 that the children of enslaved women were legally deemed slaves and, thus, also the property of their owner, in practice this was the de facto law of the land prior to 1662.

63. Morgan, *Laboring Women: Reproduction and Gender in New World Slavery*, 3.

64. "County Court Records of Accomack-Northampton, Virginia 1640–1645," folio 150.

65. Ralph T. Whitelaw, *Virginia's Eastern Shore*, 2 vols., vol. I (Richmond: Virginia Historical Society, 1951), 108.

66. "Northampton County Virginia Record Book: Deeds, Wills, Ect., 1657–1666," 104.

67. As an example of the cost of African versus European laborers, the estate inventory of William Burdett showed that his eight-year-old enslaved girl (no name recorded) was valued at three thousand pounds of tobacco, while his twelve-year-old boy servant with eight years of service remaining was valued at one thousand pounds of tobacco. "County Court Records of Accomack-Northampton, Virginia 1640–1645," 423.

68. "York County, Virginia Records, 1638–1644." The cost of Black male servants averaged around two thousand seven hundred pounds of tobacco.

69. Ibid.

70. David Eltis, Stephen D. Behrendt, David Richardson, and Herbert S. Klein, *The Trans-Atlantic Slave Trade: A Database on CD-ROM* (Cambridge, 1999).

71. Susan Westbury, "Slaves of Colonial Virginia: Where They Came From," *William and Mary Quarterly* 42, no. 3 (1985): 228–37. According to Westbury, enslaved persons came to colonial Virginia by three routes: directly from Africa, from Africa with a protracted stay in the West Indies, and from other mainland British colonies.

72. Jarvis, "In the Eye of All Trade: Maritime Revolution and the Transformation of Bermudian Society, 1618–1800," 151.

73. "Ives Rich Papers," 214–15, 233–34.

74. Gomez, *Exchanging Our Country Marks*, 192–93.

75. Miller, *Kings and Kinsmen: Early Mbundu States in Angola*, 43.

76. "County Court Records of Accomack-Northampton, Virginia 1640–1645," 423.

77. Ibid.

78. Hening, ed., *The Statutes at Large; Being a Collection of All the Laws of Virginia, from the First Session of the Legislature in the Year 1619*, I: 242.

79. Jacqueline Jones, "'My Mother Was Much of a Woman': Black Women, Work, and the Family under Slavery," *Feminist Studies* 8, no. 2 (1982): 239.

80. Kingsbury, *The Records of the Virginia Company of London: The Court Book, from the Manuscript in the Library of Congress*, 399.

81. Barbour, *The Complete Works of Captain John Smith, 1580–1631*, II: 618. "York County, Virginia Records, 1638–1644." The cost of Black male servants averaged around two thousand seven hundred pounds of tobacco.

82. Emily J. Salmon and Edward D. C. Campbell Jr., eds. *The Hornbook of Virginia History: A Ready-Reference Guide to the People, Places and Past*, 4th ed. (Richmond: The Library of Virginia, 1994), 13. For statistics on White male immigration rates see James Horn, *Adapting to a New World: English Society in the Seventeenth-Century Chesapeake* (Chapel Hill: University of North Carolina Press, 1994), 137.

83. Salmon, *The Hornbook of Virginia History: A Ready-Reference Guide to the People, Places and Past*, 14.

84. Kingsbury, *The Records of the Virginia Company of London: The Court Book, from the Manuscript in the Library of Congress*, I: 256–57.

85. Ibid. Here the term "planted" means people settling in a colonized area.

86. Wesley Frank Craven, *White, Red, and Black: Seventeenth-Century Virginia* (Charlottesville: The University Press of Virginia, 1971), 5.

87. Linda Kerber, "The Republican Mother: Women and the Enlightenment-an American Perspective," *The American Quarterly* 28, no. 2 (Summer 1976): 188. According to Kerber during the Enlightenment period the Republican ideology included a domestic role for women as "Republican Mothers" that defined their relationship to the state in the making of civic culture. Here I use Kerber's analysis of the "Republican Mother" to explain how White women participated in the making of American Whiteness through their domestic roles that supported the development of a White civil society in seventeenth-century Virginia.

88. H. R. McIlwaine, "The Maids Who Came to Virginia in 1620 and 1621 for Husbands," in *The Reviewer* 1 (April 1, 1921): 105–13. Also see *Virginia Magazine of History and Biography*, VII, 364–67, for population estimates.

89. McCartney, *Virginia Immigrants and Adventurers 1607–1635: A Biographical Dictionary*, 87, 423, 749.

90. Nora Miller Turman, *George Yeardley: Governor of Virginia and Organizer of the General Assembly in 1619* (Richmond: Garrett and Massie, Inc., 1959), 130. The records indicate that Mrs. Yeardley often hosted parties and received guest into their home as part of her official role as Virginia's gubernatorial first lady.

91. Jester, *Adventures of Purse and Person, 1607–1625*, 49.

92. Brown, *Good Wives, Nasty Wenches, and Anxious Patriarchs: Gender, Race, and Power in Colonial Virginia*, 117.

93. Rodney, *How Europe Underdeveloped Africa*, 88.

94. "Northampton County, Virginia Deeds, Wills, Etc., 1654–1657 Book 5." In 1656 Grace-Susanna would have been eleven and Jane five. Records indicate that John Waltham was a one-year-old in 1640.

95. Nell Marion Nugent, *Cavaliers and Pioneers: Abstracts of Virginia Land Patents and Grants, 1623–1800*, vol. I (Richmond: Press of The Dietz Printing Co., 1934), 183.

96. Walter Johnson, *Soul by Soul: Life Inside the Antebellum Slave Market* (Cambridge: Harvard University Press, 1999), 86.

97. Brown, *Good Wives, Nasty Wenches, and Anxious Patriarchs: Gender, Race, and Power in Colonial Virginia*, chapter 1. Hening, *Statutes*: III: 86–88.

98. Cheryl I. Harris, "Finding Sojourner's Truth: Race, Gender, and the Institution of Property," *Cardozo Law Review* 18, no. 2 (1996): 312–13.

99. Morrison, *Playing in the Dark: Whiteness and the Literary Imagination*, 9, 31–59. Morrison in her reading of Whiteness indicates that it became defined by its opposite, Blackness. My analysis of seventeenth-century Virginia indicates that lower-class Whites defined themselves in opposition to Blacks because of the impermanence of their bondage and in doing so sought to align themselves with elite Whites in using enslavement as a means to define their social position.

100. Texts that argue Bacon's Rebellion as an example of African/poor European solidarity include: Allen, *The Invention of the White Race: Racial Oppression and Social Control*, I; Morgan, *American Slavery, American Freedom: The Ordeal of Colonial Virginia*.

101. Paul Lovejoy, in his book, *Transformations in Slavery* (1983), stressed that the external demand for African slaves manifested in the transatlantic slave trade and impacted the growth and development of indigenous slavery in Africa. John Thornton, on the other hand, in his equally important work, *Africa and the Africans and the Making of the Atlantic World, 1400–1800* (1992), contends that external slave trades, like the transatlantic commerce, actually emerged from the native institutions of slavery that was deeply embedded in various African societies. Scholars debate the volume of the trade, the regional and ethnic origins of the exported population, and the sex and age profiles of slaves and their impact on African history and slavery in the Americas.

Chapter 3

From Slave Pen to Plantation

The Making of American Whiteness in the Built Environment, 1618–1634

Until now, the making of American Whiteness has focused on the intragroup dynamics among various classes of Europeans and how through the process of colonization, conquest and enslavement European settlers in Virginia embraced White supremacy and used this ideology as the basis for constructing civil society. That said, constructing, and more importantly growing and maintaining, a society based on White supremacy involved more than ideology: it involved physical institutions and structures that made White supremacy manifest in everyday life. And to do so, one had to look no further than the international system of slavery and its built environment.

Long before English settlers first occupied Virginia in 1607, European nations active in the international system of slavery had provided privateers and explorers a blueprint for a physical environment that advanced White supremacy through the colonization, conquest and enslavement of African people and Africa. The Portuguese, after they made the attempt in 1565 to conquer kingdoms in the Angola region of West Central Africa, erected forts and castles to maintain control of fallen territories. And in just over a ten-year span, the buildings grew more sophisticated in size and design to include castles that enabled the storage and sale of enslaved Africans.[1] Other approaches to European domiciliation of the region during this period were the use of Portuguese laborers to build temporary fortifications to guard against surprise offensives by the Mbundu peoples of Angola who were defending their lands.

It was from this prehistory that Virginia Company officials learned from their European predecessors the power of the physical environment to effectuate White supremacy. So when attempting to colonize Virginia, instead of erecting forts and castles like the Portuguese did to achieve European domination, colonial settlers constructed cookie-cutter settlements to establish White supremacy in the colony.[2] But like their Portuguese counterparts, Virginia leaders also used poorer European laborers to build protective barriers to help achieve control over the area. Examples include Virginia Company officials directing early settlers to construct fortified communities in order to avoid attack by indigenous peoples defending their lands and ordering Virginia's first inhabitants not to "settle in woodsy areas as it may act as a cover for your enemies" attacks.[3] Then, as tensions eased, Virginia colonists were instructed to encroach even farther onto Native American lands to build homes, plantations, churches and courthouses to strengthen their territorial control.

Colonists' fear of Native American retaliation against their invasion was real, and constructing buildings along with a racial narrative that assuaged and channeled this fear was equally real and was part of the reason for casting the indigenous population of Virginia as the enemy. The other part was that it served as propaganda to justify the "arrogant imposition" of the European settlers onto Confederate Powhatan land.[4] Virginia leaders also invented rhetoric around the idea of Native peoples as "savages" in order to validate the regular breach of Europeans onto indigenous lands. Such labels, combined with promises of wealth and prosperity, supplied the Virginia Company with the ideological framework that convinced the European colonists to occupy Native areas and to "expect success from God" as they built cities, towns, plantations and churches that facilitated the colonization of Virginia into a White society over the existing Powhatan one.[5]

So, with the ideology of White supremacy in place in both the psyche of Virginia residents and in the understanding of the infrastructure needed for creating a White civil society, Virginia Company officials updated the Portuguese program of erecting specific styles of buildings that facilitated conquest with their own spatial designs that improved colonization. For Virginia, this meant that the layout of communities was structured in a centrifugal pattern that was more conducive to institutionalizing White supremacy. This form had communities constructed with large plantation settlements at the center and with all other buildings (homes, churches and courthouses) seated outward from the plantations to better control the behavior of residents.[6] The concept for this design was similar to the English parish system.[7]

In England, parishes were local units of government, sometimes comprised of only a few hundred acres.[8] In 1618, the Virginia Company ordered that the assemblage of the colony's plantation settlements be divided into parishes, with the plantation owner (usually one of its investors) as the commander of each parish, to better establish power in the hands of the White upper class.[9]

Through 1629, approximately thirteen parish districts housed the colony's more than twelve hundred inhabitants.[10] These parishes were located in Virginia's five boroughs: James City, Elizabeth City, Charles City, Henrico, and the Eastern Shore.[11] Seated on each settlement was a parish church.[12]

Inside of every church was a local court. Each parish church had a staff of priests, vestrymen and churchwardens who were charged with supervising the day-to-day activities of community residents, including prosecuting any immoral activities.[13] And even though each commander had jurisdictional authority over members of his parish, each parish had a church official who held complementary jurisdictional power with the plantation owner/commander.

The New World configuration of the parish system, with its array of homes, plantation settlements, churches, courthouses and officers who oversaw them, mirrored the built environment and organizational structure of transatlantic slave trading outposts. They too facilitated the subjugation and surveillance of White indentured servants, indigenous people and enslaved Africans by wealthy Europeans, just as slave castles, slave pens and forts promoted the subjugation and surveillance of the indigenous peoples of West Central Africa by European nations and their proletariat. The efficiency of seating colonial institutions in every parish around specific settlements allowed Virginia planters to create a White-dominated society through the ability to use the built environment to oversee the governance of the everyday life of area residents, similar to how locating slave pens at the ocean side allowed Portuguese slave merchants to better govern and control the freedom and movement of their indentured servants and enslaved Africans.

That said, White civil society found its hegemonic footing with this centrifugal configuration eleven years after the first fort was erected in Jamestown, when a group of settlers formed Martin's Hundred, one of the first organized plantation communities in Virginia managed by large planters to carry out the Virginia Company's program of White rule.[14] Martin's Hundred was an eighty thousand acre settlement located in James City.[15] It was founded in 1618 by a group of private adventurers, "The Society of Martin's Hundred," named after Richard Martin, an attorney for the Virginia Company.[16] The 1624 census indicates that twenty-seven persons were living in Martin's Hundred, all of European ancestry, eleven of whom we know were indentured servants.[17] By 1712, Martin's Hundred ceased to exist as a separate locale, and was incorporated into a larger area called Merchant's Hundred.[18]

William Harwood, who arrived in Virginia in 1620, was a planter and the commander of Martin's Hundred. Harwood had only been in Virginia for less than one year when the Virginia Company made him leader of Martin's Hundred, which speaks to his wealth and stature prior to his arrival as well as to his buy-in to the racial engineering of the Virginia Company.[19] As commander, it was Harwood's job to discipline the actions of the residents living in this community. His responsibilities included preserving the area's fortifications and ensuring that the community was supplied with the basic provisions for survival: food, clothing, tools and livestock. As the head of

Martin's Hundred, Harwood had immense power over the day-to-day lives of the residents. Besides overseeing the community's supply of food, livestock and weaponry, Harwood also chose the church officials who would assist him in policing the actions of the people under his charge, which for decades was the tactic used for maintaining a White civil society. It was also within the purview of Harwood's authority to dole out privileges to selected residents, such as determining which settlers were allowed to send their children to the elite East India School.[20]

In supervising plantation communities like Martin's Hundred, commanders such as Harwood were curators in the development of Virginia into a White society using organizational and constructional methods and principles that were passed down from the international system of slavery. And like the role European slave traders played in West Central Africa for their governments nearly a century before, plantation commanders like Harwood were equally indispensable to Virginia's growth and development, namely for helping to institutionalize the social hierarchy of Virginia as White, wealthy and male. For instance, men like Harwood controlled the day-to-day lives of enslaved Africans and European indentured servants who immigrated to or passed through the global system of slavery en route to Virginia. This was done by organizing the community's social and physical structures around the plantation, which streamlined the living spaces of parish residents into manageable units that were in close physical proximity to the commanders' homes. This allowed wealthy planters like Harwood, as it had Portuguese slave agents, to better monitor the behavior of their indentured servants and enslaved Africans.

The nexus of the built environment of the parish system and the plantation to the legacy and growth of the international system of slavery becomes clearer in 1619, one year after the formation of Martin's Hundred, with the arrival of the first two groups of enslaved Africans in Virginia. One of those persons was a woman named Angelo, an African who arrived in Virginia on the *Treasurer* destined for the plantation of Captain William Pierce in the James City parish. When the ship anchored in late August or early September 1619 at the docks of Old Point Comfort, Angelo was greeted by her owner, Pierce, and his son-in-law, John Rolfe. Seeing the two White men on the Virginia waterfront awaiting her arrival must have been an ominous sight and sign for Angelo, considering how eerily similar this scene must have been to the one at the port of Luanda, Angola, before her journey to North America.

Angelo's last visions of her homeland after capture were probably similar to Equiano's: "The first object which saluted my eyes when I arrived on the coast was the sea, and a slave ship, which was then riding at anchor, and waiting for its cargo."[21] How horrifying it must have been for Angelo to experience the same exploitive geographical environs in Virginia that she had left behind on the coast of West Africa, except that in this case Pierce was her owner instead of a slave agent, and rather than being housed in a slave pen or castle, she would reside on his plantation. Thus, Angelo's first experience in Virginia reflected the racial and physical landscape of the international system of slavery that she left behind in Luanda: being held captive by White men in an area they constructed to subjugate her.

The first physical structure that Angelo likely encountered while living on Pierce's plantation that mirrored the slave pens in Luanda was the slave quarters. On February 16, 1624, Angelo was recorded as residing in Jamestown in a home or a part of a home designated for Pierce's servants and enslaved persons. The 1624 census indicates that there was only one house on Pierce's settlement. If this was the case, then Angelo and Pierce's three European indentured servants, "Thomas Smith 17 yeares, Henery Bradford aged 35 yeres, and Ester Ederife a maid servant," all lived in the home with Pierce and his wife, Jone.[22] Typically, separate living spaces were constructed to house servants and enslaved persons when there were more than four persons residing on a plantation.[23] However, when plantations had only one house, as it appears was the case for Pierce, then European servants and enslaved persons shared the inferior portion of the home. In either case, the isolation of servants and enslaved persons in a specific part of the main house served a similar purpose as the slave pens of Luanda: it helped planters control the movement of their servants and slaves—making it difficult for them to avoid surveillance.[24]

We have no way of knowing how the internal dynamics of these living arrangements impacted Angelo, but we do know something about the social rank accorded to European servants over bonded Africans in Virginia society. Because the international system of slavery was evolving to be such a powerful tool for communicating Whiteness and social position to its participants, including in the built environment, we know that Smith, Bradford and Ederife were ranked higher on Pierce's plantation than Angelo, given their European ancestry and indentured status. As was mentioned previously, European servants were rated above Africans in the international system of slavery and in Virginia because they volunteered their labor for a fixed period of time to advance the progress of colonization. The term of service for European indentured servants was typically five to seven years, while for bonded Africans the time spent in servitude was indefinite and subject to the prerogatives of their enslaver. Moreover, for Whites, their temporary servitude reflected their lack of economic success, whereas for Blacks, bondage reflected assumptions about their debased humanity relative to Whites, which resulted in the indeterminate appropriation of their labor for the enrichment of the planter and Virginia society as a whole.

For these reasons, Angelo's position in the ballooning international system of slavery made her socially subordinate to her roommates Smith, Bradford and Ederife, even though Angelo was expected to work the fields as a laborer on par, if not higher, with the White men (Smith and Bradford), while the maidservant Ederife, although indentured, was probably being groomed for marriage by Mrs. Pierce, given that the social engineering of the day encouraged planters' wives to care for the White female servants and widows under her charge until they were married to White men.[25] Thus, the physical spaces of the plantation landscape regulated and reproduced the uneven social relations among Whites and among Whites and Blacks that developed in the international system of slavery, one in which Angelo was ranked below all of Pierce's European servants.

Although details of Angelo's life are scant, the geography of the plantation allows us to speculate about how she experienced her surroundings as she traveled out from Pierce's home. One of the many things that Angelo probably did when she stepped out of Pierce's home was to "take inventory of the plantation and its arrangement to consider how best to navigate this landscape."[26] Once outside, Angelo likely observed that the landscape was organized hierarchically, with Pierce's home at the center and a procession of other structures—houses, settlements, churches and courthouses—seated around it. Scholars would call this setup the "White landscape" because of the manner in which such spaces and places affirmed the culture and values of the Europeans who organized and inhabited these areas.[27] To offset this racial and spatial imbalance, perhaps Angelo reinterpreted this landscape from the perspective of Black persons living in the area.[28]

Census records indicate that most of the African people in Virginia in the early 1620s during the time Angelo was enslaved on Pierce's settlement were owned by approximately seven planters.[29] Angelo may have met some of these Black people in the wooded areas or on the trails and paths between their plantations.[30] Angelo would recognize aspects of African culture in these persons, perhaps via their dialect or distinctive markings or hair styles. If they could communicate with each other, maybe Angelo told of her location and her living conditions and perhaps they shared the same information with her. For example, had she met the seven enslaved Africans (two women, four men and one child) who lived on Abraham Peirsey's settlement, which was located near Pierce's home, it was probable that they discussed the ups and downs of sharing living space with White servants. Unlike Pierce's single dwelling, Peirsey's land contained ten dwellings on it, at least one of which was likely used as servants' quarters to house his seven enslaved Africans and twenty-nine European indentured servants.[31]

The use of the term "quarters," when referring to housing for servants, regularly appeared in the county records during the first half of the seventeenth century.[32] As mentioned earlier, separate living quarters were generally constructed on plantations that housed four or more servants and enslaved persons.[33] Relegating servants and enslaved persons to a specific location or to nearby buildings close to the commander's home allowed planters to more easily detect absences, particularly of African persons. Indeed, the Black skin of Angelo stood in stark contrast to that of her roommates Smith, Bradford and Ederife, and thus any indiscretions committed by her would be all the more noticeable because her pigmentation made her actions all the more conspicuous than it did for the Whites. However, just as Black skin was sometimes a burden, at other times it could be a comfort, for it likely drew Blacks like Angelo and those enslaved by Peirsey and other planters together.

Of the twelve hundred persons living in Virginia in 1624, just over fifty were of African ancestry.[34] Thus when Blacks came across one another in their travels, their African features were no doubt a sight for sore eyes.[35] It was possible that these women, men and children gravitated to each other looking for guidance and acceptance. And for the Africans who were "fortunate enough" to be enslaved with other Blacks, like those on Peirsey's settlement, they undoubtedly grew close, forming familial like bonds because of their common condition. Usually, these bonds would develop in the slave quarters or while at work or during travel. Inside the servants' quarters on Peirsey's settlement, the seven "Negros," as they were called in the 1624 muster, probably addressed one another by their African names, which was both affirming and empowering. African names were regarded as subversive within the plantation community and in the international system of slavery. To mitigate the uplifting effect that self-affirming African cultural practices like indigenous names had for Black people, White people created the term "Negro" and other epithets during this era and used them into the mid- to late twentieth century to communicate their slanderous interpretation of the personhood (or lack thereof) of Blacks.

Despite all this, the slave quarters and the outdoor spaces of Peirsey's settlement could still facilitate bonding and a culture of resistance if the two women, four men and one child who were enslaved there could keep alive the languages, rituals and other ties to their African past.[36] In these spaces, Black women and men surely learned to combine aspects of their ethnic customs to instruct their children and each other on how best to handle their master. Perhaps too, the women and men shared what Patricia Hill Collins called "outsider-within knowledge" about life on other plantations.[37] The spaces out-of-doors of the plantation are an excellent source for examining how enslaved persons incorporated the landscape of plantation, including the houses, fields and the woodlands adjoining it, to meet their needs in spite of the subjugating intent of the vernacular, organizational, institutional and structural environs of the Virginia landscape.[38]

Perhaps the outsider-within knowledge of Africans developed from their interpretation of the institutional order of the parish church. Like plantation settlements, the rise in the power of the parish church was comparable to the rising power of the international system of slavery. Just as the Portuguese made a conscious decision to attack Angolan kingdoms with a view toward territorial conquest using the Christian church, so too did English leaders use this institution to facilitate the colonization of Virginia.

For instance, in 1571, the Portuguese assigned its first governor, Paulo Dias, the responsibility of building a church dedicated to promoting the conquest of Angolan territories. In addition, the Royal Charter ordered the establishment of a church in the region with "all the necessary furnishings, ornaments, and vestments" that expressed the felt superiority of Portuguese religious traditions over the Angolan traditions. More important, the charter dictated that church doctrine be used to facilitate the Portuguese's enslavement objectives. One provision stated that "before slaves were certified as true captives and shipped to the mother country, the necessary justifications should be made in accordance with ecclesiastical instructions."[39]

As Portugal's most potent rival in Angola during this period, England still nonetheless emulated Portugal in its use of the church as a means for establishing White rule when settling Virginia. It was in churches like St. Mary's, where the hegemony of White Virginians was on full display and evident for all to see, just as it had been with the Portuguese in the churches they erected in Angola.

St. Mary's was one of the first parish churches built in Virginia. It was located on a settlement called Smith's Hundred, which was the first plantation parish domiciled in the Jamestown settlement. Named after Sir Thomas Smith, the first president of the Virginia Company, the community was formed in 1618 by "The Society of Smith's Hundred," and was "the first [settlement] of any moment" in Virginia to be established at private expense.[40] This meant that individual men invested their own money in the construction of Smith's Hundred rather than receiving subsidies from the Virginia Company, which gave them more authority to manage the region as they saw fit.

The construction cost for St. Mary's church was partially funded by Mrs. Mary Robinson of London, who gave two hundred shillings "toward the helpe of the poor people in Virginia, towards the building of a church and reducinge them to the knowledge of God's word."[41] In recognition of her patronage, the church came to be known as "St. Mary's church in Smith's Hundred."[42] Yet, despite the esteem that Mrs. Robinson was held in, it was the men (planters and high-ranking government officials) who garnered the most recognition at St. Mary's.

The most common scene in early Virginia churches like St. Mary's was not that of women and men engaged in worship, but the parading of planters and other male officials around the church with elaborate regalia to flaunt their authority. Dell Upton, historian of architecture and material culture, offers vivid testimony of such scenes. According to Upton, planters and government officials in early Virginia would enter the sanctuary in a formal procession, accompanied by a guard of attendants. These important men were then seated apart from other parishioners in private pews that were cushioned for their comfort.

According to Upton, the tradition of the processional of leading White males took place throughout the colonial period. It first included the colony's governors, like Sir Thomas Gates (Virginia's first governor), and then later grew to include influential planters. Large planters like Abraham Peirsey, with lots of servants and enslaved persons, were paraded into the sanctuary and conspicuously seated apart from those without such assets.[43] Moreover, it was standard during this period, Upton explains, for the pews of large planters to be cushioned and embroidered with elaborate detail to distinguish these planter's stature over not only his White servants and the Black people he enslaved, who all sat adjacent to him on hard benches, but also to distinguish him from those White congregants who were less wealthy and likewise seated apart from them.[44]

Cushioned pews were only one of the many conspicuous displays of power and stature that set Virginia planters, governors and other high-ranking men apart from other parishioners. Worshiping with fine church artifacts was also an integral part of the trappings provided to these men. For instance, Governor Gates was provided with a table and a cloth and with a velvet cushion to be used when kneeling to pray.[45] According to Upton, the governor's prayer cushions were embellished with long tassels at the corners to contrast their stature from that of laymen. These artifacts provided a fitting backdrop to the White supremacy that seamlessly melded with other carefully selected symbols of authority that adorned parish churches such as a "bible and prayer books in folio, communion vessels, cloths to cover the pulpit and an alter table and a cushion for the pulpit and a bell."[46] Visually, such ornaments not only emphasized godliness but also submission to plantation authority.

The pomp of parading officials, of private pews and embroidered cushions, ultimately leads us to the parish church's connection to the growth of the international system of slavery because these elaborate symbols of power and piety were purchased with tax proceeds collected from planters based on the number of enslaved laborers, male and female, and the number of White male servants over sixteen years of age they owned.[47] The bottom line was that "every parish church [in Virginia] of which there is a record was constructed entirely from taxes" on enslaved and servant labor, linking the parish church and plantation settlements in Virginia to the development and expansion of the transatlantic slave trade and its built environment.[48]

Since the early seventeenth century, taxes (known then as "tithes") were collected from planters on individuals in their household who were legally identified as able to perform taxable or "tithable" labor. The labor of Black women and men and White men, the three groups crucial to a country's success in the international system of slavery, were all tithable. On the other hand, White women, who were equally important in this matrix, were not tithable because they were considered to be the householders' dependents.

As previously mentioned, the issue of female labor, both Black and White, was central to the institutional history of slavery in Virginia. And as stated, we can trace this history to various pieces of legislation, such as the 1643 law that taxed Black women's labor the same as any man while exempting White female labor from this regulation, and the 1662 statute, which imposed on the children of an enslaved woman the same status.[49] The increase in tax revenues as a result of an increase in the taxable population as a consequence of this legislation allows us to visibly connect the transatlantic slave trade to one of early Virginia's most sacred institutions, the parish church. What a powerful message it must have sent that the building and ornamentation of the parish church was financed by proceeds from taxes derived from laborers imported (directly or indirectly) through the international system of slavery and that the most revered and sacred symbols of piety (the Bible, communion vessels, cloths to cover the pulpit and the alter table, prayer cushions and bells), which engendered deference to the parish church from the common settler, were all purchased with revenues from enslaved labor. In effect, these sacred symbols cultivated allegiance to historical systems of European domination like slavery and colonization. Visually and physically, the environment of the parish church was and for centuries has been an important metaphor and nexus for global systems of exploitation.[50]

Although there was no specific record of Black tithables in the early seventeenth century, we do have information on the number of Black headrights, that is, those persons for whom a planter paid for their transportation into the colony. This allows us to safely speculate the degree to which the transatlantic slave trade underwrote the development of Virginia churches. Data collected between 1632 and 1661 from the record books of Northampton, York, Northumberland, Lancaster and Charles City counties indicate that one hundred five Blacks were imported into Virginia by thirty different men. In 1639, one man, George Minifee, imported fifteen enslaved persons, which constituted the largest number of Blacks known to be imported by one individual in the first half of the seventeenth century.[51] During this period these thirty men also imported four hundred fifty-three European servants into the colony under the headrights program. Assuming that most of the Black imports were either enslaved or at least sixteen years of age, the legal age at which White labor was taxable, then roughly twenty percent of the proceeds used to build, outfit and ornament parish churches was derived from enslaved labor.

The use of revenues from enslaved labor in the early seventeenth century to help finance the construction of parish churches was perhaps the strongest institutional link to the rise of the transatlantic slave trade save for the plantation. Both having emerged out of conquest and colonization, the plantation and the church together advanced an aspect of White supremacy through the built environment that was rooted in the principles of an expanding international system of slavery. Planters and high-ranking officials embodied this history as they paraded in and out of church service and as they sat in private pews with embroidered cushions reserved for their exclusive use and knelt at elaborate prayer tables. Not surprisingly, such displays of authority also supplied poor and middling parishioners with a framework for understanding their Whiteness, one that they shared directly and indirectly with wealthier Europeans who participated in the transatlantic slave trade.

Although many White Virginians in the early seventeenth century may not have perceived their racial identity as many do today, they clearly understood the markers of Whiteness generated by the racial inequalities that existed in the parish church as a byproduct of the slave trade. For example, White parishioners in this era undoubtedly viewed their social station through the lens of where they sat in church, such that being moved up a row or nearer to large planters was tangible evidence of a rise in their stature. Thus, if high-ranking planters and politicians were seated so as to convey their rank in the community, then perhaps European servants who were likewise set apart in some fashion from enslaved Africans took some pride in their relative stature. This assumption would hold true for Abraham Peirsey's twenty-nine European indentured servants, who likely sat in an order that represented their elevated status over his seven "Negroes." Similarly, Pierce's servants, Smith, Bradford and Ederife, probably took satisfaction in the fact that they would have better seats in the church than Angelo had.

Besides class and race, parishioners were also likely seated by gender, which leads us to speculate whether Black women like Angelo were seated apart from White women like her mistress, Mrs. Jone Pierce, and even Ms. Ederife, Pierce's White female servant.[52] If so, then once again Black women were singled out as subordinate in rank to White women, including to indentured White women, just as the 1643 tax law has shown.[53] Seating by gender and class also meant that Angelo could be separated from enslaved Black men as well. What did the "Black" section of the church (female or male) look like? What was its proximity to White servants? How did Black people perceive this set up, including the parading of planters and all the church artifacts? We will never know, but one can imagine that they did have views about this scene, probably measuring their own social station against the backdrop of this hierarchal arrangement of European servants and planters by class and gender. To this end, the seating arrangement in the parish church reminds us that the church was a satellite of the plantation hierarchy, and the sorting of where one sat in the pews by race, class and gender reinforced the White supremacy inherent in both the church and the plantation structure that rose out of the international system of slavery and its built environment.

Seating parishioners by race, class and gender was managed by a team of church officers: churchwardens, vestrymen, clergy and a parish clerk. Each position was equally important in upholding the racial hierarchy of Whiteness that was instilled in the organization of parish districts. But none was more important to understanding the features of the parish church that reflected the influence of the international system of slavery on the intra-racial politics of Whiteness in Virginia than the churchwarden. Churchwardens were the chief investigative officers of parish churches. The Virginia Company ordered every parish to have two churchwardens, each with a different level of experience. The name "churchwarden" was synonymous in authority with an overseer, whose power to police the actions of area residents was ordained by the Virginia Company. We find mention of churchwardens in Virginia records as early as 1619, the same year in which enslaved African women and men arrived in Virginia.[54] Many of the early churchwardens were former tenant laborers and duty boys in the Sandys program, one of the organizations that were foundational in perpetuating the colony's Whiteness along class lines.[55] As such, churchwardens embodied the possibilities of upward mobility for former European indentured servants while also reflecting the evolving politics of forming a White civil society.

Some of the duties a churchwarden was charged to investigate were accusations of fornication, adultery, drunkenness, abusive and blasphemous speaking, absences from church, Sabbath breaking and other moral violations, such as those outlined in this 1631 oath for churchwardens:

> YOU shall sweare that you shall make presentments of all such persons as shall lead a prophayne or ungodlie life, of such as shall be common swearers, drunkards or blasphemers, that shall ordinarilie profane the saboth dayes or contemne Gods holy word or sacraments. You shall also present all adulterers or fornicators, or shall as abuse theire neighbors by slanderinge tale carryinge or back bitinge, or that shall not behave themselves orderlie and soberlie in the church duringe devyne servise. likewise they shall present such maysters and mistrisses as shall be delinquent in the catechisinge the youth and ignorant persons. So helpe yow God![56]

This oath institutionalized the authority of churchwardens to police the residents of parish communities in a way that was on par with slaveholders. For example, in 1619, the Virginia General Assembly endowed churchwardens with the authority to monitor church attendance and to punish violators based on the racial ranking of White over Black that they appropriated from the international system of slavery.[57] For instance, the Assembly ordered that the punishment for free White men who missed church be three shillings, while for enslaved Africans it was a whipping.[58]

Churchwardens enjoyed a wide range of latitude in investigating the aforementioned transgressions, which created a fair amount of anxiety, submissiveness and perhaps even a sense of class envy and admiration by some residents of parish communities. For instance, being a churchwarden offered men in this position the opportunity to rub elbows with the upper class, since it was they who were responsible for collecting the tithe (or tax) from planters on every enslaved female and male and every male indentured servant over sixteen years of age. Within this context, the churchwarden was a junior position of authority to large planters that was necessary for the maintenance of a White civil society, and as such was one that surely reaped certain kinds of benefits from this type of mentorship. For instance, maybe during his interactions with planters, churchwardens learned how to buy and sell enslaved persons, particularly Black females. Or perhaps churchwardens curried favors with planters (who tried all sorts of schemes to avoid paying taxes on their servants) by deliberately failing to record newly acquired servants and enslaved persons on the tax rolls.

It is likely that some planters and government officials who participated in the growth of the transatlantic slave trade probably spoke candidly with churchwardens about African people and their aptitude for things like fieldwork, while others may have commented on the religious reasons for the enslavement of Blacks. The closeness with which churchwardens worked with planters in collecting taxes on enslaved and indentured labor probably supplied them with opportunities to take advantage of their insider status, thus reminding us that the opportunities for upward mobility born out of the growth of the international system of slavery had its rewards for poor Whites.

But Virginia's connection to an advancing international system of slavery alone cannot account for the power of the churchwarden. It was also the acceptance of his legitimacy by other members of society that gave the churchwarden position its authority. For in a society with a rigid pecking order, like that in Virginia, deference to churchwardens was probably motivated by self-interest and even self-preservation, especially since many wardens brought charges against those deemed in violation of the colony's many laws and customs. Against this backdrop, the international system of slavery created new opportunities for former indentured servants to not only move up in social rank, but, through the duties of the churchwarden post, to participate with elites in governing Virginia as a White supremacist society.

The importance of the churchwarden position for upholding the planta-tion hierarchy took on significant meaning in the day-to-day life of ordinary women and men because churchwardens were able use the parish system's codes of conduct, like mandatory church attendance, as a pretext to mine information about the goings on of community members. Moreover, the churchwarden's jurisdiction also positioned him to easily disseminate official notices and proclamations and orders on behalf of the General Assembly, which provided him an opportunity to obtain the intelligence necessary to police the actions of parish residents and to enforce the racial hierar-chy of Virginia.[59] Thus, churchwardens were the eyes, ears and arm of the government.

Churchwardens probably learned about many of the offenses being com-mitted through casual conversation with parish residents before and after church service. These exchanges would often take place in the churchyard, where neighbors likely met to discuss the latest news and gossip and some-times even to transact business.[60] It was probably in the churchyard that a churchwarden learned of Hugh Davis's affair with a Black woman in 1630 (mentioned in chapter 2), an offense for which Davis was prosecuted in a parish court for "lying with a Negro."[61] Such examples illustrate the degree to which churchwardens could make use of the captive milieu of the churchyard to detect criminal behavior on behalf of residents.

In spite of the constant surveillance that parish residents were under by churchwardens, parishioners generally looked forward to attending church service because it provided relief from the isolation of life in widely separated farms and plantations. As such, church service was the public center of social interaction in most parish communities. For example, it was probably in the churchyard that Angelo got to meet other Blacks who may have lived in the parish district. Perhaps she had noticed them along the paths that crisscrossed the trails that led to the church. In such instances, the churchyard offered a legitimate place within the White landscape for Blacks to commune without much scrutiny. The churchyard was also part of the Black landscape when Black persons appropriated the usual function of this milieu to meet their social and political needs. In this context, we can think of the churchyard as melding crosscutting Black and White racial formations from the private life of the plantation with the public life of the church service.

For Whites, the public and private dichotomy of the churchyard took on different meanings depending on one's class. For planters who conducted business with other planters in the churchyard, this public space was where the thirty largest importers of enslaved persons could congregate with their slaveholding peers to discuss the ins and outs of planting and mastery before parading into the sanctuary.[62] For European indentured servants, the churchyard held dual meanings in that the public space of the churchyard reminded servants of their subordinate rank within Whiteness and of their temporary bondage. Here a double consciousness existed for poor Whites when interacting with Africans and planters.[63] For example, when servants like Smith, Bradford and Ederife engaged in friendly repartee with Angelo or other enslaved Blacks, the churchyard was a place of camaraderie with fellow workers, despite their elevated rank and race in Virginia's pecking order. Yet when eyeing the churchwarden commiserating with planters, the churchyard became a place to behold the transformative possibilities available to European servants once their term of service expired. Within this framework, bondage and upward mobility were all part of European servants' immersion into both worlds, one Black and one White, and one that sometimes relegated them to the periphery of these groups.

The phenomena of being "in-between" on the part of European servants showed up in the political discourse of the colony's civil war, Bacon's Rebellion. Nathaniel Bacon articulated the frustration of working-class European men in 1676 over the lack of unfettered access to the frontier lands that were settled and occupied by Native Americans. The rhetoric used by Bacon to articulate poor and propertyless White men's dissatisfaction with government officials curtailing their opportunities to likewise make propriety claims to Native American land reveals an acute understanding of the expectations of Whiteness that suggests that White workers had faith that the plantation structure would ultimately work to their benefit. Indeed, it would appear that the observations of early European servants about the racial hierarchy of the churchyard, with Blacks at one end, planters at the other and them in the middle, anticipated not only the grievances that led to their support of Bacon's Rebellion but also their decision to side with the planter elite and forgo interracial class solidarity with the few Black men who participated in the rebellion.[64]

In the first few decades of the colony when indentured servants were still struggling to prove their legitimacy as members of the dominant group, the churchwarden post offered former European servants an opportunity to integrate into the privileged class. Such was the case for George Parker Jr., who was a churchwarden of the Upper Parish in Northampton County in the early 1650s. In 1649, at the age of sixteen, Parker and his older brother Robert were indentured servants to Robert Barlow. The records show that by the age of seventeen, Parker obtained his freedom.[65] We do not know the circumstances surrounding his freedom, nor do we know how it was that one year after obtaining his freedom, at the age of eighteen, George had the means to pay for the transportation of nine servants into the colony, which netted him four hundred fifty acres of land.[66] No matter; we do know that four years later, in 1654, Parker was a churchwarden, and during this time he was awarded thirteen hundred acres for bringing twenty-six more persons into the colony, one of whom was his wife, Florence Cade Parker.[67] The people that Parker sponsored were considered to be his taxable property, whereas his wife was not because free White women were legal dependents of the householder.[68]

Besides the land he received for paying for the transportation of his wife and servants into the colony, Parker and his brother Robert also inherited land and money from their father, George Parker Sr., an early seventeenth century settler of Virginia known as an Old Adventurer. His father's standing in the community probably accounted for the speed of his appointment as church-warden.[69] George Parker Jr.'s wealth in servants also probably facilitated his rise to the level of commander of his parish district in 1658.[70] Not long after that, in 1661, Parker Jr. purchased seventeen enslaved persons and acquired six more indentured servants, for which he received another thirteen hundred acres of land.[71]

Parker's entry into slaveholding occurred as the enslaved population in Virginia was growing at a rate of about sixty per year, swelling from roughly fifty in 1625, to three hundred in 1649, to about two thousand in 1670.[72] The example of Parker's life as a former indentured servant turned churchwarden and enslaver makes him an interesting model for observing how the church codified race, class and gender relations of the plantation that were set by the perspectives of the built environment extracted out of the international system of slavery.

Besides collecting taxes from planters on enslaved and indentured laborers, another of the many duties required of a churchwarden was the investigation of acts of fornication. Specifically, parish churches worried about affairs that produced a child out of wedlock, a condition known as bastardy. Given that the parish church was responsible for setting and enforcing a standard of moral conduct for its members, parish officials were anxious about how the actions of the residents under their charge reflected upon the social and racial order they were attempting to control. Moreover, because the welfare of "bastard" children sometimes fell upon the parish, churchwardens took great pains to stay abreast of rumored indiscretions, especially those that undermined race and class lines, like sexual relations between indentured European men and bonded African women. It was such concerns that moved the James City churchwarden in 1640 to investigate rumors of fornication between Robert Sweat, a White servant, and an African woman. The result of the inquiry led to Sweat being ordered "in the forenoon [to] do public pen-ance at a church in James City for having a child with a Negro woman."[73]

In 1649, a similar concern may have been behind the Norfolk parish churchwarden's prosecution of William Watt, a White servant, for forni-cating with "Cornelius Lloyd's Negro Woman, Mary."[74] With the Sweat and Watt cases, churchwardens became enforcers of the colony's efforts to preserve White racial purity when attempting to police the anti-Black law against miscegenation. Equally as important and not at all contradictory to the White supremacy woven into the miscegenation laws were the ones that made Black women's laboring bodies vehicles of White people's prosperity, as did the law in 1643 that made African women's labor the legal equivalent of men's and the one in 1662 that assigned slave status to children based on the status of the mother. Churchwardens likely learned to make sense of the variants of White supremacy and the anti-Blackness inherent in these laws from their up close and personal relationship with planters while policing and enforcing of all these regulations. That said, these cases stand as further evidence of the importance of the parish church in replicating and advancing the White supremacy that extended from the international system of slavery into Virginia society and its built environment.

Even as churchwardens came to model the possibilities of advancement available to former European indentured servants, they were not the only sanctioning body in the parish church that assisted in maintaining the racial pecking order of White over Black in the colony. The other was the parish vestry. Similar to a board of directors with judicial powers, the vestry was a small committee of officials, including churchwardens and ministers, who were responsible for overseeing the business of their parish.[75] And like churchwardens, their positions also provide insight into the rise of White racial identity—and the role of the church as an extension of that identity—that was connected to the built environment and plantation culture via the international system of slavery.

The mention of vestries appears in colonial records as early as 1624. Initially, they were established because of a scarcity of ministers in the colony—there were only ten in 1662—and the need for effective church leadership in the newly formed parishes and counties.[76] The vestry's duties included the appointment of clergymen, making decisions about land boundaries, working with churchwardens in adjudicating charges like adultery and fornication, and organizing care for the indigent in their parishes.[77] Vestrymen also levied the taxes on tithable laborers (that of enslaved Black women and men and White male servants over the age of sixteen) which the churchwardens were sent to collect. Thus, like churchwardens, vestrymen were an extension of the Virginia government in the administration of a White civil society.

The General Assembly institutionalized the authority of the vestry in 1634 when it ordered that each parish should have one.[78] The law read:

> There shall be a vestrie held in each parish, for the makeing of the leavies and assessments for such use as are requisite and necessary for the repairing of the churches, etc. and that there be yearly chosen two or more churchwardens in every parish. That the most men be chosen and joyned to the minister and churchwardens to be of that vestrie.[79]

As the law stated, each parish's vestry was to be composed of prominent men in the community, usually large planters and slaveholders. As such, vestrymen were more than sympathetic to the sovereignty of planters to exert control over their bonded laborers without interference from government officials. For instance, in 1624 vestrymen helped push through a law barring a governor from appropriating private servants and enslaved laborers for "his own service," a victory that illustrates the degree to which the capacity of the international system of slavery grew to shape Virginia's intra-racial public policy battles around property rights, the cornerstone of American freedoms that presaged the Civil War and other internal conflicts for centuries to come.[80] Moreover, it shows just how much the interests of Virginia's churches were intertwined with the culture of the plantation around property rights and Whiteness, concepts that at once prefigure New World settlement as far back as the sixteenth century and the beginning of the transatlantic slave trade.[81]

Vestrymen were also charged with selecting the parish minister, who was as much as any person an extension of the continued influence of the international system of slavery in Virginia society, especially because clergymen were exempted from paying taxes on as many as six of their indentured servants or enslaved women, men and children.[82] This policy would have applied to Reverend William Cotton, a minister who had been living in Virginia since 1632, and who owned two enslaved men, Sampson and Domingo.[83] Like most ministers of today, Cotton's salary was paid by the members of the church in which he officiated. Thus, as a slaveholder and a minister, Cotton in these capacities represented a convergence of White supremacy, the church and the international system of slavery. And accepting the salary and the tax exemptions that came with parish ministry made him beholden to planters and other high-ranking officials in the community, which allows one to view clergymen likewise as junior partners of Virginia elites. For instance, Cotton could find himself unemployed if he failed to uphold the White supremacy of plantation culture. However, if he managed his parishioners as well as his enslaved persons and indentured servants in accordance with the White supremacist customs of Virginia, then he would be given his remunerative and social due as chief servant of the house of God and of the parish at large.

The Virginia Company clearly felt that the church and its clergy were essential to maintaining a White civil society, so much so that a minster was selected by the Virginia Company to be in the delegation of the first one hundred seventy-two original settlers of Virginia.[84] The position of clergy, as host and servant to planters and parishioners, was set in such high esteem that it was illegal to disparage one without sufficient proof.[85] One resident, Stephen Charlton, mentioned in chapter 2, learned this lesson the hard way in 1634 when he was punished for slandering Reverend Cotton. As punishment, Charlton was ordered "for the Syd offense [to] buyld a pare off Stocks and

Sett In them three Severall Sabouth days in the tyme of Dyvine Servis and their aske Mr. Cotton foregiveness."[86] Charlton's punishment was an example of the parish minister's stature and the parish church's authority in civil society. That said, the salary and tax breaks that he received on his enslaved and indentured persons made it inevitable that ministers were answerable to planters, and by extension, to the international system of slavery.

The offices of the parish church (clergy, vestry and churchwarden) were positions in the social structure of Virginia that were reserved for White men, even when there were Black men of comparable background. Even poor men of European ancestry had access to avenues of power through parish church positions, like churchwardens and vestrymen, that were most always unavailable to men of African descent. William Burdett, the owner of "Caine the Negro," was a man who benefited from such a system.

Burdett arrived in Virginia in 1615 aboard the *Susan* at age sixteen as an indentured servant. He was listed in the 1624 muster as the servant of Captain William and Margaret Epps of the Eastern Shore.[87] In spite of Burdett's lowly beginning as an indentured servant of the Eppses, by 1639 he was appointed to the Vestry in Accomacke County.[88] Before he died in 1643, he had amassed at least one thousand five hundred acres of land, had at least nine confirmed servants and enslaved persons, and had been appointed as a Burgess to represent Accomack County in the General Assembly.[89] Like many court officials during this time, including the aforementioned George Parker Jr., who was appointed churchwarden in 1654, Burdett's European ancestry was one factor that accounted for his selection to the vestry, the other being his wealth in physical and human property, which he acquired after his release from his indenture. These same privileges, however, were not extended across racial lines to similarly situated men of African ancestry, such as Anthony Johnson, mentioned in chapter 2.

Anthony Johnson, like Burdett, was also listed in the 1624 muster as a "servant." Johnson was a member of Edward Bennett's household in Warrosquyoak, a settlement just outside James City.[90] Most historians conclude that Johnson arrived in Virginia in 1621 as a captive in the transatlantic slave trade.[91] Yet, it appears that by the mid-1640s, Johnson and his wife, Mary, were free. During the same period as Burdett, Johnson was known to have owned at least five indentured servants and an enslaved man named John Casar. And, like Burdett, Johnson was awarded land from the Virginia government under the headrights program for paying the transportation of laborers into the colony.[92] In Johnson's case, it was three hundred-fifty acres of land.[93] Despite his accomplishments and relative wealth, the records do not indicate that Anthony Johnson was selected as a vestryman. Such an omission suggests that he was not selected, particularly given the fullness of the era's records on Johnson and his high degree of prominence. In the early 1660s

(1661 or 1662) Johnson relocated to Somerset County, Maryland, perhaps because it offered more fruitful opportunities than Virginia given the extent of anti-Blackness at the time.[94]

Although the wealth of Johnson was rare for a Black man during the mid- to late seventeenth century, the juxtaposition of the lives of Anthony Johnson and William Burdett is apropos for demonstrating how the racial politics of the burgeoning international system of slavery shaped Virginia society. That a byproduct of the international system of slavery also provided opportunities for White servants to advance to offices like the vestry because of their elevated social position speaks to the role the international system of slavery had in making American Whiteness. Moreover, given that indefinite bondage and slavery, which was the exclusive province of Africans, also ensured that upward mobility for Blacks in Virginia lagged severely behind indentured Whites, whose length of servitude was fixed and legally temporary, evidences not only the centrality of slavery in the making of American Whiteness but also its concomitant anti-Blackness.

So, by the time of Johnson's and Burdett's rise in Virginia, the colony had been active in the international system of slavery for nearly half a century, which meant that the anti-Blackness and White supremacy in Virginia had several decades to become institutionalized and therefore persons of African ancestry had much less opportunity to amass the economic, social and political capital needed to break through the systemic racism in the colony. Thus, even though both Johnson and Burdett came to Virginia in bondage, both were owners of human property and modest parcels of land, and both were apparently well-liked, the byproduct of a social order heavily shaped by the tenets of Whiteness and the anti-Blackness of a developing international system of slavery meant that Burdett rather than Johnson was selected to the vestry.[95] And although Johnson's accomplishments were remarkable, his exclusion from the upper reaches of political power as a Black man was not. The politics of Whiteness and anti-Blackness in a colony influenced by the schemes of a growing international system of slavery dictated the terms of Johnson's limited access to Virginia's most sacred institutions.

Until now, Anthony Johnson's accomplishments have been used by historians of early America to argue against the influence of the international system of slavery in producing racism against Blacks and against it producing the racial categories of White and Black in Virginia prior to 1660.[96] Yet Johnson's lived experience, especially when measured against similarly situated European men like Burdett, provides evidence to the contrary. It speaks clearly of the impact the international system of slavery had in shaping Virginia as a White society, particularly since so many of Virginia's founding institutions (plantations and churches) were modeled on concepts that settlers learned from their experience in and knowledge of the transatlantic slave trade. And yet in Johnson, we are able to see how despite the efforts of these institutions (plantations and churches) to systematically restrict the opportunities of Black people, they were still able to survive and express their independence in a society that was highly influenced by White supremacy and the growing scope of the international system of slavery in Virginia society.

Another anomaly at the time that made Johnson remarkable was that he purchased his freedom. In doing so, Johnson demonstrated the resiliency of Black people and their willingness to push back against Virginia's White supremacist social structure. And although it took several years for Johnson to accumulate the funds to purchase his freedom, every penny he saved from his arrival in Virginia in 1621 to his freedom in the 1640s was more than an act of resistance; it was an appropriation of the very policies designed to restrict him being used for his own benefit and, concomitantly, for the benefit of Black folk in Virginia.

In the early seventeenth century, many African peoples, including Johnson, financed their freedom by selling livestock.[97] Yet, purchasing one's freedom in this manner was made difficult by prohibitions against "truck and trade" with Blacks. Just as the Virginia Company instructed colonists in 1612 not to trade with Native groups in order to discourage the formation of intimate relations and formal alliances, so too did leaders routinely outlaw trade with Blacks out of fear that it would undermine the colony's growing institution of slavery.[98] For example, in March 1644, planter William Andrews petitioned the court to block truck and trade with his enslaved man. His request was upheld by a Northampton County magistrate in a ruling that stated that "no man shall Truck or Trade with John his Negro, upon penalty or the forfeiture of what he or they do truck, trade, barter, buy or sell with said Negro."[99] Truck and trade laws were an important way in which planters used local courts along with a cadre of other institutions under their authority to assist them in subjugating African peoples.

As it was with the parish churches, local courts likewise were part of a network of institutions in Virginia that were influenced by the expanding orbit of the built environment that came out of the international system of slavery. The enforcement of trade restrictions with Blacks was one example of how the courts were used by planters to institutionalize the subjugation of their enslaved property. This process was made easier because area courts were seated on plantations, with the hearings taking place inside parish churches. Consequently, the institutionalized racism of the court system grew organically out of the structure of parish districts being organized around the plantation, leading courts during this era to be appropriately referred to as parish courts.

There were three parish courts in 1623, one in Charles City, one in Elizabeth City and one in James City.[100] Parish courts were the forerunner to county courts, which first began in 1634.[101] The physical closeness of parish courts to the plantation meant that the courts' organizational structure generally mirrored the intra-racial hierarchy of the plantation, meaning most of the court justices were slaveholders and most of its clerks were former indentured servants. In fact, the influence of planters onto local courts was so institutionalized that sometimes court sessions were held in their homes. Often the presiding judge was a plantation commander, like the aforementioned William Harwood, or some other large planter or slaveholder. For example, in 1637, court sessions were held in the homes of Stephen Charlton and Argoll Yeardley.[102] Undoubtedly, some of the courtroom visitors and participants may have even worked for these men. If this was the case, then the courthouse culture also replicated the anti-Blackness and the intra-racial dynamics of Whiteness of the plantation that grew out of the international system of slavery and its built environment.

For instance, we know that persons of African ancestry were generally excluded from holding court positions. This shows that Virginia's judiciary was influenced by the politics of the international system of slavery—particularly since the court was managed by owners of large plantations and slaveholders. The obvious byproduct of this interdependency (the court system and slaveholding) was the strict judicial scrutiny given to the enforcement of things like trade restrictions with bonded Blacks that were designed to thwart opportunities for Black freedom and independence. Thus, when Anthony Johnson purchased four head of livestock from four different planters between May 1647 and December 1648, he was probably in violation of this regulation.[103] Johnson likely used his "outsider-within knowledge" of the White landscape to circumvent the authority of the courts when he sold his livestock, and in doing so he cleverly found a way around the laws against trading with "Negroes" and thereby secured his and his family's freedom despite these rules.[104]

Johnson's knowledge of White people was gained by living and working with them, an awareness that allowed him to convince planters like John Pott, Edward Douglas, James Berry and James Winberry to sell him the cattle that ultimately financed his freedom.[105] Yet Johnson's knowledge of the value of livestock was probably not gained just from his experiences in Virginia but also from his life in West Africa. Perhaps Pott, Douglas, Berry and Winberry did not know that Johnson and other Blacks were well versed in animal husbandry prior to arriving in Virginia.

Like most Black women and men living in Virginia prior to 1640, Johnson was born in Africa and likely arrived in Virginia by way of the Luanda seaport, which meant that he possessed any number of agricultural skills before ever having set foot in North America. According to Joseph Miller, the Mbundu people of Angola, for example, tended chickens, goats, sheep and cattle.[106] In addition to domestic animals, Miller posits that Mbundu men hunted for wild game with bows, arrows and traps throughout the year and with fire toward the end of the year. The dry months also provided opportunities for fishing. Such proficiencies undoubtedly served Johnson well in Virginia, which, as early as 1621, was home to an "abundance of cattle and hogs both wild and domestic."[107] One early seventeenth-century planter, Peter Arondelle, noted that the colony was "soe well furnished with all sorts of provisions as well as with Cattle that any laborious honest man many in a shorte time become ritche in this Country."[108] Over the twenty-year period from slavery to freedom, Johnson clearly made use of his prior farming knowledge to exploit the agricultural environment of Virginia toward gaining his and his family's freedom from enslavement and their eventual prosperity.

During his time in bondage, Johnson also relied on his friendships with other African people to get around the rules against Whites trading with Blacks. Two Black men named Richard and John Johnson (likely no relation to Anthony Johnson) were important in Johnson's life in this regard, so much so that Johnson named his two sons, Richard and John, after these men. The census records do not show that these two Black men, Richard and John, were enslaved with Johnson on the Bennett plantation.[109] So it was likely that the men became friends while living on separate plantations, getting acquainted while moving in and around their masters' plantations or in their parish churchyards. It was somewhere in this spatial milieu that the men would have exchanged information about how to obtain their freedom. Maybe Richard and John knew that Pott, Douglas, Berry and Winberry were the type of White men who could be fooled into selling cattle to Blacks or perhaps Richard and John perceived the men to be sympathetic to the plight of Black peoples. Such enlightened knowledge of the complexities of race on plantation life reminds us that the path from slavery to freedom is not walked alone. Often one is assisted by other people (Black, White and indigenous), who provide aid and assistance along the way during the journey to freedom. To this end, Johnson's road to freedom and prosperity depended on his pooling his resources and mastering the finer points of navigating the Black and White (and indigenous) landscapes of Virginia. However, for each success Johnson had in circumventing the plantation hierarchy, there were equally forceful attempts by Whites to prevent Johnson from upsetting the social order of Virginia that was highly influenced by the racist politics of a developing international system of slavery.

Although Anthony Johnson was one of the more famously documented Africans who possessed many of the visible trappings of wealth (servants, a slave and land), there was considerable evidence to suggest that despite his accomplishments, his success led to him leaving or being forced out of Virginia in the early 1660s because he disrupted the social order and crossed many of the racial boundaries that were set to preserve a system of White supremacy.

As an African man who was also a slaveholder, Anthony Johnson held a status that few men in Virginia of his background occupied prior to 1660. Many White leaders of Northampton County may have challenged Johnson's authority precisely because he was an African man who was also a slave-holder, which could have been what prompted churchwarden George Parker Jr. and his brother Robert, in November 1654, to lure Johnson's slave, John Casar, to their nearby plantation to work for them.[110] Johnson later sued the Parkers and regained custody of Casar.

Many scholars of the early seventeenth century hold out Anthony Johnson's legal victory as exemplary of the lack of anti-Black racism in Virginia. That because he was a slaveholder who was granted similar defer-ence in the courts as White men of similar status, that there was no anti-Black racism against Johnson in particular and in the colony in general. What is missing, however, in the many discussions about Johnson is a more nuanced assessment of Johnson's life as slaveholder and its significance to our under-standing of Whiteness and Blackness in Virginia during this era. Specifically, the legal challenge Johnson made against the Parkers over their presumed propriety to his human property enhances our understanding of the cultural distinction between Whites and Blacks during this era regarding "slavery" that is overlooked in this dispute. As I will discuss in more detail in chapter 4, the complex distinctions between a "slave" as a commodity and a "slave" as a member of one's household are what was at stake on the one hand, in Johnson's response to the Parkers theft of Casar, and the Eurocentric frame-work of race in early America that is championed in the historiography, on the other.

G. Ugo Nwokeji tells us in his book, *The Slave Trade and Culture in the Bight of Biafra*, that households in many West African communities consisted of a variety of persons who held a variety of statuses. A household, accord-ing to Nwokeji, included "the nuclear family, the polygynous family, and other persons or families, who could be slaves, refugees, long-term guests, or clients."[111] In seeking to usurp Johnson's patriarchal authority over his house-hold, the Parker brothers' actions reveal a European perspective of social rela-tions that was prevalent in the international system of slavery, one that did not contemplate the degree of familial assimilation that persons under Johnson's charge likely held. So, when Parker reported in November 1654 that "Richard Johnson Negrowe and a Negrowe woman of the family of Anthony Johnson Negrowe" were engaged in fornication, he was ignorant of the complexities of the domestic relationships that were common in societies in West Central Africa and likely in the Johnson household.[112]

Therefore, whether it was because of jealousy, contempt or ignorance, the attacks against Johnson's human property by the Parkers suggest that Johnson's station as head of household challenged strongly held New World ideas about patriarchy and the sophistication of African people and societies that had been wrongly interpreted by Whites who worked in the international system of slavery.

Cheryl Harris's analysis of the colony's early history of property rights may be useful in explaining the context of Parker's actions within a society so heavily influenced by mounting incidents of colonialism within the international system of slavery.[113] Harris contends that historical systems of domination, such as conquest, removal and the extermination of Native American life and culture, produced a system in America whereby only White possession of land was validated as the basis of property rights, a paradigm that was formed long before the arrival of Africans in Virginia. In fact, this paradigm was manifest in European encounters with Blacks in West Central Africa as early as the fifteenth century, leading to four centuries of enslavement and the exploitation of the labor and lands of Black peoples. Within this context, Anthony Johnson, as landowner and "slave master," violated long-established European ideologies about Black male patriarchy, which turned New World Europeans' assumptions about property rights as the exclusive domain of White men on its head. As a result, Johnson and his family were targeted and harassed until they eventually relocated.

Examples include several failed attempts by White men to swindle land from Johnson's sons. One instance in 1654 involved Anthony Johnson's nineteen-year-old son, John Johnson's, attempt to patent five hundred fifty acres of land on the south side of Pungoteague Creek.[114] Having not received confirmation of this transaction, Johnson inquired into the matter and discovered that the sheriff, through ignorance or malice, had sent the patent to a European man also named John Johnson.[115] The European Johnson refused to acknowledge the error and return the paperwork, claiming that he was the rightful owner of the property. The African Johnson eventually prevailed in court, but only after the testimony of the powerful planter Edmund Scarburgh, who had actually surveyed the land, confirmed that the acreage did, in fact, belong to the African John Johnson.[116] Given the racial politics of Virginia society at the time, the African Johnson would probably not have triumphed in the courts without the help of the influential Scarburgh. That said, the fact that some Whites like Scarburgh would at times be of assistance to Blacks in their freedom struggles does not mitigate the jurisdictional claim to property rights that Harris suggests undergirded White supremacy and racial hierarchies.[117] Thus, the ruthless actions taken against the Johnson family suggest that racialized notions about property ownership and patriarchy may have been behind White men's attempts to challenge Black men's right to amass large amounts of land and servants.

This may have been why other White men also tried to steal land from the Johnsons. In 1658, a man named Matthew Pippen successfully stole land from Anthony Johnson's other son, Richard. In this instance, Pippen beat Richard Johnson out of one hundred acres of land by patenting property for which Johnson could not prove ownership in the form of a paper document, and afterward, boldly lived next to Johnson for the next five years despite his prior occupancy.[118] It is from this context that we can understand the various attempts by White men to make proprietary claims against the property of the Johnson men as an attempt to preserve the domain of property rights and mastery exclusively for Europeans. Thus, we can now situate George Parker Jr.'s and his brother's challenge to Anthony Johnson's patriarchal rights over his land and human property within the playbook of American Whiteness.

Despite these actions, Johnson continued to petition the courts, an institution designed to subordinate him, in order to have his property rights legally recognized. Besides successfully suing Parker in 1654 over Casar and forcing Parker to return his human property, Johnson also won a reprieve from his taxes in 1652 after his home had been destroyed in a fire.[119] Such examples reveal the extent to which Johnson was able to circumvent Virginia's institutions in order to mitigate, albeit temporarily, attacks against his personal freedoms and property. How did Johnson develop his strategies of resistance? The next chapter examines the early history of resistance by African peoples to the subordinating forces of Virginia society. Some of their resistance strategies can be traced back to West African social systems, many of which were refashioned to meet the needs of the New World. This next chapter located such resistance tactics within the context of precolonial West African cultural systems. What did indigenous African resistance tactics look like in early Virginia? More important, how did it work to alleviate their circumstances and, in some cases, free Black people?

NOTES

1. Birmingham, *Trade and Conflict in Angola: The Mbundu and Their Neighbours under the Influence of the Portuguese 1483–1790*, 46.

2. Dell Upton, *Holy Things and Profane: Anglican Parish Churches in Colonial Virginia* (Cambridge: MIT Press, 1986), 5.

3. Barbour, *The Jamestown Voyages under the First Charter, 1606–1609*, I, II, I: 24.

4. Blackburn, *The Making of New World Slavery: From the Baroque to the Modern, 1492–1800*, 33.

5. Barbour, *The Jamestown Voyages under the First Charter, 1606–1609*, I, II, I: 36–37.

6. Kingsbury, *The Records of the Virginia Company of London: The Court Book, from the Manuscript in the Library of Congress*, III: 98; Cynthia Miller Leonard, ed., *The General Assembly of Virginia: A Bicentennial Register of Members, July 20, 1619–January 11, 1978* (Richmond: Virginia State Library, 1978), ix. I ground my analysis of the buildings housed on plantation settlements (homes, churches and courthouses) as a system of social control in the work of Theodore Allen, *The Invention of the White Race: Racial Oppression and Social Control*, I, I: 52–70.

7. Charles Francis Cooke, *Parish Lines Diocese of Virginia* (Richmond: Virginia State Library, 1967), 4; Charles E. Hatch, *The First Seventeen Years: Virginia, 1607–1624* (Charlottesville: University of Virginia Press 1957), 19.

8. Upton, *Holy Things and Profane: Anglican Parish Churches in Colonial Virginia*, 8.

9. George MacLaren Brydon, *Parish Lines in Diocese of Virginia*, 4. By 1662, there were between forty-five and forty-eight parishes districts. Roger Green, *Virginia's Cure* (London: W. Godbid for Henry Brome, 1662).

10. Cooke, *Parish Lines Diocese of Virginia*, 43–46, 195–98, 263–68. Population figures taken from Evarts B. Greene and Virginia D. Harrington, *American Population before the Federal Census of 1790* (New York: Columbia University Press, 1932), 135–36, show roughly twelve hundred inhabitants in Virginia in 1624 and about twenty-six hundred in 1630.

11. Kingsbury, *The Records of the Virginia Company of London: The Court Book, from the Manuscript in the Library of Congress*, III: 100.

12. Rebecca A. Goetz, "From Potential Christians to Hereditary Heathens: Religion and Race in the Early Chesapeake, 1590–1740" (Dissertation, Harvard University, 2006), 34. English Protestantism was the religion practiced by the overwhelming majority of Virginians in the early decades of the seventeenth century.

13. Morgan, *American Slavery, American Freedom*, 61. Prior to 1634, parish commanders made up Virginia's local judiciary.

14. George Carrington Mason, *Colonial Churches of Tidewater Virginia* (Richmond: Whittet and Shepperson, 1945), 2; Cooke, *Parish Lines Diocese of Virginia*, 5. The term "hundred" is a geographical term loosely referring to an area that was inhabited by a hundred families.

15. *Colonial Records of Virginia*, 48.

16. Alexander Brown, D. C. L., *The First Republic in America* (New York: Russell and Russell, 1898), 275.

17. Jester, *Adventures of Purse and Person, 1607–1625*, 43–44.

18. H. R. McIlwaine, *Executive Journals of the Council of Colonial Virginia*, vol. VI (Richmond: Virginia State Library, 1925–1966), III: 316; IV: 237, 285.

19. Susan M. Kingsbury, ed., *Records of the Virginia Company of London*, 4 vols., vol. I (Washington, D.C.: Government Printing Office, 1906, 1933), I: 382–83, 479. The February 1624 muster listed Harwood as a single head of household with three houses, one boat and six European indentured servants.

20. Ibid., IV: 562–67.

21. Robert J. Allison, ed., *The Interesting Narrative of Olaudah Equiano, or Gustavus Vasa, the African* (London: 1789), 91–94.

22. Jester, *Adventures of Purse and Person, 1607–1625*, 29.

23. J. Douglas Deal, *Race and Class in Colonial Virginia: Indians, Englishmen, and Africans on the Eastern Shore During the Seventeenth Century* (New York: Garland Publishing, Inc., 1993), 106.

24. Robert K. Fitts, "The Landscapes of Northern Bondage," in *Cabin, Quarter, Plantation: Architecture and Landscapes of North American Slavery*, eds. Clifton Ellis and Rebecca Ginsburg (1996), 198.

25. Kingsbury, *The Records of the Virginia Company of London: The Court Book, from the Manuscript in the Library of Congress*, I: 256–7.

26. Upton, "White and Black Landscapes in Eighteenth-Century Virginia," 135.

27. Dell Upton's important article "White and Black Landscapes in Eighteenth-Century Virginia" offers excellent analysis of the White landscape from which to analyze the racial dynamics of space and place.

28. See Clifton Ellis and Rebecca Ginsburg, eds., *Cabin, Quarter, Plantation: Architecture and Landscapes of North American Slavery* (New Haven: Yale University Press, 2010). See this publication for several essays on Black persons' interpretations of subjugating landscapes.

29. Those planters included the aforementioned Edward Bennett, Abraham Peirsey and George Yeardley.

30. Jester, *Adventures of Purse and Person, 1607–1625*, 22, 27, 29, 34, 46, 49, 62.

31. Ibid., 22.

32. See "County Court Records of Accomack-Northampton, Virginia 1640–1645," 204, 457; "Northampton County Virginia Record Book: Orders, Deeds, Wills, Ect., 1645–1651, Book 3," folio 116.

33. Deal, *Race and Class in Colonial Virginia: Indians, Englishmen, and Africans on the Eastern Shore During the Seventeenth Century*, 106.

34. Sluiter, "New Light on the '20. And Odd Negroes' Arriving in Virginia, August 1619," 396.

35. Evarts B. Greene and Virginia D. Harrington, *American Population before the Federal Census of 1790* (New York: Columbia University Press, 1932), 135–36.

36. For texts that elucidate the role of slave quarters as a site for both community building and developing resistance strategies see Gerald W. Mullin, *Flight and Rebellion: Slave Resistance in Eighteenth Century Virginia* (New York: Oxford University Press 1972), 219. Also see John W. Blassingame, *The Slave Community: Plantation Life in the Antebellum South* (New York: Oxford University Press, 1972).

37. Patricia Hill Collins, *Fighting Words: Black Women in Search for Justice* (Minneapolis: University of Minnesota Press, 1998), 5–8. According to Collins, "outsider-within knowledge" is gaining knowledge about or of the dominant group without gaining the full power accorded to that group.

38. Barbara Heath, "Space and Place within Plantation Quarters in Virginia, 1700–1825," in *Cabin, Quarter, Plantation: Architecture and Landscapes of North American Slavery*, eds. Clifton Ellis and Rebecca Ginsburg (New Haven: Yale University Press, 2010), 169.

39. Birmingham, *Trade and Conflict in Angola: The Mbundu and Their Neighbours under the Influence of the Portuguese 1483–1790*, 47.

40. *Virginia Historical Collections,* VII: 65. For information about Thomas Smith see Whitelaw, *Virginia's Eastern Shore,* I, I: 48.

41. Brown, *The First Republic in America,* 275.

42. George Carrington Mason, *Colonial Churches of Tidewater Virginia* (Richmond: Whittet and Shepperson, 1945).

43. Upton, *Holy Things and Profane: Anglican Parish Churches in Colonial Virginia,* 181.

44. Ibid., 175–96.

45. Ibid., 154.

46. Ibid., 139.

47. Ibid., 15.

48. Ibid.

49. Hening, ed., *The Statutes at Large: Being a Collection of all the Laws of Virginia, from the First Session of the Legislature in the Year 1619,* I: 242, II: 26.

50. Robert P. Jones, *White Too Long: The Legacy of White Supremacy in American Christianity* (New York: Simon & Schuster, 2020), 4. Jones argues White Christians have constructed and sustained a project of protecting White supremacy and opposing Black equality that has framed the entire American story.

51. Conway Robinson, "Notes from the Council and General Court Records," in *Robinson Notes* (Richmond: Virginia Historical Society).

52. Upton, *Holy Things and Profane: Anglican Parish Churches in Colonial Virginia,* 180.

53. Hening, ed., *The Statutes at Large; Being a Collection of All the Laws of Virginia, from the First Session of the Legislature in the Year 1619,* I: 243. The statute reads in part as follows: "Be it also enacted and confirmed there be tenn pounds of tob'o. per poll & a bushell of corne per poll paid to the ministers within the severall parishes of the collony for all tithable persons, that is to say, as well for all youths of sixteen years of age as vpwards, as also for all negro women at the age of sixteen years."

54. Oliver P. Chitwood, *Justice in Colonial Virginia* (New York: Da Capo Press, 1971), 84.

55. For further elaboration on the Sandys program, see chapter 2 of this book.

56. Hening, ed., *The Statutes at Large; Being a Collection of All the Laws of Virginia, from the First Session of the Legislature in the Year 1619,* I: 56.

57. Philip Alexander Bruce, *Institutional History of Virginia in the Seventeenth Century,* 2 vols., vol. I (New York: The Knickerbocker Press, 1910), 28–29.

58. Ibid.

59. James Morton Smith, ed., *Seventeenth-Century America: Essays in Colonial History* (Chapel Hill: The University of North Carolina Press, 1959).

60. Ibid., 128.

61. Hening, ed., *The Statutes at Large; Being a Collection of All the Laws of Virginia, from the First Session of the Legislature in the Year 1619,* I: 146.

62. Upton, "White and Black Landscapes in Eighteenth-Century Virginia," 130–31.

63. W. E. B. Du Bois, *The Souls of Black Folk* (New York: Vintage, 1989). "Double consciousness" is the term coined by Du Bois that I use in this text to refer to the ways American Blacks have lived in a society that has historically repressed and devalued them such that it became difficult for them to unify their Black identity with the American identity. I reframe this term to refer to a mental state of European indentured servants in early seventeenth century Virginia, who were trying to take on a White identity despite not quite possessing qualities of Whiteness held by wealthier colonists and a reluctance to identify with enslaved Africans.

64. Scholars such as Breen and Innes, *Myne Owne Ground*, 5, suggest that before Bacon's Rebellion there was a real possibility of an integrated society of Blacks and Whites. Also see Kathleen Brown's *Good Wives, Nasty Wenches, and Anxious Patriarchs*, and Edmund Morgan's *American Slavery, American Freedom: The Ordeal of Colonial Virginia*.

65. Stella Pickett Hardy, *Colonial Families of the Southern States of America: A History and Genealogy of Colonial Families Who Settled in the Colonies Prior to the Revolution* (Baltimore: Genealogical Publishing Company, 1968), 409. Nugent, *Cavaliers and Pioneers: Abstracts of Virginia Land Patents and Grants, 1623–1800*, I, 185.

66. Nugent, *Cavaliers and Pioneers: Abstracts of Virginia Land Patents and Grants, 1623–1800*, 193.

67. Ibid., 307.

68. "Northampton County Virginia, Orders, Deeds & Wills 1651–1654 Book 4," 227. Headrights are persons who had their transportation into the colony paid for by another person. In doing so, the sponsor would be granted fifty acres of land per person.

69. His father's will stipulated that George was to receive twenty shillings at age twenty-one. George Parker Sr. was born in Southampton, England. He later became a judge in the Accomack County, Virginia, court before he died in 1640. For an important discussion on the rise and selection of certain men to high-ranking positions in Virginia, see Charles S. Sydnor, *Gentlemen Freeholders: Political Practices in Washington's Virginia* (Chapel Hill: University of North Carolina Press, 1952).

70. "Northampton County Order Book, 1657–1664, Book 8," folio 19.

71. Nugent, *Cavaliers and Pioneers: Abstracts of Virginia Land Patents and Grants, 1623–1800*, I, 400.

72. Craven, *White, Red, and Black: Seventeenth-Century Virginia*, 85–86.

73. Henry R. McIlwaine, *Minutes of the Council and General Court of Colonial Virginia with Notes and Excerpts from Original Council and General Court Records, into 1683, Now Lost* (Richmond: The Colonial Press, Everett Waddey Co., 1622–1632, 1670–1676), 477.

74. "Lower Norfolk County Order Book, 1646–1650," 113a.

75. Bruce, *Institutional History of Virginia in the Seventeenth Century*, I, 55. Sometimes there were up to twelve vestrymen per parish church.

76. Smith, *Seventeenth-Century America: Essays in Colonial History*, 139.

77. Cooke, *Parish Lines Diocese of Virginia*, 10–11.

78. Hening, ed., *The Statutes at Large; Being a Collection of All the Laws of Virginia, from the First Session of the Legislature in the Year 1619*, I: 204. Charles Maclaren Brydon, *Virginia's Mother Church and the Political Conditions under Which It Grew* (Richmond: Virginia Historical Society, 1947), 93.

79. Hening, ed., *The Statutes at Large; Being a Collection of All the Laws of Virginia, from the First Session of the Legislature in the Year 1619*, I: 240.

80. Ibid., I: 124. At the time, Sir Francis Wyatt was the governor of Virginia.

81. Cheryl I. Harris, "Whiteness as Property," *Harvard Law Review* 106, no. 8 (1993).

82. Ibid., I: 124, 424.

83. Jennings C. Wise, *Ye Kingdome of Accawmacke or the Eastern Shore of Virginia in the Seventeenth Century* (Richmond: The Bell Book and Stationary Company, 1911), 286.

84. Upton, *Holy Things and Profane: Anglican Parish Churches in Colonial Virginia*, 5.

85. Hening, ed., *The Statutes at Large; Being a Collection of All the Laws of Virginia, from the First Session of the Legislature in the Year 1619*, I: 124.

86. "Northampton/Accomacke County, Virginia Orders, Deeds and Wills: Book I, 1632–1640," 4.

87. Jester, *Adventures of Purse and Person, 1607–1625*, 66.

88. "Northampton Accomacke County, Virginia Orders, Deeds and Wills: Book I, 1632–1640."

89. "County Court Records of Accomack-Northampton, Virginia 1640–1645." These figures were based on his November 13, 1643, estate inventory. Burdett was appointed to the House of Burgess in 1641.

90. Jester, *Adventures of Purse and Person, 1607–1625*, 46. Warrosquyoak was the namesake of an indigenous group in the Powhatan Confederacy. On the proximity of Burdett and Johnson to one another during the 1620s, Warrosquyoak was a neighboring county close to Accomacke County.

91. For scholars who make this claim, see Breen and Innes, *Myne Owne Ground*, and Deal, *Race and Class in Colonial Virginia*.

92. Under the headright program, a person would receive fifty acres of land for paying another person's (or their own) transportation to Virginia.

93. "Northampton County Virginia, Orders, Deeds & Wills 1651–1654 Book 4," folio 37.

94. Somerset County Judicial Record, 1671–1675, 159–61.

95. We can claim that Johnson was held in high esteem because after a fire in February 1653, the county court decided to help the Johnsons out financially based on their tenure in the colony by exempting the women in his household from all public taxes and levies. "Northampton County Virginia, Orders, Deeds & Wills 1651–1654 Book 4," folio 161. As for Burdett, his selection to the House of Burgesses illustrates the respect he held in the community.

96. The work of Breen and Innes, *Myne Owne Ground*, is one of the most notable of works that argues Johnson's life as a free African was proof that the international system of slavery did not produce racial categories prior to 1660.

97. Strachey, *For the Colony in Virgnea Brittania: Lawes Divine, Morall, and Martiall*, 10–17, 21, 24–27.

98. William Strachey, ed., *The Historie of Travell into Virginia Britania, 1612* (London: The University Press, Glasgow, 1953), 64.

99. "County Court Records of Accomack-Northampton, Virginia 1640–1645," 330.

100. Hening, ed., *The Statutes at Large: Being a Collection of All the Laws of Virginia, from the First Session of the Legislature in the Year 1619*, I: 246.

101. Salmon, *The Hornbook of Virginia History: A Ready-Reference Guide to the People, Places and Past*, 55.

102. Whitelaw, *Virginia's Eastern Shore*, I: 246. See chapter 2 of this book for additional references on Stephen Charlton.

103. "Northampton County Virginia Record Book: Orders, Deeds, Wills, Ect., 1645–1651, Book 3," f.75; "Northampton County Virginia, Orders, Deeds & Wills 1651–1654 Book 4," 123. Johnson was thought to be free by the 1640s, since it was then that he acquired his slave, John Casar.

104. Hill Collins, *Fighting Words: Black Women in Search for Justice*, 5–8. According to Collins, "outsider-within knowledge" is gaining knowledge about or of the dominant group without gaining the full power accorded to that group.

105. "Northampton County Virginia Record Book: Orders, Deeds, Wills, Ect., 1645–1651, Book 3," f.75; "Northampton County Virginia, Orders, Deeds & Wills 1651–1654 Book 4."

106. Joseph C. Miller, *Kings and Kinsmen: Early Mbundu States in Angola* (New York: Oxford University Press, 1976), 36.

107. Kingsbury, *The Records of the Virginia Company of London: The Court Book, from the Manuscript in the Library of Congress*, III: 587–89.

108. Ibid.

109. Land Patents of Virginia, 1652–1655, Book no. 3, 294; "Northampton County Virginia Record Book: Deeds, Wills, Ect., 1657–1666," 23.

110. NCo SW 1654–5, f.35; and NCo DW 1651–4, 226-f.226.

111. G. Ugo Nwokeji, *The Slave Trade and Culture in the Bight of Biafra: An African Society in the Atlantic World* (New York: Cambridge University Press 2010), 121.

112. "Northampton County Virginia Record Book: Orders, Deeds, Wills, Ect., 1654–55," V:55; "Northampton County Virginia, Record Book: Orders, Deeds & Wills, Ect., 1655–1668, 21.

113. Cheryl I. Harris, "Whiteness as Property," *Harvard Law Review* 106, no. 8 (1993): 1714.

114. "Northampton County Virginia, Orders, Deeds & Wills 1651–54 Book 4," f.103. Pungoteague Creek was thought to be the first African community in America. It was said to be made up of more than a dozen native Africans. Writers' Program of the Works Project Administration, *The Negro in Virginia* (New York: Hastings House, 1940), 11.

115. Deal, *Race and Class in Colonial Virginia: Indians, Englishmen, and Africans on the Eastern Shore During the Seventeenth Century*, 220–21. "Northampton County Virginia Record Book: Deeds, Wills, Ect., 1657–1666," 57–58. "Northampton County Virginia, Orders, Deeds & Wills 1651–1654 Book 4," f. 200.

116. Scarburgh was one of the fifteen planters that owned ten or more servants and/or enslaved persons in Virginia. Others include William Tucker, Edward Bennett, Abraham Piersey, George Yeardley and George Menifie.

117. Blumer, "Race Prejudice as a Sense of Group Position," 222.

118. Nell Marion Nugent, *Cavaliers and Pioneers: A Calendar of Virginia Land Grants, 1623–1800*, vol. I (Richmond: Library of Virginia, 1934), 296, 532. Whitelaw, *Virginia's Eastern Shore*, I, I: 699. This land was known to have been in the Johnson family for several years. It was not clear what happened to the patent. According to Cheryl Harris, "Whiteness as Property," *Harvard Law Review* 106, no. 8 (1993): 1714, rights in property are intertwined and conflated with race.

119. "Northampton County Virginia, Orders, Deeds & Wills 1651–1654 Book 4," folio 161, p.161. Howard Mackey, and Marlen A. Groves, ed., *Northhampton Country Virginia Record Book: Deeds, wills, Ect., 1655–1657*, vol. VI, VII–VIII (Rockport: Picton Press, 2002), 72.

Chapter 4

From Freedom Suits to Fictive Kin

African Resistance to White Supremacy in Colonial Virginia, 1619–1660

Precolonial West African social systems powerfully shaped the nature of Black people's responses to enslavement and White supremacy in Virginia during the early decades of the seventeenth century. Long before the first African people set foot in the New World, West African social systems were an effective tool for managing struggles with European people who traveled along the coast of West Central Africa in the fifteenth and sixteenth centuries looking for people to enslave. Intense trade negotiations between greedy European merchants and eager African rulers during this period supplied ordinary Black people in these regions with crucial information about the ways of White folks that they would combine with their own knowledge systems to manipulate European traders.

For example, in bargaining for European goods, ethnic leaders of West Central Africa would often appeal to the vanities of European traders in an attempt to gain an edge in negotiations. Like in 1504, when the Mbundu peoples of Angola tolerated Portuguese proselytizing in order to maintain cooperative trade relations.[1] In fact, some ethnic leaders welcomed, and even courted, Portuguese missionaries into their communities for political and commercial purposes. In 1577, for instance, one ruler, Ngola Inene, even went so far as request to be baptized by Jesuit missionaries in order to promote diplomatic relations between the Mbundu people and the Portuguese.[2] But as the Portuguese began to exploit the internal warfare taking place in the Angola region over European consumer goods, and as the global demand for enslaved Africans led to Angola being targeted by Europeans as a major source in the trade of human beings—one that continued until the nineteenth century, with over three million enslaved persons shipped from this region alone—African rulers eventually abandoned Christianity as a diplomatic strategy but continued the internal fighting brought on by the social and economic disruption as a result of European demand for slaves.[3]

Despite the short-lived success of the Mbundu peoples in fooling European merchants about their religious beliefs, African peoples grew effective at appealing to the cultural sensibilities of European peoples in order to gain a strategic edge in various types of negotiations. This strategy laid the foundation for subsequent interactions with White people in the New World, especially for the approximately three hundred Black persons in Virginia through 1650, nearly all of whom were born in Africa and captured and exported from the port in Luanda, and thus were quite familiar with the conceits of Europeans from their interactions with slave traders.

Although most of the three hundred or so Blacks in Virginia in the early seventeenth century were enslaved, they were nonetheless empowered to resist the enslavement and oppression by Whites by recreating the successful maneuvers used by African peoples in precolonial West Africa to meet their needs in the New World. A signal of this adaptation was found in the advent of freedom suits, petitions by enslaved African persons seeking freedom through the courts.

During the first half of the seventeenth century, lawsuits by Blacks that manipulated Virginia's White supremacist legal and religious institutions were the standard, even as freedom suits and other resistance strategies that played one slaveholder against another were becoming more common, especially if an enslaved child was involved. One of the more documented seventeenth-century freedom suits was the one brought on by the aforementioned Elizabeth Key.

Elizabeth Key initiated her freedom lawsuit in 1655 on the grounds that she was a Christian and of English ancestry.[4] Born of a free English father and an enslaved African mother, Key cleverly appropriated these powerful European titles as part of her legal strategy to argue the idea that Christianity and Englishness could include persons of African ancestry and thereby prohibit her enslavement.[5] Key's freedom suit was indicative of the acculturation progress that African people had made after three decades of living, working and slaving under White folks in the New World.[6] So much so that after only twenty-five years of life, Key was savvy enough about European ideologies to refashion the meaning of staid social and racial identities like Christianity and Englishness to her advantage, just as her forbearers in Africa had done with Christianity nearly a century before.[7]

Like the Mbundu people of Angola, Christianity held a variety of meanings and uses for most Black persons in early Virginia. To many in the Angolan region, Christianity was seen as just another religious order or as a means that allowed them to become freer.[8] Similarly, African peoples in early Virginia interpreted the biblical message of salvation for the soul with their own ideas about liberation for the body, and used this combination of religious and secular doctrine to form the basis of their resistance strategy.[9] This was in stark contrast to European people, who saw in Christianity not only a spiritual philosophy but also one in which to rationalize their social position and justify their acts of conquest and enslavement against the so-called heathens of Africa (and, of course, the indigenous people of the New World) well into the nineteenth century and beyond. Key, in her freedom suit, astutely recognized the contradiction and gaps in the social construction of Christianity and Englishness as it applied her enslavement, and found in her heritage a legal loophole through which to reconceptualize Christianity and Englishness to meet her own idea of freedom in the hopes of being incorporated into Virginia's White civil society without prejudice.

In this chapter, I argue that the indigenous social systems of precolonial West Africa provided the enslaved Black persons who arrived in early Virginia with the framework for interpreting, reinterpreting, negotiating and in some cases outwitting the Eurocentric bureaucracy of Virginia's institutions, including those religious and legal policies that were fundamental to their oppression in ways that are also foundational to understanding the making of American Whiteness. How did Blacks employ indigenous African-based cultural systems to manipulate the White supremacist landscape of Virginia? African peoples found ways to transfer the culture of their African homelands onto their surroundings in Virginia, and oral traditions were one cultural form from their precolonial past that African peoples used to advance their freedom struggles.

Oral traditions were perhaps the strongest and most enduring indigenous West African cultural practice in the New World and in the seventeenth century that was used by Blacks to resist White supremacy. Oral traditions were a method by which women and men communicated knowledge of White folks to each other, and it was the medium by which memories of their kingdom and ethnic traditions were kept alive.

The use of the oral tradition to combat the institutional racism and White supremacy of Virginia provided stability to the community of African peoples trying to survive the early decades of the colony and the trauma of the Middle Passage. We see evidence of the stabilizing force that oral traditions had in the life of African people from the lived experience of the previously mentioned Anthony Johnson and his family, one of the more documented Black families in early American history.

In 1677, Anthony Johnson's grandson, John Johnson Jr., named his forty-four-acre estate in Somerset County, Maryland, Angola. We should not underestimate the value that the name Angola had in making the memory of a pre-European contact African past real and affirming. Equally, and perhaps more important, we should not underestimate the value the name Angola had as a source into the perceptions of early Africans that illustrates "who they thought they were," or "where they hailed from in Africa," particularly since most embarked out of the port in Luanda, Angola.[10]

We do not know the exact birth places of the Africans aboard any of the European slave ships that brought hundreds of thousands of Black people to the New World. But because of their common embarkation point, Johnson Jr.'s invocation of the name Angola suggests a broad regional identity of shared descent that connected him to the many thousands of Black persons that passed through the European slave trading port in Luanda, some of whom likely ended up in Virginia (and Maryland).

Clearly, Anthony Johnson had planted the seeds of an Angolan identity into his family legacy using the oral tradition. And even though John Johnson Jr.'s actions occurred in Maryland in the third quarter of the seventeenth century, presumably the process of transmitting the notion of Angola as the family's place of origin began while they were still in Virginia, where Anthony Johnson undoubtedly described the region to his son John Johnson Sr., who, in turn, likely passed the details onto John Johnson Jr.

Anthony Johnson died seven years before his grandson honored the memory of his life by naming his estate Angola.[11] Yet, for all the numerous essays and monographs about his wealth and prosperity, perhaps Anthony Johnson's greatest achievement, one that is absent in the American historiography on Johnson, was instilling a connection to precolonial Angola into the hearts and minds of his children. Arriving in Virginia in 1621, probably having departed from the Luanda port in Angola, Anthony Johnson must have provided vivid and detailed information about his homeland to his son John Johnson Sr. for it to have made such a searing impression on John Johnson Jr. Thus, we can reasonably assume that Anthony Johnson's oral stories were steeped in powerful messages about West African culture and, as a result, the literal and figurative meaning of Angola was therefore a readily available counternarrative for his family to use to mitigate the negative impact that European social and legal practices could have on his family's psyche.

Since the mid-1500s, the Mbundu peoples in the Angola region used a variety of oral traditions (testimonies about the family tree, proverbs and songs) for the purposes of preserving a family's lineal history.[12] Oral traditions were probably used for similar purposes by African peoples in Virginia, particularly during life's dramatic transitions: at birth, before marriage, at death or other important moments. Such events afforded the community of African-born adults in the New World the opportunity to utilize oral teachings to instill rich cultural imaginary of their country into the spirit of their children (just as Anthony Johnson did with his family) that replaced the oppressive European imagery and symbols of Virginia and its institutions.

The naming of the estate after a location so important to Black people in the transition from freedom to enslavement confirms not only the success of Anthony Johnson's child-rearing efforts but also the durability of West African oral traditions as a means and method to communicate to succeeding generations the beauty of Angolan life before European contact and before the horrors of the transatlantic slave trade. So much so that the telling and retelling about life in the Angolan region left an imprint in the hearts and minds of Anthony Johnson's children and grandchildren in a way that allowed the region to flourish as a "well spring to which [his] descendents could return in times of doubt to be refreshed" or to pay homage during times of celebration, such as marriage, the purchase of land or the birth of a child.[13]

The emergence of Angola as an alternate geography to Maryland and Virginia took shape decades before John Johnson Jr. was ever born. Anthony Johnson and his wife, Mary, who arrived in Virginia in 1622, probably shared stories of their African homeland and their lineal customs with each other while enslaved on the plantation of Edward Bennett. Perhaps Johnson told Mary of how in Africa he hunted for wild game with bows, arrows and traps throughout the year to provide food for the group.[14] Maybe Mary Johnson recounted information about her matrilineal heritage and how she worked the land she stood to inherit to produce millet and sorghum for her family.[15] Such exchanges about their life in the Angola region most likely occurred out of the earshot of their owner Bennett and his ten European servants.[16] Conceivably, these stories were told at night, after a long day of work, or when traveling in and around the plantation or on the way to church or in the churchyard.

By the 1640s, when the Johnsons were free and living on their own land, they were at liberty to discuss Angola openly, raising their sons John and Richard with all sorts of accounts about the region and perhaps even sharing their experiences with other African peoples who traveled past their home or with their invited guests. As landowners, the Johnsons were enfranchised to give Angola as prominent a place in their home as they wanted. Consequently, they probably spoke a lot about Angola around their "slave," John Casar, who himself likely hailed from this region. Not surprisingly, scholars of early America have tended to emphasize the fact that Johnson owned a slave when discussing his standing in Virginia as if to demonstrate the colony's racial equality.[17] This narrow analysis of Johnson's household is shortsighted and incomplete, and it fails to take into account the context of the term "slave" that Johnson was raised with across the Atlantic in Africa.

Perhaps Casar was what G. Ugo Nwokeji called "a person of the household," meaning "persons or families who [were] slaves" that were incorporated into the nuclear family, rather than a "market slave," who was treated like a commodity.[18] The degree of kinship in precolonial West African families with those that historians have labeled a "slave" allows us to see

Johnson's relationship with Casar through a more diasporic and nuanced understanding of African cultural retentions. It is from this context that we come to understand the influence that West African cultural traditions held in shaping the experiences of the Johnsons in Virginia and ultimately for his grandson in Maryland. Thus, one can imagine any number of physical spaces or structures within the Black landscapes of Virginia that were given names that signaled knowledge or invocations of a precolonial African past. And for the Johnsons and other African people in Virginia or Maryland, the name "Angola" symbolized a Black space in a larger White one that could offset the mounting effects of legislation in a White civil society that made it increasingly difficult for Black people to remain free.[19] Therefore, from Johnson's grandson's act of naming his estate Angola, we learn how oral traditions facilitated an emotional attachment to the region such that Angola became his, and perhaps other Black persons', most salient cultural reference.[20]

Just as Anthony Johnson provided his children with oral accounts of Angola that offered an alternative geography to the New World, one that ultimately framed their view of themselves and Virginia society, so too did Elizabeth Key's mother perhaps provide her with stories of how the Mbundu people used Christian conversion to further trade relations with the Portuguese.[21] Little is known about Key's mother except that she gave birth to Elizabeth in 1630 and that she was listed as a slave in the 1655 General Assembly committee report.[22] Other references in this report show Key's mother as the "Negro woman with Childe" that led to Thomas Key being fined for impregnating her.[23] Despite the scant details about her mother, Key's birth year, 1630, suggests her mother likewise embarked from the Luanda port in Angola, as did almost all the other Black persons in Virginia prior to 1650. Therefore, she probably raised Elizabeth with the insights and values that she grew up with in the Angola region.[24] As such, it was not surprising that Elizabeth knew the value that European peoples placed on Christianity, nor was it surprising that she employed this knowledge in crafting her freedom strategy.

Oral tradition was a link between the descendants of the Angola region in the New World and their forbearers on the African continent.[25] This connection was maintained by the steadily increasing population of African peoples in Virginia: fifty or so in 1625, three hundred in 1649, roughly two thousand in 1670 and nearly six thousand by the turn of the century, about half of whom were African-born.[26] At this rate, information about West Africa would continue to saturate Virginia. Consequently, knowledge gained from oral accounts about Angolan kingdoms would undoubtedly influence the children of these captive people, who ultimately would be central figures in the struggle for Black freedom at the turn of the century.

Perhaps the greatest value of oral traditions for African peoples in the early decades of Virginia was the transmission of resistance strategies from one generation to the next, especially about how to transcend enslavement and oppression, build community and outwit White folks. In this vein, oral stories provided Black peoples with the means of looking at the organization of Virginia in a way "that made [their] exploitation of the social system [seem] possible."[27]

Negotiating Virginia's institutions of social control (courthouses, churches and plantations) armed with knowledge gained from oral sources allowed Black persons to manipulate these institutions so that the spaces they occupied, as well as the surrounding areas, were less threatening to free and enslaved Black people. Often, oral sources allowed African peoples to know as much about Virginia's culture and its institutions as did many Europeans. Recounting stories of other Black persons who had found loopholes in the system helped encourage others to replicate those proven strategies. Evidence from freedom lawsuits between 1641 and 1655 offers several examples of Black peoples exploiting gaps in Virginia's institutional structure to gain their freedom or that of a family member.

Elizabeth Key's 1655 freedom suit illustrates one model for reorienting our perspective about just how much African people understood the racial politics of White civil society in the New World. As a strategy for self-emancipation, Key's freedom suit circumvented her enslavement and stamped her membership in Virginia society as a free Black woman by exploiting the colony's bias for Englishness and Christianity. Other resistance models include the manipulation of the colony's religiosity and plantation structure in order to gain the freedom of a loved one, like John Graweere did in his 1641 lawsuit to regain custody of his enslaved daughter. His suit took place fourteen years before Key's lawsuit, clearly showing the endurance and viability of oral traditions as a resistance strategy for Black people in Virginia in their struggle to be free from enslavement.

John Graweere was an African "servant" of a planter named William Evans. On March 31, 1641, he brought suit against a Robert Sheppard for custody of his daughter, whose mother was enslaved by Sheppard.[28] Despite his bonded status, Graweere had a relative amount of freedom with Evans in that he was permitted to raise hogs and keep half of the profits from their increase.[29] This measure of freedom is what probably made it possible for Graweere to have fathered a child by a "negro maid servant" on Sheppard's plantation.[30] Moreover, it was possible that Graweere's regular presence on his plantation initially helped Sheppard feel comfortable enough with him to consent to allowing him to purchase his daughter's freedom. But, for reasons that are unclear in the record, Sheppard in the end refused to release the child to Graweere. Nonetheless, on March 31, 1641, the General court ruled in Graweere's favor, agreeing that the child "be free from the said Sheppard or his assign and to be and remain at the disposing and education of the said

Graweere and the child's godfather [Evans] who undertaketh to see it brought up in the Christian religion."[31]

The case provides an important framework for reconstructing the history of freedom suits, revealing how African peoples used them to manipulate the social structure of Virginia in an effort to obtain the freedom of a loved one. We have no way of knowing the circumstances that led Graweere to elicit the help of Evans in the lawsuit. However, we do know that the plantation system of Virginia dictated that an enslaved person could not obtain sole custody of his or her child without a White slaveholder approving the exchange, a fact that Graweere and his wife used to their advantage by involving Evans.

We can assume that the decision to involve Evans was one that Graweere and the child's mother made together, realizing that the best chance for their daughter's freedom ultimately lay with Graweere working with Evans given their collegial relationship, rather than with the child's mother, who was bonded to Sheppard—particularly since Evans had already allowed Graweere to earn money on the side. The couple undoubtedly knew that the court would not recognize the paternal rights of an enslaved person, given the influence of slaveholders on the judiciary, with many of the court judges and officers owning slaves themselves.[32]

In fact, high-level officers in Virginia owned seventy-seven percent of all enslaved persons imported in Virginia between the 1630s and 1640s.[33] Moreover, between 1651 and 1680, sixty-one percent of planters owned between five and nine slaves.[34] This data confirms that Graweere and his wife stood little chance in the courts without the assistance of a White person. Had Graweere or his wife been European, the decision about the child's custody would need not have been litigated in the courts because, unlike bonded Black women, the status of the children of White female servants was determined by the father, in contradistinction to the 1662 law that made the children of enslaved Black women enslaved also. And more importantly, the condition of White people's bondage was by law temporary and fixed. So given these circumstances, Graweere and his wife probably used Evans to circumvent Virginia's racist paternity laws and customs that applied only to the children of enslaved Blacks in the hopes that in the end, including Evans in the custody arrangement would provide a more direct route to their daughter's freedom. Thus, to increase the probability of their daughter's freedom, Graweere and his wife had to find a way to get Evans to sponsor a freedom suit on behalf of their child.

The records do not tell us why Evans stood up for Graweere in the freedom suit. Perhaps Graweere agreed to work harder, maybe even hire himself out and give the proceeds to Evans. Or, Evans could have just been a nice man who intended to free Graweere anyway and, therefore, decided to help him obtain his child's freedom as a gift for all his free labor. We have no way of knowing for sure, but what we do know is that this case laid the foundation for other freedom suits like Elizabeth Key's that appropriated the cultural values of Europeans in order to circumvent the institutionally racist and White supremacist barriers to Black freedom.

The seeming incongruence of a freedom strategy that includes moving a female child from one slave master to another is not so far-fetched if we take into account that Graweere and the child's mother were likely reared in a matrilineal society like the Mbundu people of Angola, the country where most of the earliest Africans in the New World embarked. Among the Mbundu, girls were usually born in their father's lineal village, often remaining there until marriage.[35] Even after marriage, women in matrilineal societies sometimes lived with their husband's relatives, returning to their mother's village only after they ceased to bear children or after becoming divorced or widowed. Perhaps this was the context in which the couple sought the help of Evans. If so, then the release of their daughter into the custody of Graweere by way of Evans demonstrates the sophistication with which Black people reinterpreted matrilineal customs in Africa to sidestep the White supremacist customs and laws of Virginia society as they related to the children of enslaved Black women. By adapting their understanding of common matrilineal practices to circumvent the racist Eurocentric paternity system of Virginia (Englishness and Christianity) that African people had to contend with, Graweere and his daughter's mother were able to exploit the White identity politics of the colony in order to further the possibility of freedom for their daughter and thereby increase her chances for independence.

Another man, Mihill Gowen, also got his owner to help him obtain custody of his child. In 1655, the same year that Key brought her freedom suit, Gowen followed a pattern similar to that of Graweere to gain custody of his son, William.[36] In this case, Anne Barnhouse turned the child over to him without a court battle. Nonetheless, the cases were strikingly similar in one regard. Like Graweere's and Key's lawsuits, Gowen had to negotiate the politics of Christianity and Englishness before the transfer could take place. This meant that not only did the child need to be baptized in the Christian faith, but also that a White man had to support the exchange. Barnhouse acknowledges these conditions when she declared that: "I Anne Barnhouse hath given unto Mihill Gowen Negro hee being att this time Servant unto Robert Stafford a male child borne of my negro Prosa being baptized by Mr. Edward Johnson . . . [and] I the said Anne Barnhouse doth bind myself never to trouble or demand my Service of the said Mihill or his said Sonne William."[37]

Like the Graweere case, Robert Stafford, Gowen's master, had to support the reassignment of Gowen's son, William. Although the release of Gowen's son was not the result of a court order, it did require a sworn affidavit to certify the transfer. Also like Graweere's daughter, it appears that the fact that Gowen's son was baptized was an important precondition to his release, all of which elucidates the significance that the close proximity of churches and courthouses to plantation settlements had in the regulation of Black enslavement and White supremacy in Virginia. But more importantly, the case reveals the high degree of knowledge African peoples had about the Eurocentric institutions of Virginia and how to circumvent their bureaucracy. Undoubtedly, the oral tradition held an important function in disseminating information to those in the Black community about loopholes in the colonial system.

The records do not indicate why Ann Barnhouse decided to release Gowen's son, William, to him and Stafford. Perhaps Barnhouse did it as a favor to Gowen, or perhaps the child was released as part of a financial arrangement between her and Stafford. Either way, because William had been baptized in the Christian faith and because he would be under the charge of a White male master (Stafford), William was allowed to be reunited with his father. Consequently, the possibility of William's freedom was established through Stafford, showing the degree to which Christianity, Englishness and maleness together were not only an identity but also racial and status markers that could provide or prohibit freedom depending on one's ancestry. In this context, Elizabeth Key's appropriation of these titles becomes an important lens through which to observe how Black peoples played these constructs to their advantage when possible.

The transfer of Black children held in bondage from one planter to another who was possibly more lenient represents a reorientation of how Black peoples adapted to New World bondage systems in order to achieve freedom. However, it gets us no closer to understanding why the children in the Graweere and Gowen cases were transferred from their enslaved mothers to their enslaved fathers. Perhaps in Virginia, like in West Africa, enslaved Black women were highly valued by planters because they could produce more children and thereby increase the slaveholder's pool of free laborers. This combined with the fact that Black women were expected to work as hard as the men, and because they could also produce children, meant that it was less likely that a Black woman would be manumitted before a Black man. If this was the case, then Black couples probably made a calculated decision to push their masters to release their children to the father in the hopes that their offspring would be freed sooner.

The strategy of freeing a child to its father was informed by the realities of the enslavement system in Virginia. It may also have been informed by West African social practices. Black women in Virginia may have pressed for the release of their children to their father because it was common in some matrilineal societies that children grew up away from their mother's lineal family, only to return when they got older. Thus, Prossa, the mother of William, may have felt safe in turning over her child to Gowen and his master because she also believed that the child may return to her down the road, if and when he became free.

The seeming incompatibility of a freedom strategy that required a mother to give up custody of her child is not so strange when it is considered within the context of other tough choices that many African women had to make in their homelands regarding marriage, settlement and child-rearing in order to retain some control over their lives.[38] For example, matrilineal Mbundu societies that required women to raise their children in the lineage of their husbands also required women to relinquish their rights of inheritance. That said, these requirements did not detract Mbundu women from their duty to their children or their duty as a wife in her husband's lineage.[39] In this vein, Prossa's and Graweere's wives both made difficult decisions about the fate of their children in order to retain some control over their future, even as they themselves faced permanent bondage.

By contrast, bonded European women held complete authority over the freedom of their children during the entire term of their indenture. And unlike enslaved Black women, the children of European women remained with them even after their term of service expired. Enslaved Black women like Prossa's, Gowan's and Graweere's wives were forced to find a way around the apparatus of the plantation system in order to retain some authority over their children's future. Thus, whether it was by moving into a new lineage community in Angola or transferring the custody of a child to another planter in Virginia in the hopes that it would hasten their child's freedom, the choices of Black women during the seventeenth century were never the same as those of White women. As a result, it was probable that enslaved Black women in early Virginia drew on their experiences in Africa and in Angola in order to protect their children, who were innocent victims of the colony's internal slave trading, and in doing so, they likely shared information about the interworking of area courts with one another so as to mitigate their family's oppression.

The enslavement of Graweere's and Gowans's children was not the earliest known case of children being held as slaves in Virginia. In 1624, two children were known to have been enslaved, both of whom were listed with their parents in that year's muster.[40] Abraham Piersey's record lists one of these children in an entry that simply read "Negro Woman and a young Child of hers."[41] The other enslaved child was William, the son of Isabella and Anthony. They were recorded in the muster of William Tucker as "Antoney Negro: Isabell Negro: and William theire Child Baptised."[42] These records suggest that Virginia practiced the enslavement of children as early as 1619, given that most of the Black peoples listed in the 1624 muster were thought to be among the first to have arrived in Virginia.

Other cases of child enslavement, previously mentioned in chapter 2, occurred in the 1640s. One instance had Stephen Charlton in 1645 gifting a two-year-old "Negro childe" to his sister, and the other, which also involved Charlton, was in 1646 when he purchased a "Negro woman and a boy."[43] Both cases were indicative of a pattern of children being enslaved in the early part of the century.

All told, these cases of child enslavement, including the enslavement of Graweere's daughter in 1641 and Gowan's son in 1655, occurred years before the enactment of the 1662 law that made a child's slave status contingent on the mother's status.[44] This suggests that slavery in Virginia was more common and more pernicious and more systematic during this period than has been recognized by scholars of early American history.

The transfer of enslaved children from one planter to another in the hopes that they would become free sooner marked the emergence of a new approach in the resistance strategies of African people in the early seventeenth century. Attempts to protect children from indefinite bondage likewise offer unique insight into early African people's perceptions about family that point to another important precolonial African social system besides oral traditions that was used in Virginia to mitigate the ravages of enslavement: the concept of lineages.

Lineages were a social system that organized groups of people based on descent. Depending on whether the lineage structure was matrilineal or patrilineal, family members moved in and out of lineal groups at various moments of their life such as birth, marriage or the death of a spouse.[45] Lineages also allowed women, men and children who had lost their natal attachments to be incorporated into a new group as kin.[46]

The prior knowledge of lineage systems and the understanding of its utility for facilitating the management and incorporation of people moving into and out of the family supplied most early "Angolans" in Virginia with a framework for creating and maintaining familial ties with those who had been sold or separated as a result of the vagrancies of the colony's internal system of slave trading. So much so that by the middle of the seventeenth century, we find that the earliest arriving Africans, like Angelo and Anthony and Mary Johnson, did not develop their sense of belonging from a spatial connection to the colony's plantations, churches and courthouses like Europeans settlers. Rather, evidence suggests that African peoples found closeness and acceptance in a host of personal relationships that mirrored the lineal and affinity arrangements that were prevalent in precolonial Angolan communities.

As early as the sixteenth century, Angolan kingdoms of West Central Africa, the region where nearly all of the early Blacks in Virginia originated or at least embarked, organized their societies around a series of lineal relationships: fathers-sons, husbands-wives, daughters, brothers, nieces, nephews and outsiders, all of whom were incorporated into the group through a variety of pathways including marriage or as a concubine, pawn or slave.[47] Rooted in this structure was the genealogical history of the group, which formed the basis of belonging and acceptance. Early African peoples in Virginia drew on this knowledge and used it to reinterpret the White supremacist social system of slavery that existed in the New World to create new relations between enslaved (and free) Black persons, transforming the notion of what constituted family.

For example, as a consequence of the separation and dislocation of families that resulted from the transatlantic slave trade, persons of African descent in Virginia reformulated familial categories to include non-biological relations such as fictive mothers, fathers, daughters and sons. This helped to mitigate the trauma caused by Whites as a result of external and internal slave trading in the colony that regularly separated Black families. Thus, the creation of fictive kinships proclaimed the emergence of the West African lineage system reconstructed in Virginia to facilitate the formation of family ties between enslaved people of different ethnic groups not related by blood.

According to Rebecca Ginsburg, negotiating Virginia using a set of overlapping social systems and cultural forms like lineages and oral traditions demonstrated the "geographical intelligence" of Black women and men in Virginia.[48] This geographical intelligence allowed Black people like Graweere and Gowan to define family in a way that was more consistent with the familial arrangements in West Central Africa, leaving open the possibility that indigenous approaches to creating family ties could make institutions of the White landscape—the courthouses, churches and plantations—less threatening.

The process of creating new familial relations began during the experience of the Middle Passage, a shared experience of shock and upheaval that laid the groundwork for the creation of a variety of familial relationships between enslaved Black women, men and children from various ethnic groups who were shipped out of the port in Luanda on European vessels to the Americas. According to Walter Hawthorne, enslaved persons out of Angola who arrived in Brazil in the sixteenth century on the same ship often called each other *malungo*, a Mbundu word for "ancient authority symbols brought by ancestors from the sea."[49] For those who landed in Brazil together, the name "malungo" suggests that these persons saw each other as more than just shipmates; the name demonstrates their understanding of their ancestral connection created through their common origins and common condition of being enslaved captives in the transatlantic slave trade.

Just as shipmates from various ethnic Angolan kingdoms in Brazil were connected through their experience together in the Middle Passage, so too were early Africans in Virginia. Despite their obvious ethnic differences, the women, men and children who left Angola out of the seaport in Luanda were more like family members than strangers because of the horrific trauma they experienced together aboard European slave ships. As such, fictive kinships were perhaps the most common and strongest formal program developed by women and men of African ancestry in Virginia that most closely adhered to the sanctity of the indigenous cultural form of lineage systems.

Fictive kinships were a type of familial relationship that developed between Blacks in Virginia with persons who were not related by blood. These persons often stood in for relatives who could not be present as a result of ruptures in families that occurred because of the external and internal slave trading systems in the colony. Enduring familial bonds, already a strong cultural value of African women and men reared under lineage systems, paved the way for fictive kinship to take root in Virginia, allowing those sold away from loved ones to develop new family ties while retaining biological ones in spite of being separated. Emanuel and Frances Driggus probably drew on fictive relationships to sustain them while they were separated from their children on at least two occasions by their enslaver, Francis Pott.

Francis Pott was part of an emerging cadre of up-and-coming European planters in the 1640s who participated in local and transatlantic slave trading as a means to build and create wealth. As the numbers of enslaved Africans increased throughout that period (two hundred nine enslaved persons were imported into Virginia between 1635 and 1656), owning slaves for Whites became associated with prosperity, wealth and stature.[50] Taking advantage of the uptick in slave trading in the era, Pott had purchased at least twelve Black persons by 1650. Eight were children, five of them girls, including Elizabeth and Jane, the daughters of Emanuel and Frances Driggus.[51] Ironically or tragically, Pott bought Elizabeth and Jane from Robert Sheppard, the same man who enslaved the aforementioned wife and daughter of John Graweere. A court document dated May 27, 1645, certifying Pott's purchase of Elizabeth and Jane is detailed in the following affidavit:

> I Francis Pott has taken to service two daughters of my Negro Emanuel Drigus to serve and be with my heirs, the named Elizabeth Drigus, around 8 years old to serve 13 years which will be completed and ended on the first day of March in the yeare of our Lord God One thousand six hundred and fifty eight in which time she will be around only sixteene years of age (or there abouts) old, and the other child named Jane Dregis being about 1 year old to serve I Francis Pott as they did Elizabeth until they are 30 years old, if she do live that long, to be completed May 1, 1674.[52]

This source provides us with much information about Virginia's institution of slavery. It reveals information about the buying and selling of Black children, the prospects of intergenerational wealth among Whites created out of enslaving Black people and the power of a planter to control the fate of Black peoples. What the source does not provide, however, is information about the circumstances that led to Elizabeth and Jane being separated from their family or how Emanuel and Frances coped during the separation.

Pott's declaration of purchase was typical of the county court records of the 1640s in its failure to offer insights into the views of those African peoples who were affected by local slave trading. After having survived the traumas of the Middle Passage, we know that early Africans in Virginia had definite ideas about the transatlantic slave trade.[53] That said, we cannot regret sufficiently the inadequacy of early seventeenth documents to tell the story of New World slavery in ways that include the perspective of Blacks.[54] Scholars have noted that documents alone cannot tell the full story of the New World slavery, its connection to Africa or the continents role in the development of African American culture.[55] Although county records do provide evidence of the many instances when the Driggus family was separated as a result of local slave trading, much still remains unclear.

For instance, a survey of the records shows that a separation occurred in 1647, when Emanuel and Frances were sold by Pott to Stephen Charlton, leaving their two daughters Elizabeth and Jane alone again on Pott's plantation.[56] In December 1652, Emanuel and Frances were repurchased by Pott, and the family was reunited back on his plantation.[57] In 1657, there was further upheaval in the family when two of the Driggus's other children, Ann, aged nine or ten, and Edward, aged three or four, were sold.[58] Ann was sold to John Pannell "for ever" for five thousand pounds of tobacco.[59] Edward was said to have been sold to Henry Armitrading "for [his] whole life."[60]

Despite this basic information, the records do not indicate when Emanuel and Frances or their children became free. Several documents suggest that by 1658, when Pott died, the family was free.[61] Moreover, records do not provide insights about Emanuel's and Frances's perspectives on being enslaved or sold away from their children and friends. As such, we are left to read against the grain of early seventeenth century documents that White slaveholders provided to local county officials to understand how it was that the Drigguses or other Black people survived enslavement and separations. In the absence of records showing the views of African peoples regarding the upheavals suffered under Virginia's enslavement system, fictive kinships offer an important counter-framework for some understanding of the outlook of early Africans: information that is all but absent in colonial era historiographic documents.

The circumstances that Emanuel and Frances Driggus found themselves in were illustrative of the wild upheavals endured by many enslaved Black families in the early seventeenth century. Sometimes plantations like Pott's, Charlton's and Sheppard's were a revolving door of slaveholding activities—buying, selling, trading and the hiring out—of enslaved women, men and children to fulfill a variety of personal, economic and social needs and whims of slaveholders. Recurring separations of families and friends surely reminded early Africans of the dire consequences of the transatlantic slave trade, and it also throws light on the importance of overlapping West African cultural traditions and social formations like oral traditions and lineage systems that Black persons in seventeenth century Virginia recreated to stay connected and survive these upheavals.

The threat and reality of separation must have broken down any ethnic differences or divisions that may have existed between African peoples, leading to the formation of alliances between disparate groups of Black peoples. Thus, an interest in maintaining some sort of familial associations under such uncertain conditions provided the context for fictive kinships to take root as a modified form of West African lineage systems.

For example, in the wake of the barriers to the maintenance and creation of biological kinships that resulted from the transatlantic slave trade, early Africans in Virginia reinterpreted the lineage system and developed fictive mothers, fathers, daughters and sons in order to mitigate the trauma arising from sale and separation. In instances where children were separated from their biological parents, Black parents relied on other Black peoples to look after their children. In the case of Emanuel and Frances Driggus, the couple depended on a group of surrogate parents to take care of Elizabeth and Jane. We have no way of knowing, for example, exactly who assumed the role of mother for the girls while they were apart from their parents. Perhaps it was a woman like the one who cared for Frederick Douglass, "a feeble woman too old for field labor," or maybe it was a network of providers, female and male, who became acting parents for Elizabeth and Jane.[62] Whatever the arrangement, someone assumed the parental role for the girls. Why? Perhaps it was a conscious recognition of their own vulnerable position at the margins of Virginia society that led African people, who themselves were fearful of being caught in similar circumstances, to assist in the care of a motherless or fatherless child.

We do not know for how long Elizabeth and Jane were separated from their parents before Pott purchased them in May 1645. Given their ages at that time, age eight and one, respectively, it is safe to assume that it was for a short period of time. There were occasions, though, when the family was separated for an extended length of time. One separation lasted five years, from 1647 to 1652, which in the life of a child is a very long time. During this long separation, Elizabeth would have turned fifteen, which meant that she entered puberty and was transitioning into a young lady without her parents around to assist her. For Elizabeth, this reality meant that her surrogate mother would teach her about the changes that her body was experiencing as a young adolescent. The most common lessons in this regard would have revolved around her menstrual cycle, pregnancy and motherhood.

The enslaved Black people on Pott's plantation were also probably charged with integrating Elizabeth into the work force and then teaching her about life under slavery. With her parents having been sold after the 1643 law, which made Black women's (but not White women's) labor taxable, we can assume at the very least that Elizabeth's work duties were not much different or any less strenuous from those of a fifteen-year-old boy, Black or White. Her work regime might have entailed lots of chopping and hoeing. Perhaps she received more specialized instructions on crop management and animal husbandry. Or maybe her surrogate parents even shared with her some of the horticultural practices that they used in Angola that they modified for the environment of Virginia.

An enslaved girl like Elizabeth entering puberty had to be taught skills of self-preservation to prevent her from "falling prey to the licentious [White and Black] men" on Pott's plantation.[63] Neither of her biological parents could assist her in such matters. Thus, any teachings on how to protect herself from the sexual overtures of men would have had to come from the women and men of the enslaved Black community on the plantation where she resided.

The literature on child enslavement tells us that enslaved girls and boys had "virtually no childhood because they entered the work force early and as a result were subjected to arbitrary plantation authority, punishments and separations."[64] Thus, it was up to surrogate parents to teach children in their care the ways of White people (and Blacks) in the area.

Jane was only three when her parents were sold. The nature of the parenting provided by her surrogates during the five years that she was apart from her mother and father probably entailed more nurturing, given her young age, than it did for Elizabeth. Some enslaved woman on Pott's plantation mothered Jane for several years, which meant she had to be taught many of the childhood basics such as bathing, toilet training and manners by a surrogate. Jane probably spent the majority of her time at play. However, as the progeny of an enslaved family, she was ultimately under the jurisdiction of Pott even after her parents returned. Nonetheless, it was the responsibility of her surrogate parents to teach Jane about the plantation's pecking order: Pott, his wife, his children, his European servants and then enslaved Black peoples. As such, Jane had to be instructed that conversations among Black persons were not to be discussed with Whites.[65] So, by the time the family was reunited in 1652, Elizabeth and Jane would have been schooled in the particulars of Virginia's institution of enslavement by their fictive parents. As the institution of enslavement in Virginia continued to grow, importing enslaved Africans at a rate of about sixty persons a year during this period, increasingly the persons charged with raising Black children would be fictive kin.[66]

The enslaved community's interest in the rearing of Elizabeth and Jane led not only to the formation of fictive kinships, but presumably to the creation of an "underground railroad" of formal and informal communication between Pott's plantation and Charlton's that allowed Emanuel and Frances to keep up with their daughters' development during the years they were separated.[67] In the spaces and places between the plantations, perhaps women and men found ways to provide regular updates to Emanuel and Frances about how the girls were doing. Maybe the parents occasionally were able to sneak back to visit with the girls without being detected. Conceivably, their interactions were like those of Frederick Douglass's mother: "very short in duration and at night."[68] Or perhaps the parents had a chance to talk with the girls in the churchyard or along the paths to the parish church. Either way, such networks of communication were undoubtedly part of the environment of enslaved Africans, one that was largely unknown to White persons and, therefore, part of the terrain of the Black landscape. Fictive kinships were a conscious investment by Black people in the security of Black families against the horrors of the slave trade and, as such, they paved the way for a Black space to exist in and around Pott's and other slaveholder's plantations.

The bonds that developed between Elizabeth and Jane and their caretakers probably were not undone when their parents returned. Conceivably, their relationship evolved into that of niece-aunt or niece-uncle. Thus, the fluidity of fictive relations created permanent bonds and a perpetual kinship system between Black peoples across the plantation landscape that was similar to those that existed among the Mbundu peoples of Angola who, while moving in and out of lineage groups, maintained immutable affinities to their former village.[69] With this in mind, any effort to compile a history of early Africans in Virginia must begin by introducing their cultural practices and ways of life in Africa (before they had contact with Europeans) into any discussion about the various methods Black peoples used to survive oppression and build community in the New World, particularly while in bondage.

Fictive kinships were one strategy born out of an interpretation of Virginia's White civil society that allowed free and enslaved people to use the theories of indigenous African lineage systems to construct enduring bonds of attachment that held Black people together during the absence of biological family members who were regularly sold. The Driggus family, like other enslaved African families, undoubtedly relied on fictive kinships during their years of bondage as well as while free. And as one of the multiple intelligences used to combat enslavement, the formation of fictive kinships permitted early African peoples to survive the exploitive and White supremacist institutions that made up Virginia's plantation system. Therefore, we can assume that while Emanuel and Frances were separated from Elizabeth and Jane from 1647 to 1652, they knew that a collegial fictive kinship system was likely on the plantation where their daughters were enslaved.

African lineage systems and the transatlantic slave trade were mutually constitutive explanations for the emergence of fictive kinships in early Virginia. For Black peoples reared in lineage systems in precolonial West African nations like Angola, the familial separation that came with New World enslavement was the social equivalent in of "social death," that is, being without kin.[70] And fictive kinships helped to rectify this situation because the sale of loved ones united the entire Black community in maintaining some form of familial attachment across time and space regardless of whether the transaction involved a blood relative. An unfortunate case in point was when Emanuel and Frances Driggus had the unpleasant experience of witnessing the effect of the sale of another family's child in their cohort one year prior to the sale of their daughters.

In November 1646, Emanuel and Frances were present when the children of one of their enslaved comrades, a woman named Marchant, were sold while Francis Pott was in England on business. During this time, Pott directed his nephew John to sell Marchant's daughter and son, Pew and William, to pay off a debt.[71] Like Elizabeth and Jane, Pew and William were young when they were sold away from their mother; Pew was about five years old, and her brother William was about three. In this case, they were sold to another slaveholder in the area, a man named John Browne. And like Elizabeth and Jane, Pew and William's nurturing, comfort and rearing became the responsibility of surrogate mothers and fathers on John Browne's plantation.

Although it would be another year before Elizabeth and Jane Driggus were separated from their parents, the sale of Marchant's children was no doubt seared into the hearts and minds of Emanuel and Frances, illustrating not only the vulnerability of their family to the avarice of planters and slave traders but also the impact such sales had on the entire Black community. Thus, the selling of Black peoples by Whites is a reminder of the peril that nearly all descendants of Africa faced during the early decades of the seventeenth century, out of which indigenous West African cultural practices such as fictive kinship systems and oral traditions were enacted as a mitigation strategy.

Did observing Marchant's grief prepare Emanuel and Frances Driggus for the hurt they would feel in the next year from being separated from their children? Probably not. Although, the pain of separation they felt was possibly modulated to some degree by the community custom of enslaved Black adults looking after the enslaved Black children on their plantation.

Fictive kinships in the form of enslaved Black adults acting as surrogate parents to enslaved Black children, with its emphasis on nurturing and rearing those separated from their biological parents, might have been a natural response to the threat of being sold. That said, the kind of shared sacrifice that fictive kinship brought to unify Black people in support of Black children also existed between Black adults, many of whom formed sibling-like bonds with one another while enslaved. Often, these bonds extended to efforts to obtain one's freedom or the freedom of one's spouse and children.

Self-purchase was the most common way for enslaved women and men like Marchant and the Drigguses to be able to free themselves and their children. Usually, the terms of manumission were some combination of extra work, such as hiring out one's services to another planter and using the proceeds toward self-purchase, or by the sale of livestock or crops. Emanuel Driggus probably received assistance from one of his close friends on Pott's plantation to help finance his and his family's freedom. Most likely his help came from his friend and fellow enslaved comrade named Bashawe Farnando. The friendship between Driggus and Farnando spanned over a decade, and from it we can track how sibling-like kinships developed between adults over time through the ups and downs of enslavement.

The brotherly relationship between Farnando and Driggus began in 1645, when the men were part of the group of enslaved persons Pott brought with him to the Eastern Shore region of Virginia.[72] Farnando and the Drigguses, as well as Pott's other enslaved persons and indentured servants, all lived on a fifteen hundred acre plot of land in an area of Northampton County called Magotha Bay.[73] In 1658, Pott purchased another thirty-five hundred acres before his death that year. With such large landholdings and holdings of White servants and enslaved Black persons, Pott probably owned several homes, including servants' quarters, which was typical of planters who held four or more persons in bondage. It was probably in these living quarters that Driggus and Farnando got to know each other really well, perhaps discussing the myriad of changes that they experienced together as enslaved persons.

For example, in October 1646, Frances and Emanuel Driggus and Bashawe Farnando were used as collateral in a debt Pott owed to his cousin, Mary Menifie, the widow of the large planter (also known in the era as a Great Planter) George Menifie.[74] Although their time in bondage with Menifie was short because they were later sold to Pott's brother-in-law, Stephen Charlton, in March 1647, Barshawe nonetheless experienced the trauma of Virginia's enslavement system with Emanuel and Frances and thus could testify not only to the obvious anguish he felt under the circumstances but also to the hurt and pain the couple felt while separated from their children.[75]

Like time spent in a foxhole during war, going through stints of enslavement together produced bonds and intimacies that broke down any social distinctions, such as those of ethnicity, age or gender. We have no way of knowing about where in Angola that Emanuel Driggus and Bashawe Farnando had lived before being shipped out of the port in Luanda on European slave ships or what their ethnic or lineal affiliations were. However, we do know that the experience of enslavement, such as what the two men shared for over a decade while enslaved together on Pott's plantation, created a permanent kinship between them in much the same way it did with nonrelatives who were brought into a Mbundu lineage group and, over time, came to be thought of as family.

Examples likely included Emanuel Driggus confiding his agony to Farnando at being separated from his children during the short time they were held as collateral by Menefie. Later, when Driggus and his wife Frances were sold to Charlton in 1647, in what ended up being a five-year stretch, maybe the pain of separation was so great that two men began to dream, plan and seek out the counsel of other Blacks regarding to how to best go about gaining their freedom.

Although the records kept by his enslavers do not include references about Bashawe Farnando that suggest that he was a brother, son, husband or a father, it would be a mistake to assume that he did not hold close attachments with other Blacks before he was enslaved by Pott or while on Pott's plantation. Undoubtedly, he and the entire Black community where he lived felt a sense of loss after his being sold. Thus, the profound sense of detachment felt by Farnando and Driggus while away from loved ones probably hastened their closeness and propelled them to help each other become free.

The regularity in the number of enslaved Black persons being imported into the area between 1635 and 1656 set in motion several changes between adults over the course of the many decades of bondage that became important to the formation of the kinship between them, namely, enslaved African peoples collaborating in their freedom struggles.[76] The most common cooperation between fictive kin came in the form of pooling resources like livestock and crops to fund manumission. Driggus and Farnando helped each other in this manner. Ironically, their enslaver, Frances Pott, supplied the men with their first animal that perhaps unwittingly provided the means for them to effect their own emancipation.

The records show that upon arriving in Northampton County in 1645, Pott "delivered unto [his] servant Emanuel Driggus a black cow and a red calf forever with all their increase to dispose of in his lifetime or after his death."[77] On the same day, Pott also "gave unto [his] Negro Mann Bashawe Ffanndo one red cow calf, and the said calfe is Bashawe's with its increase forever."[78] These animals would jump-start and ultimately underwrite Driggus and Farnando's quest for freedom and, in the process, create a brotherly alliance between them that was precipitated not only by their experiences together in bondage but also by their aptitude for raising livestock and cultivating crops.[79]

The records do not indicate why Pott bestowed the animals to Driggus and Farnando. Perhaps it was a reward for their free labor, or maybe the men had made an arrangement with Pott, as did many enslaved persons, to secure their freedom using the proceeds from the sale of their animals. If so, then the five years spent together on the plantation of Charlton could have been part of an arrangement between all four of the men, in which Pott hired out Driggus and Farnando to work for Charlton with an agreement that part of their earnings went toward their manumission. We have no way of knowing for sure, but what we do know is that while with Charlton, the two men continued to accumulate more livestock.[80] For example, on April 22, 1647, a Northampton County planter named John Roberts sold Emanuel Driggus "one black heifor aged 2 ½ . . . and [likewise assigned a] heifor and all her increase to Barshaw Farnando and his heirs."[81]

By 1652, the amount of livestock owned by Driggus and Farnando had grown so large that Pott and Charlton were compelled to acknowledge the legality of the men's considerable holdings, given the local prohibitions against trading with Black persons. In an affidavit certifying their awareness of the men's collection of animals, Pott and Charlton professed to the court that their enslaved workers, Driggus and Farnando,

> Have cartaine cattle, hogs, and poultrye nowe in their possession the which they have lawfullie gotten, and purchased in their service formelie under the said Capt. Pott, and since augmented and increased under the service of Capt. Stephen Charlton. . . . [These] are the proper goods of the abovesaid Negroes and . . . they maye freely dispose of them either in their life tyme or att their death.[82]

This declaration admitting that Driggus and Farnando had lawfully accumulated livestock over the course of seven years lends support to the idea that Pott and Charlton permitted their buildup of cattle. The initial motives for the men's accumulation of animals are unknown, although one can guess that Pott and Charlton were aware of the fact that the sale of their animals could help Driggus and Farnando buy their freedom. Nonetheless, their collection of livestock over the years shows that Driggus and Farnando possessed the means to buy their freedom. One could imagine the collaboration that ensued between Driggus and Farnando included such decisions as which animals to buy: a cow or a bull, or a calf or a heifer.

The going rate for a ten-year-old cow during this period was around five hundred pounds of tobacco, and a young cow with her calf cost about six hundred pounds tobacco.[83] Such prices made self-purchase feasible, given that a Virginia mistress named Jane Eltonhead charged her enslaved man, Francis Payne, whom I will discuss later in this chapter, "fifteen hundred pounds of tobacco" for his freedom.[84] This price may have been prohibitive if one had to work alone to accumulate this much tobacco. However, by pooling their resources, Driggus and Farnando had a real chance of buying their freedom and the freedom of their family. This was particularly so because between 1645 and 1652, the men had combined their assets to acquire several heads of cattle as well as some hogs and poultry, which, at a cost of several hundred pounds of tobacco each, could indeed help to finance their freedom.

If Driggus and Farnando were planning to use the animals to fund their freedom, then the men may have had to be careful not to be too public about their intentions for fear of offending the sensibilities of conservative planters who supported the colony's "no trade with Negros" policy mentioned in the previous chapter. The possibility of Driggus and Farnando using their live-stock to finance their manumission was clearly on the mind of Pott and may have been what prompted him to file a petition on August, 18, 1654, ordering that the "inhabitants of Northampton County take notice not to truck, trade, buy, sell, or bargain with any of his Negro servants without his consent."[85] We get a sense of the general anxiety Pott felt over the potential loss of the people he enslaved in an earlier letter written to his nephew, John, while he was away in England. Needing money to settle a debt, Pott in 1646 directed John to pay the bill with tobacco or land, but not his slaves. According to Francis Pott, he would "rather parte with any thinge or all I have besides; then with my Negroes."[86] Knowing this would have made it all the more crucial for Driggus and Farnando to stick together and play down their intentions of using the animals to purchase their freedom.

We will never know exactly what prompted Pott's admonition to the residents of Northampton County. However, we do know that many plant-ers relied on the labor of enslaved people to finance their lifestyles. And the trade in animals with enterprising Blacks created opportunities for their free-dom that upset Virginia's social order of White over Black and its lucrative internal slave trading system, which helps one to understand why Pott may have been anxious about White residents engaging in this manner with those he enslaved. That said, Pott's directive attests to the progress that African peoples made in the procurement of animals as a means to win their freedom and independence.

The bondage experiences of Driggus and Farnando offer scholars of early American enslavement a perspective on social relationships between Black adults that is mostly absent in the historical record. These alliances were very different from those formed between free and indentured Whites, who mostly came to Virginia of their own volition with family or to be with family and thus the need to create fictive kinships as a survival or resistance strategy was superfluous. However, for persons of African descent, fictive kinships outline the many contours of affect between Black persons enslaved together, be it during the Middle Passage or on a plantation in the New World.

Although much of the development of fictive kinships among the enslaved Blacks can be traced to the struggle to overcome the deleterious impact of Virginia's slave trading system, fictive kinships also formed the basis of a cohesive Black community. Fictive kinships provided early Africans in Virginia with a defense against the sale and separation of loved ones, and doing so organized disparate groups of Black peoples around a common goal of freedom. Caring for children and assisting one another in freedom struggles laid the foundation for a united Black community, which expanded throughout the seventeenth century. The recognition that livestock was the currency of freedom encouraged Black women and men to pool their vast agricultural knowledge that was initially gained in precolonial West Africa and then used in Virginia to increase the probability of their freedom. The growth in enslaved Black peoples arriving in Virginia between 1635 and 1656, meanwhile, compelled women and men to pursue additional revenue generating sources for gaining freedom besides the accumulation and sale of livestock.[87] As the dominant cash crop of the region, tobacco also became an important commodity in the freedom aspirations of African women and men.

Just as tobacco and slavery were linked together, so too were tobacco and freedom. Tobacco dominated Virginia's agriculture scene for most of the seventeenth century, beginning around 1613.[88] In 1630, workers harvested four hundred thousand pounds from Virginia tobacco crops, and by 1660, tobacco yields exceeded fifteen million pounds.[89] Tobacco also served as Virginia's principal currency for much of the century. So much was this so that on March 27, 1637, an Accomack County court ordered all debts to be paid in the form of tobacco.[90]

Most African peoples in Virginia hailed from societies steeped in agrarian culture, which meant that many of them were able to master the science of tobacco production rather quickly. In fact, many arrived in Virginia already highly skilled in tobacco culture. For instance, as early as the sixteenth century, enslaved African peoples had "cured tobacco in Cuba, Hispaniola and the northern coast of Venesuala, and in other Spanish colonies."[91] So by the time the first Africans had arrived in the British colony of Bermuda in 1613, Africans had nearly a century of experience in tobacco cultivation under their belts. It was not a coincidence then that Bermuda's immediate rise as a world leader in tobacco production can be attributed to the acumen of African women and men.[92] The aptitude of African peoples in tobacco production was so extensive that the Bermuda "assembly denied Blacks the right to buy, sell or barter tobacco without the knowledge or consent of their master" for fear of undermining its system of enslavement.[93] The successful early experiences of cultivating tobacco crops in the New World enshrined in succeeding generations of Black people a discourse about freedom that included tobacco.

African people's facility for agronomics and its use as a New World freedom strategy has its basis in precolonial West Africa. Since the fifteenth century, various groups of African peoples grounded their social and economic independence around agricultural production. For example, the Balanta peoples of Upper Guinea established a market in rice production to trade the war captives that ultimately underwrote their independence.[94] And, in what is now Sierra Leone, some unfree persons in bondage sold a variety of other crops to purchase their freedom.[95] Likewise, some women acted as market makers for the agricultural goods they produced, including initiating trade with merchants outside of their ethnic group.[96] Overall, it was rather common for many African ethnic groups to include market-based strategies in their plans to surmount threats to their independence. Thus, the idea that agricultural skills could translate into freedom and opportunity for free and enslaved Black persons in early Virginia overlapped with those people in other agrarian societies in West Africa who likewise sought independence through agricultural markets.

Tobacco emerged as a potent economic discourse for Black and White peoples in Virginia in the early seventeenth century, many of whom formed their ideals about freedom and enslavement around this crucial commodity. Markets were made around the buying and selling of Black peoples using tobacco as the currency. In the 1640s, for example, African females put up for sale by European traders cost around twenty-five hundred pounds of tobacco.[97] Planter William Burdett's estate inventory valued "one negro girle about 8 years old at 2000 pounds of tobacco," which was twice the value of any one of his White servants, female or male.[98] As was mentioned earlier, one of Emanuel Driggus's daughters, Ann, was sold to John Pannell for a startling five thousand pounds of tobacco.[99] However, in as much as tobacco was the currency used to enslave Black peoples, it also was a key to their manumission. Thus, knowledge about the political economy of tobacco had personal consequences for Black Virginians.

The arrival of newly imported slaves from the Americas during the early decades of the seventeenth century made it all the more likely that Black peoples in Virginia would understand the value of tobacco vis-à-vis their own freedom. Francis Payne, an enslaved African man, who himself was valued at twenty-four hundred pounds of tobacco in an appraisal of his deceased owner's estate, understood the market value of tobacco and used the proceeds from the sale of tobacco crops to purchase his freedom and, eventually, the freedom of his entire family.[100]

Payne's road to freedom began nearly twenty years after his arrival in Virginia when, on May 13, 1649, he struck an agreement with his mistress that set the terms of his eventual freedom. The agreement between them read as follows:

I Jane Eltonhead wife to William Eltonhead do covenant and agree to and with francis payne my Negro Servant (hee being parte of the Estate belonging to my children) as followeth first that I the said Jane do resign all my right of this insueing crop that he is now working, warranting him to enjoy the same (crop) quietly for any trouble or molestation that nay or can arise for any persons. . . . Likewise I do authorize him to use the best means lawful be and can for the further bettering of the said crop.[101]

The document leaves us with the impression that Payne was fully in charge of this land and could do with it whatever he deemed to be suitable to extract the most personal value from it. As such, the record helps us to understand how tobacco was used to bring about freedom for enslaved (and free) Black peoples in the middle decades of the seventeenth century.

Mrs. Eltonhead left Payne in charge of the plantation after she moved to Maryland with her husband William, which attests to her confidence in his agricultural skills. Payne's adeptness at tobacco farming could have come from his experiences in Bermuda or from time spent in Spanish colonies if he had been enslaved there, as many Africans were before arriving in Virginia. A more likely scenario was that he learned how to manage tobacco crops from his experience with an agronomic process called "shifting cultivation," which was commonly practiced by farmers in the Angolan region of West Africa to increase the yields from their crops.[102]

In the sixteenth century, the Mbundu peoples of Angola, the region where most Blacks in early Virginia originated, rotated varieties of millet and sorghum crops from one area of land to another every few years in order to refresh the soil and increase harvests. Such practices translated very well in Virginia with tobacco crops, which, over time, drained the soil of its fertility and likewise required frequent rotation.[103] Most European colonists lacked an agrarian tradition and knowledge of tobacco production. In contrast, many enslaved Blacks had a highly developed set of agronomic skills. Thus, with tobacco being the most valuable export of Virginia for much of the seventeenth century, adroit Black farmers like Payne enjoyed a greater amount of latitude from enslavers like Eltonhead in managing crops.

The horticultural experiences of Black peoples in Western Africa and the Americas around tobacco production represent a "diffusion of an indigenous knowledge system" that became an especially valuable resource for negotiating the terms of their freedom.[104] For Payne, his adroitness at crop management produced "fifteen hundred pounds of tobacco and six Bushels of corne," which was enough to pay Eltonhead for his freedom.[105] Thus, whether it was rice, tobacco or livestock, indigenous African agricultural systems fueled kinship and community links between African peoples in Virginia in the mid-seventeenth century while also serving as a means for achieving freedom.

Tobacco cultivation and animal husbandry were valuable conduits to the formation of fictive kinships. And agrarian culture cemented the relationship between men like Bashawe Farnando and Emanuel Driggus, both of whom used their farming knowledge to facilitate their freedom. The brotherly closeness that developed over the years was wedded through their accumulation of livestock, which occurred around the upheavals of enslavement that they experienced together on Pott's plantation. In this context, "family" must have meant more than blood to Emanuel and Bashawe. It also included their shared experiences in captivity, such as the sale and recovery of a loved one as well as events that led to their personal freedom. This was how fictive kin relations in Virginia functioned, paralleling the lineage structures that women and men in precolonial West Africa experienced that regularly allowed nonrelatives to incorporate into the group as family.[106]

The success of fictive kinships, especially looking after children, the formation of a Black underground communication network, adult bonding around the accumulation of livestock, and the sale of marketable crops all motivated African peoples to ensure that the gains made in their struggle for freedom extended into the next generation. Free Black people, for instance, took on a moral and financial responsibility for sustaining the progress they made using a range of resistance tactics. By the mid- to late 1650s, for instance, the responsibilities of formerly enslaved women and men included bequeathing property to each other. A typical example is found in the estate records of Francis Payne. He requested in his 1659 will that his heirs sell his "mare colt" to Anthony Johnson.[107] Another example of wealth transfer between Black peoples also occurred in 1659, when Anthony Johnson's son, John Johnson Sr., along with two other African men, John Rogers and Jon Assford, requested in their wills that their heirs sell one of each of their animals and distribute the proceeds "unto John Williams and his heirs."[108]

The records do not reveal why the men wanted John Williams to inherit their animals. Maybe they knew of his efforts to negotiate the purchase his freedom or that of a loved one and knew he did not have the funds, so the men bequeathed Williams some of their livestock to ensure that he and his family would become free. Or perhaps the animals were a form of freedom dues that were meant to jump-start his life of independence. Either way, committing property to other African persons was an important manifestation in the interpretation of West African lineage systems that blurred the biological connection between heirs and, in the process, further united the Black community around the common goal of freedom.

Wills were an important vehicle that allowed Black persons to project a broad regional West African identity (particularly the Angola region) in the form of lineage systems across the Virginia landscape during the middle decades of the seventeenth century. In their most basic form, wills supplied

the framework for the continuation of fictive kinships into the next generation, muddling the lines between biological and fictive family members in the
process. In addition, bequeathing property to family, biological or fictive, was
the fruit of a life spent struggling against the upheavals of Virginia's White
supremacist society and its slave trading system.

As mentioned in previous chapters, in the 1650s, Anthony Johnson owned
roughly three hundred fifty acres of land, several servants and one slave
while in Virginia. After relocating to Maryland in the late 1660s, he likewise
acquired several hundred acres of land. Interestingly, he died in the spring
of 1670 without a will. Yet, although Johnson died intestate, his wife, Mary
Johnson, did make arrangements for the disposition of her modest estate.
"On September 3, 1672, Mary Johnson, of Somerset County, Negro, (relict of
Anthony Johnson, late of the said county, Negro, deceased), made deed of gift
for cattle to her grandchildren, viz; Anthony Johnson, son of John Johnson,
Negro, and Francis and Richard Johnson, sons of Richard Johnson."[109]

Mary Johnson's will allows us to see more clearly how inheritance marked
a new pattern in the freedom struggles of Black peoples. We can see in her
will the degree to which animal transfers facilitated the opportunity for Black
independence in the seventeenth century and beyond. Although Mary died
sometime in 1682, she left little doubt about her belief in property inheritance
as a means to sustain the freedoms she and her deceased husband Anthony
worked so hard to achieve.

When they had the means, most African peoples embraced wills as a
resistance strategy against the growing influence of the international system of slavery to relegate Blacks in Virginia to indefinite bondage. A 1670
law explicitly stating that "all servants not being Christians imported into
the colony by ship shall be slaves for their lives," made it difficult for any
person of African ancestry in Virginia to remain free.[110] In 1705, Black
persons in Virginia were made chattel through a law that declared that "all
negroe, mulatto, and Indian slaves shall be made real estate."[111] Such legislation speaks to the urgent need for self-help programs that would mitigate
the colony's growing investment in the lifetime bondage of Black peoples.
Moreover, with enslaved Africans arriving in Virginia in increasingly large
numbers, over five thousand between 1650 and 1700, fictive kinships and the
bequeathing of property would become more important to the maintenance of
a cohesive Black community.[112]

Overlapping webs of familial relations and various other resistance strategies, like freedom suites and oral traditions, firmly tied Black peoples to
one another and to the continent of Africa in a way that began to transform
Africans to African Americans beginning in the early decades of the seventeenth century. The focus on family in whatever form, biological or fictive,
was not that different from their counterparts in precolonial West Africa, who

regularly incorporated outsiders into lineal groups with little disruption to the groups' cohesiveness.[113] The concept of fictive kinships (the formation of familial like relations with persons who are not related by blood) created the foundation for unity among disparate groups of African peoples for decades to come. Thus, the degree of cohesiveness between Black peoples in a Virginia increasingly influenced by the development of the international system of slavery cannot be assessed simply by biology or ethnicity. It also resulted from the common experience of being enslaved and oppressed by Whites and the constitutive processes used by Blacks to become free. This too was a product of the burgeoning transatlantic system of slavery and the making of American Whiteness.

NOTES

1. Birmingham, *Trade and Conflict in Angola: The Mbundu and Their Neighbours under the Influence of the Portuguese 1483–1790*, 29.

2. Letter from Antonio Mendes to the General, 9 May 1583, Biblioteca Nacional do Rio de Janeiro, I: 497.

3. Birmingham, *Trade and Conflict in Angola: The Mbundu and Their Neighbours under the Influence of the Portuguese 1483–1790*, 37–38. Data on slave trade in Angola region taken from Lovejoy, *Transformations in Slavery: A History of Slavery in Africa, Second Edition*, 53. Also refer to Lovejoy for his analysis of the various factors in the transatlantic slave trade that led to the transformation of West African societies.

4. "Northumberland County Record Books, 1652–1658," 72–73, 97.

5. Hening, *The Statutes at Large; Being a Collection of All the Laws of Virginia, from the First Session of the Legislature in the Year 1619*, II: 283. This case prefigured the 1670 law that explicitly stated that "all servants not being Christians imported into the colony by ship shall be slaves for their lives." The law was enacted to quell cases such as those brought by Key in order to prevent enslaved Africans from claiming that being a Christian precluded their enslavement.

6. Another freedom suit that claimed Christianity and English ancestry was unsuccessfully filed by a man named Fernando in 1667. Warren M. Billings, "The Cases of Fernando and Elizabeth Key: A Note on the Status of Blacks in Seventeenth-Century Virginia," *The William and Mary Quarterly* 30, Third Series, no. 3 (July 1973): 468, 468.

7. Ibid. Key was born in 1630.

8. Sandra E. Greene, *Gender, Ethnicity, and Social Change on the Upper Slave Coast: A History of the Anlo-Ewe* (Portsmouth: Heinemann, 1996), 6–7.

9. Sterling Stuckey shows in *Slave Culture: Nationalist Theory and the Foundations of Black America* the variability in the success of the ruling class in the antebellum South to convert persons of African descent to Christianity, 37–38.

10. Walter Hawthorne, *From Africa to Brazil: Culture, Identity, and an Atlantic Slave Trade, 1600–1830* (New York: Cambridge University Press, 2010), 11. My reading of Hawthorne's work suggests that what African people called themselves provides insights into who they were and where in Africa they hailed from or identified with.

11. Deal, *Race and Class in Colonial Virginia: Indians, Englishmen, and Africans on the Eastern Shore During the Seventeenth Century*, 228.

12. Miller, *Kings and Kinsmen: Early Mbundu States in Angola*, 16–18.

13. P. Sterling Stuckey, "Through the Prism of Folklore: The Black Ethos in Slavery," *The Massachusetts Review* 9 (Summer 1968): 418–19. Quote made by Sterling Brown during a paper delivered before the Amistad Society in Chicago, spring 1964.

14. Miller, *Kings and Kinsmen: Early Mbundu States in Angola*, 51.

15. Greene, *Gender, Ethnicity, and Social Change on the Upper Slave Coast: A History of the Anlo-Ewe*, 3.

16. Jester, *Adventures of Purse and Person, 1607–1625*, 46.

17. For scholars who present Johnson as slaveholder in the Western sense, see Breen and Innes, *Myne Owne Ground* and Deal, *Race and Class in Colonial Virginia*.

18. Nwokeji, *The Slave Trade and Culture in the Bight of Biafra: An African Society in the Atlantic World*, 121–22.

19. A series of laws enacted in 1670, like the one that deemed lifetime servitude the "normal" condition for Black persons, made it increasingly difficult for persons of African descent to remain free. See Hening, *The Statutes at Large; Being a Collection of All the Laws of Virginia, from the First Session of the Legislature in the Year 1619*, II.

20. Here I draw on Nwokeji's work to challenge the claims by scholars such as E. Franklin Frazier, *The Negro Family in the United States* (Chicago: The University of Chicago Press, 1966), who contend that first-generation children born in the New World to African parents held no cognitive attachment to Africa and that their cultural references were "American." Nwokeji's research is also consistent with the research of Michael Gomez, *Exchanging our Country Marks*, 188–92, which found that the children of African-born parents did hold an outlook that was more African than American.

21. P. Sterling Stuckey, *Slave Culture: Nationalist Theory and the Foundations of Black America* (New York: Oxford University Press, 1987), 37–38.

22. "Northumberland County Record Books, 1652–1658," folio 66–67, 85; "Northumberland County Order Book, 1652–1665," folio 40, 46, 49.

23. Ibid.

24. Gomez, *Exchanging our Country Marks: The Transformation of African Identities in the Colonial and Antebellum South*, 192.

25. P. Sterling Stuckey, "Reflections on the Scholarship of African Origins and Influence in American Slavery," *The Journal of African American History* 91, no. 4 (Fall 2007): 10.

26. Craven, *White, Red, and Black: Seventeenth-Century Virginia*, 85–86. Philip Alexander Bruce, *Economic History of Virginia in the Seventeenth Century: An Inquiry into the Material Condition of the People, Based Upon Original and*

Contemporaneous Records (New York: Macmillan and Co., 1896), II, 108. Michael A. Gomez, *Exchanging Our Country Marks: The Transformation of African Identities in the Colonial and Antebellum South* (Chapel Hill: University of North Carolina Press, 1998), 192–93.

27. Rebecca Ginsburg, "Escaping through a Black Landscape," in *Cabin, Quarter, Plantation: Architecture and Landscapes for North American Slavery*, eds. Clifton Ellis and Rebecca Ginsburg (New Haven: Yale University Press, 2010), 55.

28. Henry R. McIlwaine, *Minutes of the Council and General Court of Colonial Virginia, 1622–1632, 1670–1676, with Notes and Excerpts from Original Council and General Court Records, into 1683, Now Lost* (Richmond: The Colonial Press, Everett Waddey Co., 1924), 477.

29. Paul C. Palmer, "Servant into Slave: The Evolution of the Legal Status of the Negro Laborer in Colonial Virginia," *The South Atlantic Quarterly* 65, no. 3 (Summer 1966): 357.

30. Robert Samuel Cope, "Slavery and Servitude in the Colony of Virginia in the Seventeenth Century" (Dissertation, Ohio State University, 1950), 14.

31. Several sources cite this case including: Cope (above), 14; McIlwaine, *Minutes of the Council and General Court of Colonial Virginia with Notes and Excerpts from Original Council and General Court Records, into 1683, Now Lost*, 477, and Palmer, "Servant into Slave: The Evolution of the Legal Status of the Negro Laborer in Colonial Virginia," 357.

32. John C. Coombs, "Building 'the Machine': The Development of Slavery and Slave Society in Early Colonial Virginia" (Dissertation, College of William and Mary, 2003), 38, 248.

33. Ibid.

34. Ibid.

35. Miller, *Kings and Kinsmen: Early Mbundu States in Angola*, 44.

36. Although Key's suit began in 1655, it was not settled until July 1659.

37. "York County, Virginia Wills, Deeds, and Orders," (1657–1659), 26.

38. Greene, *West African Narratives of Slavery: Texts from Late Nineteenth- and Twentieth Century Ghana*. I ground my analysis of the impact of the transatlantic slave trade on Black women's lives on the work by Saundra Greene that suggests that slavery and the slave trade was influenced by gender and by Black women's personal circumstances. In this way, many Black women caught in the transatlantic slave trade shared a commonality about issues such as motherhood that crossed time and space and gender.

39. Miller, *Kings and Kinsmen: Early Mbundu States in Angola*, 43–44.

40. The African peoples included in the 1624/25 muster are thought to be the "20. and odd Negroes" who arrived in Virginia aboard the *Treasurer* in 1619.

41. Jester, *Adventures of Purse and Person, 1607–1625*, 22.

42. Ibid., 49.

43. "Northampton County Virginia Record Book: Orders, Deeds, Wills, Ect., 1645–1651, Book 3," 289; Northampton County Virginia, Orders, Deeds & Wills 1651–1654 Book 4," 28.

44. Hening, *The Statutes at Large; Being a Collection of All the Laws of Virginia, from the First Session of the Legislature in the Year 1619*, II: 26.

45. Miller, *Kings and Kinsmen: Early Mbundu States in Angola*, 44.

46. The act of incorporation used by many precolonial West African ethnic groups involves movement from a marginal and unfree status in the community toward one with greater acceptance and standing. Suzanne Miers and Igor Kopytoff, eds., *Slavery in Africa: Historical and Anthropological Perspectives* (Madison: University of Wisconsin Press, 1977), 19.

47. Miller, *Kings and Kinsmen: Early Mbundu States in Angola*, 16.

48. Ellis and Ginsburg, *Cabin, Quarter, Plantation: Architecture and Landscapes of North American Slavery*, 58.

49. Hawthorne, *From Africa to Brazil: Culture, Identity, and an Atlantic Slave Trade, 1600–1830*, 132.

50. "Virginia Land Patents, 1623–1660," 41.

51. The records indicate that Pott owned at least twelve slaves: Emanuel and Frances Drigus, Bashawe Farnando, six children of the Drigguses—Elizabeth, Jane, Thomas, Frances, Edward and Ann—and a woman named Marchant and her two children, William and Pew. "Northampton County Virginia Record Book: Orders, Deeds, Wills, Ect., 1645–1651, Book 3," folio 51, p.8.

52. Ibid.

53. Here my work draws on the scholarship of Ralph Austen, "The Slave Trade as History and Memory: Confrontations of Slave Voyage Documents and Traditions" that concludes that historical memory can serve as an empirical historical source. I also draw on the work of Michael Gomez that posits that the Middle Passage was not a period of erasure of Africa for those captured and sent to the Americas, but rather the Middle Passage was a period of survival that facilitated bonding and consciousness around their Africanness.

54. LaGarrett J. King, "Black History Is Not American History: Towards a Framework of Black Historical Consciousness," *Social Education* 84, no. 6 (2020).

55. Ralph Austen, "The Slave Trade as History and Memory: Confrontations of Slaving Voyage Documents and Communal Traditions," *William and Mary Quarterly* 58, no. 1 (2001): 229–47.

56. "Northampton County Virginia, Orders, Deeds & Wills 1651–1654 Book 4," 22.

57. Ibid., folio: 81, 114, pages 82, 114.

58. Howard Mackey and Marlene A. Groves, eds., *Northampton County Virginia Record Book: Deeds, Wills, Ect., 1655–1657*, vol. VI, VII–VIII (Rockport: Picton Press, 2002), 176, 84.

59. "Northampton County Virginia, Orders, Deeds & Wills 1651–1654 Book 4," 22.

60. Mackey, *Northampton County Virginia Record Book: Deeds, Wills, Ect., 1655–1657*, 176.

61. "Northampton County Virginia Record Book: Deeds, Wills, Ect., 1657–1666," 57.

62. William L. Andrews and William S. McFeely, eds., *Narrative of the Life of Frederick Douglass, an American Slave, Written by Himself* (New York: W. W. Norton & Company, 1997), 99.

63. Deborah Gray White, *Ar'n't I a Woman?: Female Slaves in the Plantation South* (New York: W. W. Norton & Company, 1985), 96.

64. Wilma King, *Stolen Childhood: Slave Youth in Nineteenth-Century America* (Bloomington: Indiana University Press, 1995), xx.

65. White, *Ar'n't I a Woman?: Female Slaves in the Plantation South*, 93.

66. Craven, *White, Red, and Black: Seventeenth-Century Virginia*, 85–86.

67. Rebecca Ginsburg, "Escaping through a Black Landscape," in *Cabin, Quarter, Plantation: Architecture and Landscapes for North American Slavery*, eds. Clifton Ellis and Rebecca Ginsburg (New Haven: Yale University Press, 2010), 52–53.

68. Andrews, ed., *Narrative of the Life of Frederick Douglass, an American Slave, Written by Himself*, 99.

69. Miller, *Kings and Kinsmen: Early Mbundu States in Angola*, 45–46.

70. Patterson, *Slavery and Social Death: A Comparative Study*, 21. According to Patterson "social death" is when a slave is natally alienated and liminally incorporated as a marginal person who is dishonored and degraded. Kinlessness in precolonial West Africa was a state of detachment from one's biological family. Miers and Kopytoff, eds., *Slavery in Africa: Historical and Anthropological Perspectives*, chapter 1.

71. "Northampton County Virginia Record Book: Orders, Deeds, Wills, Ect., 1645–1651, Book 3," folio 51, p.8.

72. Ibid., folio 51, p.8. The records indicate that Pott owned at least twelve slaves: Emanuel and Frances Drigus, Bashawe Farnando, six children of the Drigguses—Elizabeth, Jane, Thomas, Frances, Edward and Ann—and a woman named Marchant and her two children, William and Pew.

73. Whitelaw, *Virginia's Eastern Shore*, I: 64.

74. Ibid., 182. George Menifie was at one time one of the wealthiest men in Virginia. He owned several thousand acres of land and upward of forty-five European indentured servants and fifteen slaves. "Council and General Court Records, Robinson Transcripts," 40. According to Warren M. Billings, *A Little Parliament: The Virginia General Assembly in the Seventeenth Century* (Richmond: The Library of Virginia, 2007), 89. Great Planters held most of the high ranking political positions in the General Assembly, including positions such as councilor or Burgess. Great Planters also owned lots of land, usually more than seven thousand acres. Moreover, Great Planters owned roughly seventy-seven percent of all African servants/enslaved persons in Virginia.

75. "Northampton County Virginia, Orders, Deeds & Wills 1651–1654 Book 4," folio 25, p. 28. Charlton lived about twenty miles to the north of Potts plantation. In 1652, Emanuel, Frances, and Barshawe had returned to the Pott plantation.

76. "Virginia Land Patents, 1623–1660" 41. Two hundred nine enslaved persons were imported into Virginia between 1635 and 1656.

77. "Northampton County Virginia Record Book: Orders, Deeds, Wills, Ect., 1645–1651, Book 3."

78. Ibid.

79. Breen, *"Myne Owne Ground": Race and Freedom on Virginia's Eastern Shore, 1640–1676*, 81.

80. "Northampton County Virginia Record Book: Orders, Deeds, Wills, Ect., 1645–1651, Book 3."

81. Ibid., 161.

82. "Northampton County Virginia, Orders, Deeds, & Wills 1651–1654 Book 4," folio 112, p.114.

83. Ibid., 149a, 150. Prices for cattle varied according to age and condition of the animals.

84. Ibid.

85. "Northampton County Virginia Record Book: Orders, Deeds, Wills, Ect., 1654–1655," V:47.

86. "Northampton County Virginia Record Book: Orders, Deeds, Wills, Ect., 1645–1651, Book 3," folio 95.

87. "Virginia Land Patents, 1623–1660," 41. Two hundred nine enslaved persons were imported into Virginia between 1635 and 1656.

88. Salmon, *The Hornbook of Virginia History: A Ready-Reference Guide to the People, Places and Past*, 14, 18.

89. Horn, *Adapting to a New World: English Society in the Seventeenth-Century Chesapeake*, 142.

90. "County Court Records of Accomack-Northampton, Virginia 1640–1645."

91. Jarvis, "In the Eye of All Trade: Maritime Revolution and the Transformation of Bermudian Society, 1618–1800," 153–54; Engel Sluiter, "Dutch-Spanish Rivalry in the Caribbean Area, 1594–1609," *Hispanic American Historical Review* 28 (1948): 165–96. In Hispaniola, tobacco became a favorite cash crop and was used as the local currency in the late sixteenth century.

92. Jarvis, "In the Eye of All Trade: Maritime Revolution and the Transformation of Bermudian Society, 1618–1800," 87. Bermuda led Virginia in tobacco exports until 1624.

93. Sir J. H. Lefroy, *Memorials of the Bermudas* (London, 1878–79), I: 386.

94. Walter Hawthorne, *Planting Rice and Harvesting Slaves: Transformations Along the Guinea-Bissau Coast, 1400–1900* (Portsmouth: Heinemann, 2003), 152.

95. Carol P. MacCormack, "Wono: Institutionalized Dependency in Sherbro Descent Groups," in *Slavery in Africa: Historical and Anthropological Perspectives*, eds. Suzanne Miers and Igor Kopytoff (Madison: The University of Wisconsin Press, 1977).

96. Hawthorne, *Planting Rice and Harvesting Slaves: Transformations Along the Guinea-Bissau Coast, 1400–1900*, 152.

97. "York County, Virginia Records, 1638–1644." The cost of enslaved Black men averaged around two thousand seven hundred pounds of tobacco.

98. Ibid.

99. Ibid.

100. Deal, *Race and Class in Colonial Virginia: Indians, Englishmen, and Africans on the Eastern Shore During the Seventeenth Century*, 265–66.

101. "Northampton County Virginia, Orders, Deeds, & Wills 1651–1654 Book 4," folio 118.

102. Miller, *Kings and Kinsmen: Early Mbundu States in Angola*, 44.

103. Ibid., 35.

104. Judith A. Carney, *Black Rice: The African Origins of Rice Cultivation in the Americas* (Cambridge: Harvard University Press, 2001), 2.

105. "Northampton County Virginia, Orders, Deeds, & Wills 1651–1654 Book 4."

106. Miers and Kopytoff, eds., *Slavery in Africa: Historical and Anthropological Perspectives*, 8.

107. "Northampton County Virginia Record Book: Deeds, Wills, Ect., 1657–1666," 89.

108. Ibid., 43.

109. "Anthony Johnson, Free Negro, 1622," *The Journal of Negro History* 56, no. 1 (January 1971): 71–76.

110. Hening, *The Statutes at Large; Being a Collection of All the Laws of Virginia, from the First Session of the Legislature in the Year 1619*, II: 283.

111. Ibid., III: 447–62.

112. David Eltis, "A Brief Overview of the Trans-Atlantic Slave Trade," Voyages: The Trans-Atlantic Slave Trade Data Base, http://www.slavevoyages.org/last/assessment/essay-intro-01.faces (Accessed April 27, 2008).

113. The act of incorporation, used by many precolonial West African ethnic groups, involves movement from a marginal and unfree status in the community toward one with greater acceptance and standing. Miers and Kopytoff, eds., *Slavery in Africa: Historical and Anthropological Perspectives*, 19.

Conclusion

The International System of Slavery and the Making of American Whiteness

The making of American Whiteness paralleled Virginia's growing participation in the international system of slavery in the early decades of the seventeenth century. However, it entailed more than just the act of enslaving persons of African descent. It also entailed replicating the White supremacist policies and practices of the international community that gave rise to enslavement. Intrinsic to the culture of White supremacy that was steeped in the evolving international system of slavery were a series of sordid enterprises such as colonialism, territorial expansion, religious intolerance and persecution, arrogant imposition on indigenous lands, theological justifications for slavery and racial exclusion that all focused as much on empire building as the act of enslavement.[1] Growing competition for global domination among rival European empires including Spain and Portugal encouraged England's entrance into colonialism and the burgeoning transatlantic slave trade that ultimately led to the arrival of the "20. and odd Negroes" in Virginia, marking their accession in the system of global White supremacy.

Decades before and after England entered into the advancing transatlantic slave trade, Spain and Portugal had already employed most of the principles of the international system of slavery in West Africa in the early sixteenth century. Portuguese and Spanish lawmakers and bureaucrats were key agents of power in this new imperial scheme rising among European nations that paved the way for global White supremacy to take shape in the form of colonialism and African enslavement long before the first African persons were shipped to São Tomé, Brazil or the West Indies. Confronted by the task of controlling masses of enslaved people, Portugal charted the infrastructural course for how to oppress large numbers of human beings using what we now call architectural systems of racism built into spaces like slave castles and plantations. The construction of buildings and spaces large enough to house sizable numbers of enslaved persons meant that temporary European laborers, many of whom were outcasts and criminals, were brought into colonies to perform most of the manual labor such as tilling the soil, felling the trees, breaking the rocks, planting the seeds and harvesting the crops until they were eventually supplanted by enslaved laborers.

When deciding on the most advantageous way to settle Virginia, England adopted many of the practices of White supremacy that Portugal and Spain developed in the international system of slavery. The social structure of Virginia mirrored the advances of White supremacy made in the international system of slavery through the built environment. The period between the settlement of Virginia and the arrival of the first groups of enslaved persons (1607–1619) was shaped by one essential feature that marked the colony's arrival into the rising global system of White supremacy and the international system of African slavery: the establishment of the colony's complex plantation system of governance.

In the first few decades of settlement, Virginia communities were constructed around large plantations with all other building and institutions (homes, churches and courthouses) seated outward from it. To better manage such a labyrinthine organizational system, each plantation owner was made commander over the community and given jurisdictional authority over the governance of the area. Plantations that had four or more European servants and enslaved Africans were designed with separate living quarters to help planters better oversee their movements. This arrangement mirrored the built environment of other European colonies like São Tomé, Bermuda and the West Indies in that it allowed the plantation owner to better monitor and control the behavior of their indentured servants, enslaved Africans and other inhabitants, just like European slave merchants did by organizing slave castles and forts at the ocean's edge.

The role of the Christian church in this setup held increased authority in Virginia as a consequence of the need to control the behavior of recalcitrant White laborers. During the early days of settlement, when the problem of keeping such a diverse group of European inhabitants functioning as a cohesive body loomed largest—it was indeed the initial challenge of colonialism—Virginia leaders ordered a church to be seated on each plantation. Inside every church was a local court. Each church had a staff of priests, vestrymen and churchwardens who were charged with, among other things, collecting the taxes on White servants and enslaved African laborers and supervising the day-to-day actives of community residents, including prosecuting any immoral activities.[2]

Despite these efforts at social control, it may have been the fact that wealthy planters and slaveholders were employed as the plantation court's judges and the fact that many former European indentured servants were employed as court clerks that led poorer European settlers to ultimately submit to the authority of the plantation system. And if the social position of planters and slaveholders was not enough to promote acquiescence to institutional power, then the benefit of Whiteness was, and the church and the court took great pains to reinforce the real and symbolic value of Whiteness on the plantation by conspicuously elevating large planters and politicians over not only indentured servants and enslaved persons but also over Whites who were less wealthy. The growth and development of Virginia's institutions (churches and courthouse plantations) and their concomitant bureaucracies produced a spatial environment that reflected the interests of an expanding international system of slavery, interests that facilitated colonialism and African enslavement and, especially, the compliance of European settlers, who stood to benefit the most from this White supremacist social system.

Underlying the growth of the international system of slavery and the making of American Whiteness was a new role for European immigrants, both indentured and free, as future junior partners to the wealthy elite. Initially, European indentured servants in Virginia did all the work of colonization, including assisting in the subduing of Native populations. A key to luring European immigrants to Virginia was the creation of a "heroic myth of colonization" whereby hundreds of thousands of adventurous men were asked to risk all they had to find a sponsor to Virginia or to themselves pay for some of the settlement costs in the hopes of becoming land-rich.[3] Eventually, many secured good positions like churchwardens and vestrymen, and some even received low-level political appointments, for example, as Burgesses. The rhetoric of colonization also created new ways of imagining what it meant to be European and White in a multiethnic Virginia, where identities such as Christian and English were extolled and juxtaposed to those labeled "heathen," "savage," and "negro."

In the first few decades of the seventeenth century, the making of American Whiteness included laws discouraging intimacy and trade, first with Native groups and then with African peoples, so as to invoke sharp distinctions in the minds of various classes of Europeans about their superior place as White in Virginia's pecking order. Charges of "lying with a Negro" or "running away with a Negro" were met with punishments intended to shame and humiliate European offenders. Punishments also called for fines, whippings and increases in terms of service, all in an effort to teach poor Whites their newfound social station in Virginia, which was below European elites and above Native and African persons. Even though European servants were sometimes worked as hard as enslaved Africans, the temporary nature of their servitude told them that they were not equals, a fact that plainly spelled out the connection between African slavery and the making of American Whiteness.

Whiteness clarified the colony's pecking order while also protecting European indentured servants from the real and psychological debasement of life as the lowest-ranked group of Whites in the colony. By mid-century, increases in the enslaved population—just over fifty in 1625, three hundred fifty-five in 1649, roughly two thousand in 1670, and nearly six thousand by the turn of the century, about half of whom were African-born—translated into better jobs and entry-level political posts for many former European servants who became junior partners to the White elite.[4] Despite their low rank in Virginia, the social standing of European indentured workers was on the whole supported and elevated as a social class as a consequence of an international system that promoted the expansion of European plantation economies in the Americas using enslaved African labor.

The mass migration of European peoples across the Atlantic created the conditions for American Whiteness to take root in Virginia's transition from observer to participant in the progress of the international system of slavery. With the first two shipments of enslaved persons to Virginia in 1619 that were part of a larger cargo of African peoples shared among several of the European colonies in the Americas including Bermuda, the West Indies, Barbados and Jamaica, Virginia joined with other European colonizers in expanding global Whiteness through importing enslaved African laborers.[5] The European colonies in Vera Cruz and the West Indies in particular were more than just intermediaries in Virginia's supply chain for African slaves. Global ties to slave-rich European colonies contributed to Virginia being listed as a port of call along transatlantic slave trading routes. Cargos of enslaved persons were offloaded in Virginia after having sailed directly from Africa or indirectly from Africa after a protracted stay in the West Indies or from other mainland British colonies.[6] It is not surprising, therefore, that Virginia's role in the growth of the international system of slavery developed out of a web of European connections linking it to Africa by way of England and its colonies and by way of French, Spanish and Portuguese colonies. The emergence of this modern, global Whiteness via the expansive African slave system directly impacted the evolution of indigenous forms of slavery in West Africa as well as its economic underdevelopment.[7]

Throughout the seventeenth century, participation in the explosion of the international system of slavery connected Virginia to the other European colonies that drained West Africa of its most valuable commodity: its people. The small numbers of enslaved Africans imported into Virginia in the early decades of the seventeenth century did not predict Virginia's ideology about enslaved Africans throughout the century, nor should it deter our analysis of Virginia's place in the global pipeline of European colonies in the Americas that demanded slaves from West Africa. Elite, wealth-seeking White men pushed Virginia deeper into an ever-expanding transatlantic slave trade with consistent imports of African peoples into the colony; two hundred nine enslaved persons were imported into Virginia between 1635 and 1656.[8] In doing so they were establishing Whiteness and wealth for their families with the acquisition of enslaved Africans through the international system of slavery. Indeed, acquiring slaves, especially African women, was a means by which Whiteness was produced and wealth sustained in early Virginia through laws that allowed the entire family of a slaveholder (sons, wives and daughters) to control Black women's wombs.

The history of American Whiteness and Virginia's entrance into a developing international system of slavery suggests that we reexamine our assumptions about race, which hold that the transatlantic slave trade transformed Africa but not early Virginia. Owning slaves signified prosperity among Virginia elites. Enslaved women, men, girls and boys were sold, willed and gifted to meet a variety of social and economic needs. Enslavement meant that poor and indentured Whites would have access to jobs that otherwise may not have been available.

While the African population in Virginia was relatively small compared to the numbers of Europeans, about two percent of the population in 1650, ten percent in 1670 and twenty-five percent in 1700, slavery in Virginia did not develop slowly. In fact, all known records show that the first groups of Black people to arrive in Virginia were indeed enslaved and remained in that status for many years, ensuring that the gains made by poor and indentured Whites were maintained.[9] Such a society did not reflect an isolationist and exceptional Virginia, detached from the slave trade, but an international one, which historians of early America have written about uncertainly within the context of a far-reaching European transatlantic slave trade.

Examining Virginia within an international and European imperialist framework allows us to be more certain in our articulations about the colony's White racist character when we recognize that England's colonial ambitions emerged at a time of European expansion around the world, which included African enslavement as one of the important keys to the growth of its global power.

Almost from the beginning, early Africans in Virginia recognized the colony's White supremacist social structure, its built environment and local landscape from their experiences with the Portuguese in precolonial West Africa. Black people's responses to Virginia's racist social and legal systems shifted as the move toward lifetime bondage intensified in custom and law. Black persons such Anthony Johnson and his family, Elizabeth Key, Frances and Emanuel Driggus and others used a variety of overlapping social systems and cultural forms indigenous to West Africa to manipulate the racist bureaucracy of Virginia and, in the process, mitigate their oppression. One can identify three types of indigenous West African social systems used by

Black persons in early Virginia to resist subjugation and build community: agrarian culture, oral traditions and lineage systems. These were not mutually exclusive but rather overlapped in ways that supplied disparate groups of African peoples with the tools to alleviate the fallout from the rise in external and internal European slave trading.

Throughout the seventeenth century, African peoples worked diligently to remain connected to their West African roots and to one another. The period between 1636 and 1655 brought a steady supply of new arrivals (two hundred nine enslaved persons) who, using oral traditions, helped keep the memory of "Angola" alive in the hearts and minds of Black peoples.[10] Stories were shared and information was exchanged not only about their collective connection to the Angola region but also about the happenings in Virginia. Black women and men communicated knowledge with each other about the ways of White people and they passed down successful strategies about how to exploit Virginia's racist institutions in a way that alleviated, if only temporarily, the degree of their oppression. No matter how bad the situation was, African people found ways to remain linked to their homelands using oral traditions.

Although oral traditions were the medium by which African people remained connected to each other and their homelands, the sharing of agrarian knowledge systems motivated some to undertake more ambitious acts of resistance such as self-purchase. Animal husbandry and farming skills appear to have been the leading methods for effectuating emancipation. Those women and men who were highly skilled in tobacco production or livestock management were able to earn the funds necessary to finance their freedom as well as that of friends and loved ones late into the seventeenth century. The growing success that African people employed with this freedom strategy moved a few planters to petition local courts to enforce restrictions against trading with Black persons. Large planters and government officials feared that trading with enterprising persons of African descent would undermine the growing institution of slavery in Virginia. This anti-Black legislation prompted populations of Black peoples to seek other means to mitigate the strains of bondage. Those unable to buy their freedom on their own found themselves pooling their resources with other enslaved persons. This process actually produced familial like bonds between women and men who collaborated in their freedom struggles.

By the middle of the seventeenth century, African people in Virginia began to link their bondage conditions with indigenous precolonial West African social systems in new ways. Concern for maintaining stable familial relations in the mist of the upheavals surrounding enslavement, Black people came to reconfigure their indigenous lineage system to mitigate the upheavals of Virginia's expanding external and internal slave trading. Such kinships did not necessarily reflect existing biological relations. Rather, these African people sometimes developed fictive kinships that stood in for the matrilineal and patrilineal arrangements that existed in precolonial West Africa. When the ruptures and dislocations associated with local slave trading intensified, a new era of resistance began. Black people became motivated to target the basis of their oppression and enslavement by attacking its most destructive feature, the separation of families, using fictive kinships to build new relational connections: fictive mothers, fathers, sisters and brothers.

Fictive relationships went beyond differences in gender, ethnicity and religion. These relationships represented a new form of the lineage system that mirrored the ones Black people had in West Central Africa, which provided African women and men in Virginia with a model for building a cohesive Black community. Refusing to buckle under the impediments to forming strong family bonds while enslaved, women and men relied on fictive kinships to add stability and a degree of certainty to those suffering from the immense sense of trauma and loss resulting from the sale of a loved one.

Fictive relationships meant that a so-called "family member" was waiting to assume the role of a substitute caretaker at the other end of a slave trade or that emancipation or financial gain could be legitimately had by bequeathing animals from one generation to the next in a manner consistent with matrilineal and patrilineal practices. In many ways, this new sense of family reflected the self-determination of African peoples. Their self-reliance thus reorients our understanding of Black life in early Virginia. Each of the indigenous precolonial West African social systems (oral traditions, agrarian culture and lineage systems) functioned in slightly different ways, and yet each overlapped with the other and is necessary for understanding the outlook of Black persons in the early decades of the seventeenth century.

Throughout the development of American Whiteness and the international system of slavery, African women and men in early Virginia inhabited multiple worlds. The first, the African world that existed in and around the plantations of early Virginia, connected the mostly African-born population to one another through a shared connection to the Angolan region and the seaport of Luanda where most were held before being shipped to the Americas.[11] The persons most central to this world were the nearly three hundred women, men and children living in Virginia through 1640, nearly all of whom arrived by way of the Luanda port. For this group, child-rearing entailed the reformulation of cultural forms common to the Angola region in order to cope with the environment of the White supremacist and anti-Black New World. Although the children of African-born parents may have picked up some of the habits of Virginia society, they were, nonetheless, raised with the values of their parents and scrutinized by this standard. As a consequence, these children were more African in their orientation than "American."[12]

The African people of early Virginia also inhabited a White and anti-Black world, one that viewed Africa and African peoples as a source of labor with which to fuel its public and private ambitions. Black people in Virginia understood the conceits of European persons in this regard and used them to manipulate the churches, plantations, courthouses and other spaces in and around the plantation. When negotiating in this world, either by enlisting the help of planters or playing one planter against another, a new era in Black resistance emerged: the freedom suit. Black women were key to this shift in strategy.

Racist laws, like the 1643 law that taxed African women's labor at the same rate as men and the 1662 law that established the status of children based on the condition of the mother, made it increasingly difficult for Black women or their children to become free.[13] To overcome this barrier, enslaved women and their husbands and partners looked to broker deals between opposing masters to hasten the freedom of their children. Freedom lawsuits gave voice to a growing racial consciousness of Black mothers in the early decades of the seventeenth century, who needed not only to be aware of the politics of the colony's White supremacist legal institutions but also the loopholes in the system so that they could give their children the best chance at freedom. The tension between the two worlds which African persons inhabited, the Black and the White, attributed to the agency of Black peoples in ways that highlight the White racial character of the colony during the era.

The history of American Whiteness and African slavery in Virginia appears both less exceptional and more global in orientation than we expect. The first groups of African persons imported to Virginia in the seventeenth century were commodities in a network of European nations eager to colonize the Americas that transformed the social and political order of both continents. As Paul Lovejoy puts it, Virginia's entrance into the rising international system of slavery occurred because Africa was an area of slave supply already tapped by European countries.[14] Although slavery was actually a feature in precolonial West African society, its characteristics were more dynamic than Western conceptions of the term. It was just one of many forms of unfreeness, such as pawns and concubines, that allowed people to transfer from one social group to another. Some of the special features of "slavery" in the African context included:

> The idea that slaves were property; that they were outsiders who were alien by origin or who had been denied their heritage through judicial or other sanctions; that coercion could be used at will; that their labour power was at the complete disposal of a master; that they did not have the right to their own sexuality and, by extension, to their own reproductive capacities; and that the slave status was inherited unless provision was made to ameliorate that status.[15]

When the transatlantic slave trade erupted in the fifteenth century, the indigenous African system of slavery competed with the production of trade slaves. Here is where European colonies like São Tomé, Brazil, the West Indies, Barbados, Vera Cruz, Bermuda and, finally, Virginia make their entrance. European demand for slaves, "and only slaves," produced a situation in which slavery became increasingly important to the West African economy.[16]

For African communities to meet this demand, more and more slaves had to be produced, making slavery a more prominent feature of African society rather than a peripheral one. The Kongo/Angola region of West Central Africa and the Bight of Benin, the two largest sources of slaves to North America during the seventeenth century, were drained of over one hundred twenty thousand persons and over nine thousand persons respectively in the first half of the century, in which Virginia played a small but nonetheless important part.[17]

When Virginia's leaders were settling parts of North America as a White civil society, they drew upon concepts from the growing international system of slavery such as colonialism, the conquering of indigenous lands, subduing Native peoples and the exploitation of African labor to articulate their economic and political strategy. Virginia Company officials also looked to the writings of European travelers and promoters of investment like Richard Hakluyt and John Lok to inform their pre-colonization and pre-enslavement tactics. This history is necessary for understanding the making of American Whiteness and the reality of an early Virginia connected to the rise of the international system of slavery. Thus Virginia and its political structure, its laws, its religion, its connections to other colonial powers and its links to West Central Africa all provide the framework for understanding American Whiteness within the context of the international system of slavery that was rapidly advancing during the early decades of the seventeenth century.

Many elements of American Whiteness and the international system of slavery that were present in the Virginia of the early seventeenth century persisted into the eighteenth century. For example, the number of slave disembarkations in Virginia not only continued but increased fivefold and the persistence of cohesive Black communities and African cultural traditions became even more pronounced. Concomitantly, larger percentages of former indentured servants obtained political and judicial appointments, expanding the number of White political dynasties and patronage positions into succeeding generations. However, much about Virginia's role in the expansion of the international system of slavery did change in the eighteenth century, namely the passage of the 1705 slave codes that made enslaved persons chattel, a fact that makes the turn of the century a useful focal point to observe the historical arc in the growth of Whiteness, African enslavement and the slave trade in the region.

Early in the eighteenth century, slave rebellions changed in character as the importation of enslaved persons expanded across the regions of the North American mainland. Our understanding of the perceptions of enslaved persons improved as first-person accounts of African life and the Middle Passage, such as Olaudah Equiano's 1789 autobiography, *The Interesting Narrative of the Life of Olaudah Equiano, or Gustavus Vassa, the African*, gave voice to the millions who endured the Middle Passage and the brutality of enslavement. While Virginia's population of African-born people in the eighteenth century decreased to less than fifty percent, the first generation American-born Black persons were still raised by native African parents, ensuring their cultural orientation was more African than American.[18]

Changes in the makeup of Virginia's European population in the eighteenth century also occurred as the slave exports to the New World grew to include a wider region of West Africa, namely the Gold Coast and the Bight of Biafra, leading to greater job opportunities and living conditions for all classes of White people. During the eighteenth century, European indentured servitude was nearly obsolete as a result of increases in slave imports and the expansion of territories used in the procurement of African slaves.[19] Moreover, the majority of Virginia's European population was Virginia-born, and its child mortality rate fell from thirty-nine percent to thirty-three percent.[20] The consequence of a society of free White Virginians with mostly American origins who came of age after the enactment of Virginia's 1705 slave codes was an overall increase in the number of slaveholders. Seventy-two percent of householders between 1733 and 1790 owned at least six slaves.[21] The decline of European immigrant labor and the increase in slaveholders meant that the majority of White men became landowners during the eighteenth century. Landownership was the ultimate symbol of freedom, given that the English government insisted on restricting voting rights to men who owned land. The combinations of landowning and slaveholding along with the enfranchisement of more White men became the ingredients for the republican ideals that framed the American Revolution.[22]

In the early seventeenth century, the growth and development of American Whiteness can only be understood in the context of the growth and development of the international system of slavery, from which English observations of Spain's and Portugal's actions in the Angolan region of West Central Africa provide the context for the settlement of Virginia and the structure of its institutions. Interactions with Vera Cruz, the West Indies and Bermuda supplied early Virginia with its initial shipments of enslaved Africans and facilitated its place as a port of call along the transatlantic trade route. Indeed, the rising international system of slavery reveals an early Virginia that is more connected to the development of American Whiteness and the growth of the transatlantic slave trade than the existing historical literature on early

America articulates. Perhaps increased attention to this connection might suggest new questions about White supremacy and anti-Blackness in the New World during the first few decades of the seventeenth century and, concomitantly, the twenty-first century.

NOTES

1. Blackburn, *The Making of New World Slavery: From the Baroque to the Modern, 1492–1800*, 33.

2. Morgan, *American Slavery, American Freedom*, 61.

3. Blackburn, *The Making of New World Slavery: From the Baroque to the Modern, 1492–1800*, 220.

4. Craven, *White, Red, and Black: Seventeenth-Century Virginia*, 85–86; Bruce, *Economic History of Virginia in the Seventeenth Century: An Inquiry into the Material Condition of the People, Based Upon Original and Contemporaneous Records*, II: 108; Gomez, *Exchanging Our Country Marks: The Transformation of African Identities in the Colonial and Antebellum South*, 192–93.

5. Rolfe's letter to Sandys, Jan. 1619/1620, in Susan Myra Kingsbury, ed., *The Records of the Virginia Company of London*, vol. 3 (Washington, D.C.: Government Printing Office, 1933), 243.

6. Westbury, "Slaves of Colonial Virginia: Where They Came From," 228–37.

7. Lovejoy, *Transformations in Slavery: A History of Slavery in Africa, Second Edition*, 133–35.

8. "Virginia Land Patents, 1623–1660," 41.

9. Cope, "Slavery and Servitude in the Colony of Virginia in the Seventeenth Century," 25–39.

10. "Virginia Land Patents, 1623–1660," 41.

11. Gomez, *Exchanging Our Country Marks: The Transformation of African Identities in the Colonial and Antebellum South*, 192–93.

12. Ibid.

13. Hening, *The Statutes at Large; Being a Collection of All the Laws of Virginia, from the First Session of the Legislature in the Year 1619*, I: 242, II: 26. The 1643 statute reads in part as follows: "Be it also enacted and confirmed there be tenn pounds of tob'o. per poll & a bushell of corne per poll paid to the ministers within the severall parishes of the collony for all tithable persons, that is to say, as well for all youths of sixteen years of age as vpwards, as also for all negro women at the age of sixteen years."

14. Lovejoy, *Transformations in Slavery: A History of Slavery in Africa, Second Edition*, 21.

15. Ibid., 1.

16. Rodney, *How Europe Underdeveloped Africa*, 78–79.

17. David Eltis, "A Brief Overview of the Trans-Atlantic Slave Trade," *Voyages: The Trans-Atlantic Slave Trade Data Base,* http://www.slavevoyages.org/last/assessment/essay-intro-01.faces (Accessed April 27, 2008).

18. Gomez, *Exchanging Our Country Marks: The Transformation of African Identities in the Colonial and Antebellum South,* 192.

19. Russell R. Menard, "From Servants to Slaves: The Transformation of the Chesapeake Labor System," *Southern Studies* 16 (1977): 355–90.

20. Lorena S. Walsh and Russell R. Menard, "Death in the Chesapeake: Two Life Tables for Men in Early Colonial Maryland," *Maryland Historical Magazine* LXIX (1974).

21. Nancy L. Oberseider, "A Sociodemographic Study of the Family as a Social Unit in Tidewater, Virginia, 1660–1776" (Dissertation, University of Maryland, 1975), 202–3.

22. Morgan, *American Slavery, American Freedom,* 375–76.

Bibliography

Allen, Theodore W. *The Invention of the White Race: Racial Oppression and Social Control*. 2 vols. Vol. I, New York: Verso, 1994.

———. *The Invention of the White Race: The Origin of Racial Oppression in Anglo-America*. 2 vols. Vol. II, New York: Verso, 1997.

Allison, Robert J., ed. *The Interesting Narrative of Olaudah Equiano, or Gustavus Vasa, the African*. London, 1789.

Andrews, William L., and William S. McFeely, eds. *Narrative of the Life of Frederick Douglass, an American Slave, Written by Himself*. New York: W. W. Norton & Company, 1997.

"Anthony Johnson, Free Negro, 1622." *The Journal of Negro History* 56, no. 1 (January 1971): 71–76.

Austen, Ralph. "The Slave Trade as History and Memory: Confrontations of Slaving Voyage Documents and Communal Traditions." *William and Mary Quarterly* 58, no. 1 (2001): 229–44.

Baldwin, James. *The Price of the Ticket: Collected Nonfiction, 1948–1985*. New York: St. Martin's, 1985.

———. "The White Problem." In *One Hundred Years of Emancipation*, edited by Robert A. Goodwin. Chicago: University of Chicago, The Public Affairs Conference Center, 1964.

Barbour, Philip L., ed. *The Complete Works of Captain John Smith, 1580–1631*. Vol. I. Chapel Hill: University of North Carolina Press, 1986.

———. *The Jamestown Voyages under the First Charter, 1606–1609*. 2 vols. Vol. I, II, 1969.

Bibby, Cyril. "The Power of Words." *The UNESCO Courier* VIII, no. 11 (April 1956): 24.

Billings, Warren M. "The Cases of Fernando and Elizabeth Key: A Note on the Status of Blacks in Seventeenth-Century Virginia." *The William and Mary Quarterly*, 3rd Series 30, no. 3 (July 1973): 467–74.

———. *A Little Parliament: The Virginia General Assembly in the Seventeenth Century*. Richmond: The Library of Virginia, 2007.

Birmingham, David. *Trade and Conflict in Angola: The Mbundu and Their Neighbours under the Influence of the Portuguese 1483–1790*. Oxford: Clarendon Press, 1966.

Blackburn, Robin. *The Making of New World Slavery: From the Baroque to the Modern, 1492–1800*. New York: Verso, 1997.

Blassingame, John W. *The Slave Community: Plantation Life in the Antebellum South*. New York: Oxford University Press, 1972.

Blumer, Herbert. "Race Prejudice as a Sense of Group Position." In *Race Relations: Problems and Theory*, edited by Jutsuichi Masuoka and Preston Valien, 217–27. Chapel Hill: University of North Carolina Press, 1958.

Breen, T. H., and Stephen Innes. *"Myne Owne Ground": Race and Freedom on Virginia's Eastern Shore, 1640–1676*. New York: Oxford University Press, 1980.

Brown, Alexander. *The Genesis of the United States*. Vol. II, Boston: Houghton, Mifflin, & Co., 1891.

Brown, Alexander, D. C. L. *The First Republic in America*. New York: Russell and Russell, 1898.

Brown, Kathleen M. *Good Wives, Nasty Wenches, and Anxious Patriarchs: Gender, Race, and Power in Colonial Virginia*. Chapel Hill: University of North Carolina Press, 1996.

Bruce, Philip Alexander. *Economic History of Virginia in the Seventeenth Century: An Inquiry into the Material Condition of the People, Based Upon Original and Contemporaneous Records*. New York: Macmillan and Co., 1896.

———. *Institutional History of Virginia in the Seventeenth Century*. 2 vols. Vol. I, New York: The Knickerbocker Press, 1910.

Butler, Nathaniel. "The Historye of the Bermudaes," edited by Sir J. H. Lefroy. London, 1882.

Carney, Judith A. *Black Rice: The African Origins of Rice Cultivation in the Americas*. Cambridge: Harvard University Press, 2001.

"Charles City County Court Order Book, 1658–1661."

Chitwood, Oliver P. *Justice in Colonial Virginia*. New York: Da Capo Press, 1971.

Cooke, Charles Francis. *Parish Lines Diocese of Virginia*. Richmond: Virginia State Library, 1967.

Coombs, John C. "Building 'the Machine': The Development of Slavery and Slave Society in Early Colonial Virginia." Dissertation, College of William and Mary, 2003.

Cope, Robert Samuel. "Slavery and Servitude in the Colony of Virginia in the Seventeenth Century." Dissertation, Ohio State University, 1950.

"County Court Records of Accomack-Northampton, Virginia 1640–1645."

Craven, Wesley Frank. *Dissolution of the Virginia Company: The Failure of a Colonial Experiment*. Gloucester: Peter Smith, 1964.

———. *White, Red, and Black: Seventeenth-Century Virginia*. Charlottesville: University Press of Virginia, 1971.

Curtin, Philip D. *The Atlantic Slave Trade: A Census*. Madison: University of Wisconsin Press, 1969.

Deal, J. Douglas. *Race and Class in Colonial Virginia: Indians, Englishmen, and Africans on the Eastern Shore During the Seventeenth Century*. New York: Garland Publishing, Inc., 1993.

"Decisions of the General Court." *Virginia Magazine of History and Biography*, January 1898, 233–41.

Donnan, Elizabeth. *Documents Illustrative of the History of the Slave Trade to America*. Vol. I, New York: Octagon Books, Inc., 1965.

Du Bois, W. E. B. *The Souls of Black Folk*. New York: Vintage, 1989. 1903.

Elbl, Ivana. "The Volume of Early Atlantic Slave Trade, 1450–1521." *Journal of African History* 38 (1997): 31–75.

Ellis, Clifton, and Rebecca Ginsburg, eds. *Cabin, Quarter, Plantation: Architecture and Landscapes of North American Slavery*. New Haven: Yale University Press, 2010.

Eltis, David. *The Rise of African Slavery in the Americas*. New York: Cambridge University Press, 2000.

Fitts, Robert K. "The Landscapes of Northern Bondage." In *Cabin, Quarter, Plantation: Architecture and Landscapes of North American Slavery*, edited by Clifton Ellis and Rebecca Ginsburg, 1996.

Frazier, E. Franklin. *The Negro Family in the United States*. Chicago: University of Chicago Press, 1966.

Fredrickson, George M. *The Black Image in the White Mind: The Debate on Afro-American Character and Destiny, 1817–1914*. New York: Harper & Row, 1971.

French, Peter J. *John Dee: The World of an Elizabethan Magus*. London: Routledge, 1972.

Ginsburg, Rebecca. "Escaping through a Black Landscape." In *Cabin, Quarter, Plantation: Architecture and Landscapes for North American Slavery*, edited by Clifton Ellis and Rebecca Ginsburg. New Haven: Yale University Press, 2010.

Goetz, Rebecca A. "From Potential Christians to Hereditary Heathens: Religion and Race in the Early Chesapeake, 1590–1740." Dissertation, Harvard University, 2006.

Gomez, Michael A. *Exchanging Our Country Marks: The Transformation of African Identities in the Colonial and Antebellum South*. Chapel Hill: University of North Carolina Press, 1998.

Green, Roger. *Virginia's Cure*. London: W. Godbid for Henry Brome, 1662.

Greene, Evarts B., and Virginia D. Harrington. *American Population before the Federal Census of 1790*. New York: Columbia University Press, 1932.

Greene, Sandra E. *Gender, Ethnicity, and Social Change on the Upper Slave Coast: A History of the Anlo-Ewe*. Portsmouth: Heinemann, 1996.

Guterl, Matthew Pratt. "A Note on the Word 'White.'" *American Quarterly* 56, no. 2 (June 2004): 439–44.

Hakluyt, Richard. *Divers Voyages Touching the Discovery of America*. London: Thomas Dawson, 1582.

———. *Principal Navigations of the English Nation*. London: J.M. Dent and Co., 1600.

Handlin, Oscar, and Mary. "Origins of the Southern Labor System." *William and Mary Quarterly* 7, no. 3rd Series (1950): 199–222.

Hardy, Stella Pickett. *Colonial Families of the Southern States of America: A History and Genealogy of Colonial Families Who Settled in the Colonies Prior to the Revolution.* Baltimore: Genealogical Publishing Company, 1968.

Harris, Cheryl I. "Finding Sojourner's Truth: Race, Gender, and the Institution of Property." *Cardozo Law Review* 18, no. 2 (1996): 309–409.

———. "Whiteness as Property." *Harvard Law Review* 106, no. 8 (June 1993): 1709–91.

Hart, Albert Bushnell, ed. *Era of Colonization, 1492–1689.* New York: The MacMillian Company, 1908.

Hashaw, Tim. *The Birth of Black America the First African Americans and the Pursuit of Freedom at Jamestown.* New York: Carroll & Graf Publishers, 2007.

Hatch, Charles E. *The First Seventeen Years: Virginia, 1607–1624.* Charlottesville: University of Virginia Press, 1957.

Hawthorne, Walter. *From Africa to Brazil: Culture, Identity, and an Atlantic Slave Trade, 1600–1830.* New York: Cambridge University Press, 2010.

———. *Planting Rice and Harvesting Slaves: Transformations Along the Guinea-Bissau Coast, 1400–1900.* Portsmouth: Heinemann, 2003.

Hening, William Waller, ed. *The Statutes at Large; Being a Collection of All the Laws of Virginia, from the First Session of the Legislature in the Year 1619.* 13 vols. New York: R. & W. & G. Bartow, 1823.

Heuman, G. J., and Walvin, James, eds. *The Slavery Reader.* Routledge, 2003.

Hill Collins, Patricia. *Fighting Words: Black Women in Search for Justice.* Minneapolis: University of Minnesota Press, 1998.

Horn, James. *Adapting to a New World: English Society in the Seventeenth-Century Chesapeake.* Chapel Hill: University of North Carolina Press, 1994.

———. *A Land as God Made It: Jamestown and the Birth of America.* New York: Basic Books, 2005.

Jarvis, Michael Joseph. "In the Eye of All Trade: Maritime Revolution and the Transformation of Bermudian Society, 1618–1800." Dissertation, the College of William and Mary, 1998.

Jester, Annie Lash, ed. *Adventures of Purse and Person, 1607–1625.* Princeton: Princeton University Press, 1956.

Jones, Jacqueline. "'My Mother Was Much of a Woman': Black Women, Work, and the Family under Slaver." *Feminist Studies* 8, no. 2 (Summer 1982): 235–69.

Jones, Robert P. *White Too Long: The Legacy of White Supremacy in American Christianity.* New York: Simon & Schuster, 2020.

Jordan, Winthrop D. *White over Black: American Attitudes toward the Negro, 1550–1812.* Chapel Hill: The University of North Carolina Press, 1968.

Kerber, Linda. "The Republican Mother: Women and the Enlightenment-an American Perspective." *The American Quarterly* 28, no. 2 (Summer 1976): 187–205.

King, LaGarrett J. "Black History Is Not American History: Towards a Framework of Black Historical Consciousness." *Social Education* 84, no. 6 (2020): 335–41.

King, Wilma. *Stolen Childhood: Slave Youth in Nineteenth-Century America.* Bloomington: Indiana University Press, 1995.

Kingsbury, Susan M., ed. *Records of the Virginia Company of London.* 4 vols. Vol. I. Washington: Government Printing Office, 1906, 1933.

————, ed. *The Records of the Virginia Company of London: The Court Book, from the Manuscript in the Library of Congress.* 4 vols. Washington, D.C.: Government Printing Office, 1906.

Leonard, Cynthia Miller, ed. *The General Assembly of Virginia: A Bicentennial Register of Members, July 20, 1619–January 11, 1978.* Richmond: Virginia State Library, 1978.

Ligon, Richard. *A True and Exact History of the Island of Barbados.* London, 1657.

Lovejoy, Paul E. *Transformations in Slavery: A History of Slavery in Africa, Second Edition.* Cambridge, UK: Cambridge University Press, 2000.

MacCormack, Carol P. "Wono: Institutionalized Dependency in Sherbro Descent Groups." In *Slavery in Africa: Historical and Anthropological Perspectives,* edited by Suzanne Miers and Igor Kopytoff. Madison: University of Wisconsin Press, 1977.

Mackey, Howard, and Marlene A. Groves, eds. *Northampton County Virginia Record Book: Deeds, Wills, Ect., 1655–1657.* Vol. VI, VII–VIII. Rockport: Picton Press, 2002.

Mason, George Carrington. *Colonial Churches of Tidewater Virginia.* Richmond: Whittet and Shepperson, 1945.

McCartney, Martha W. *Virginia Immigrants and Adventurers 1607–1635: A Biographical Dictionary.* Baltimore: Genealogical Publishing Co., Inc., 2007.

McIlwaine, Henry R. *Minutes of the Council and General Court of Colonial Virginia with Notes and Excerpts from Original Council and General Court Records, into 1683, Now Lost.* Richmond: The Colonial Press, Everett Waddey Co., 1622–1632, 1670–1676.

————. *Minutes of the Council and General Court of Colonial Virginia, 1622–1632, 1670–1676, with Notes and Excerpts from Original Council and General Court Records, into 1683, Now Lost.* Richmond: The Colonial Press, Everett Waddey Co., 1924.

McIntosh, Peggy. "White Privilege and Male Privilege: A Personal Account of Coming to See Correspondences through Work in Women's Studies." In *Critical White Studies: Looking Behind the Mirror,* edited by Richard Delgado and Jean Stefancic, 291. 1997: Temple University Press, 1988.

Menard, Russell R. "From Servants to Slaves: The Transformation of the Chesapeake Labor System." *Southern Studies* 14 (1977): 355–90.

————. "The Tobacco Industry in the Chesapeake Colonies, 1617–1730: An Interpretation." *Research in Economic History* 5 (1980): 109–77.

Miers, Suzanne, and Igor Kopytoff, eds. *Slavery in Africa: Historical and Anthropological Perspectives.* Madison: The University of Wisconsin Press, 1977.

Miller, Joseph C. *Kings and Kinsmen: Early Mbundu States in Angola.* New York: Oxford University Press, 1976.

Miller Turman, Nora. *George Yeardley: Governor of Virginia and Organizer of the General Assembly in 1619.* Richmond: Garrett and Massie, Inc., 1959.

Moore, Richard B. *The Name "Negro" Its Origin and Evil Use*. Baltimore: Black Classic Press, 1992.

Morgan, Edmund S. *American Slavery, American Freedom*. New York: W. W. Norton and Company, Inc., 1975.

———. *American Slavery, American Freedom: The Ordeal of Colonial Virginia*. 1st ed. New York: Norton, 1975.

Morgan, Jennifer L. *Laboring Women: Reproduction and Gender in New World Slavery*. Philadelphia: University of Pennsylvania Press, 2004.

Morrison, Toni. *Playing in the Dark: Whiteness and the Literary Imagination*. Cambridge: Harvard University Press, 1992.

Mullin, Gerald W. *Flight and Rebellion: Slave Resistance in Eighteenth Century Virginia*. New York: Oxford University Press, 1972.

"Northampton County Order Book, 1657–1664, Book 8."

"Northampton County Virginia Record Book: Deeds, Wills, Ect., 1657–1666."

"Northampton County Virginia Record Book: Orders, Deeds, Wills, Ect., 1645–1651, Book 3."

"Northampton County Virginia Record Book: Orders, Deeds, Wills, Ect., 1654–1655."

"Northampton County, Virginia Deeds, Wills, Etc., 1654–1657 Book 5."

"Northumberland County Order Book, 1652–1665."

"Northumberland County Record Books, 1652–1658."

Nugent, Nell Marion. *Cavaliers and Pioneers: A Calendar of Virginia Land Grants, 1623–1800*. Vol. I, Richmond: Library of Virginia, 1934.

———. *Cavaliers and Pioneers: Abstracts of Virginia Land Patents and Grants, 1623–1800*. Vol. I, Richmond: Press of The Dietz Printing Co., 1934.

Nwokeji, G. Ugo. *The Slave Trade and Culture in the Bight of Biafra: An African Society in the Atlantic World*. New York: Cambridge University Press, 2010.

Oberseider, Nancy L. "A Sociodemographic Study of the Family as a Social Unit in Tidewater, Virginia, 1660–1776." Dissertation, University of Maryland, 1975.

Palmer, Paul C. "Servant into Slave: The Evolution of the Legal Status of the Negro Laborer in Colonial Virginia." *The South Atlantic Quarterly* 65, no. 3 (Summer 1966): 355–70.

Patterson, Orlando. *Slavery and Social Death: A Comparative Study*. Cambridge: Harvard University Press, 1982.

Quinn, David B. *Explorers and Colonies: America, 1500–1625*. London: Hambledon Press, 1990.

Robinson, Cedric J. *Black Marxism: The Making of the Black Radical Tradition*. Chapel Hill: University of North Carolina Press, 1983. 2000.

Robinson, Conway. "Notes from the Council and General Court Records." In *Robinson Notes*. Richmond: Virginia Historical Society.

Rodney, Walter. *How Europe Underdeveloped Africa*. Washington, D.C.: Howard University Press, 1982.

Roediger, David R. *Working toward Whiteness: How America's Immigrants Became White: The Strange Journey from Ellis Island to the Suburbs*. New York, NY: Basic Books, 2005.

Salmon, Emily J., and Edward D. C. Campbell Jr., eds. *The Hornbook of Virginia History: A Ready-Reference Guide to the People, Places and Past.* 4th ed. Richmond: The Library of Virginia, 1994.

Scully, Pamela. "Rape, Race, and Colonial Culture: The Sexual Politics of Identity in the Nineteenth Century Cape Colony, South Africa." *The American Historical Review* 100, no. 2 (Apr. 1995): 335–59.

Sluiter, Engel. "Dutch-Spanish Rivalry in the Caribbean Area, 1594–1609." *Hispanic American Historical Review* 28 (1948): 165–96.

———. "New Light on the '20. And Odd Negroes' Arriving in Virginia, August 1619." *William and Mary Quarterly* 54, Third Series, no. 2 (April 1997): 295–398.

Smedley, A., and Brian D. Smedley. *Race in North America Origin and Evolution of a Worldview*, 4th ed. Boulder, CO: Westview Press, 2011.

Smith, James Morton, ed. *Seventeenth-Century America: Essays in Colonial History.* Chapel Hill: The University of North Carolina Press, 1959.

Strachey, William, ed. *The Historie of Travell into Virginia Britania, 1612.* London: The University Press, Glasgow, 1953.

Stuckey, P. Sterling. "Reflections on the Scholarship of African Origins and Influence in American Slavery." *The Journal of African American History* 91, no. 4 (Fall 2007): 425–43.

———. *Slave Culture: Nationalist Theory and the Foundations of Black America.* New York: Oxford University Press, 1987.

———. "Through the Prism of Folklore: The Black Ethos in Slavery." *The Massachusetts Review* 9 (Summer 1968): 417–37.

Sydnor, Charles S. *Gentlemen Freeholders: Political Practices in Washington's Virginia.* Chapel Hill: University of North Carolina Press, 1952.

Thorndale, William. "The Virginia Census of 1619." *Magazine of Virginia Genealogy* 33 (1995): 155–70.

Upton, Dell. *Holy Things and Profane: Anglican Parish Churches in Colonial Virginia.* Cambridge: The MIT Press, 1986.

Walsh, Lorena S., and Russell R. Menard. "Death in the Chesapeake: Two Life Tables for Men in Early Colonial Maryland." *Maryland Historical Magazine* 69 (1974): 211–27.

Westbury, Susan. "Slaves of Colonial Virginia: Where They Came From." *William and Mary Quarterly* 42, no. 3 (1985): 228–37.

White, Deborah Gray. *Ar'n't I a Woman?: Female Slaves in the Plantation South.* New York: W. W. Norton & Company, 1985.

Whitelaw, Ralph T. *Virginia's Eastern Shore.* 2 vols. Vol. I, Richmond: Virginia Historical Society, 1951.

Wilderson, Frank B. III. *Afropessimism.* New York, NY: Liveright Publishing Corporation, 2020.

Wilkerson, Isabel. *Caste: The Origins of Our Discontents.* New York: Random House, 2020.

Wise, Jennings C. *Ye Kingdome of Accawmacke or the Eastern Shore of Virginia in the Seventeenth Century*. Richmond: The Bell Book and Stationary Company, 1911.

"York County, Virginia Records, 1638–1644."

"York County, Virginia Wills, Deeds, and Orders." 1657–1659.

Index

About the Author

Carmen P. Thompson is a historian and author of *The Making of American Whiteness: The Formation of Race in Seventeenth-Century Virginia*. She earned her PhD in U.S. history from the University of Illinois Urbana-Champaign and her master of arts in African American Studies from Columbia University in New York. Dr. Thompson is a highly sought expert on race and Whiteness in America, writing the introduction to the forthcoming book, *Protest City*—a photo book that chronicles the yearlong protests in Portland, Oregon, after the murder of George Floyd by police in 2020—and co-editing and authoring articles in the peer-reviewed journal *Oregon Historical Quarterly*'s special issue on White supremacy in Oregon. She has held visiting scholar appointments at the Institute for Research in African American Studies at Columbia University in New York and in the Black Studies Department at Portland State University, and has taught a wide range of courses on the Black experience and Whiteness at Portland State University and Portland Community College.